MASCULINITIES, GENDER AND INTERNATIONAL RELATIONS

Terrell Carver and Laura Lyddon

BRISTOL
UNIVERSITY
PRESS

First published in Great Britain in 2022 by

Bristol University Press
University of Bristol
1-9 Old Park Hill
Bristol
BS2 8BB
UK
t: +44 (0)117 374 6645
e: bup-info@bristol.ac.uk

Details of international sales and distribution partners are available at
bristoluniversitypress.co.uk

British Library Cataloguing in Publication Data
A catalogue record for this book is available from the British Library

ISBN 978-1-5292-1228-0 hardcover
ISBN 987-1-5292-1229-7 paperback
ISBN 978-1-5292-1230-3 ePub
ISBN 978-1-5292-1231-0 ePdf

Cover design: Liam Roberts Design
Front cover image: ivanastar/iStock

Bristol University Press uses environmentally responsible
print partners.

Printed in Great Britain by CMP, Poole

To my parents, Mary and Dave.
LL

To the curious feminist, seriously!
TC

Contents

Detailed Contents

Acknowledgements

The authors would like to thank Bristol University Press, and in particular Stephen Wenham, who looked back on his undergraduate years at Bristol and thought there might be some exciting updates to his experiences. They would also like to thank the anonymous reviewers and a number of very helpful colleagues who very kindly read drafts and commented.

Terrell Carver is grateful to the School of Sociology, Politics & International Studies, University of Bristol, for a period of study leave during the academic year 2019–20, which was instrumental in developing this joint project. He would also like to acknowledge his affiliation as Research Associate, SA-UK Bilateral Chair in Political Theory, University of the Witwatersrand, South Africa, with particular thanks to Critical South (www.criticalsouth.blog), which posted 'The m-word', revised here for Chapter 1.

Laura Lyddon would like to give thanks to everyone who assisted and supported her with, and during, her PhD, many of whom were duly acknowledged in her thesis. In particular, she would like to thank the University of Bristol for the research scholarship that enabled her to undertake the PhD, her PhD supervisors, Terrell Carver and Paul Higate, and her PhD peers and friends: Terri-Anne Teo, Oscar Berglund, Sabine Qian, Audrey Reeves, Rupert Alcock and Natasha Carver (no relation to Terrell Carver). Special thanks and recognition also go to Olly, Sol, Zephyr and Allison.

Preface

This book is intended for anyone interested in the ways that sex, gender and sexuality define what world politics is about, not just what does or doesn't count as an 'issue' within it. To do that we confront the imbrication of militarism with masculinity at both the empirical and symbolic levels. Because our focus is not on what militarism and masculinity 'are', but rather on what they *do*, we take the reader into the secretive and securitized spaces of the global arms trade.

The global arms trade is legal under national and international law, yet the secrecy and security involved speak to a considerable legitimacy deficit. The national-corporate legitimation processes that we identify are drawn from, and reflect back on, men and masculinities, however various, thus reinforcing the gender-order hierarchy. Within that hierarchy of masculinity over femininity, there are 'nested' hierarchies through which some men, and masculinized women, dominate others in gradations of subordination and oppression.

That pyramidal power structure authorizes and deploys the everyday violence and horrendous destruction that are chronicled daily by the news media, and against which activists of all genders organize and protest all over the world. Reflecting those political movements, our concluding chapter inverts the top-down view of International Relations in order to consider the bottom-up ways that activists deploy sex, gender and sexuality when they 'trouble' and resist great-power politics.

While the academic discipline that deals most directly with great-power politics is International Relations, the concepts and issues dealt within this book are of more general interest across the humanities and social sciences. And indeed, those concepts and issues are constitutive of the lives we all lead, since sex, gender and sexuality are marginal to no one. We therefore hope that this book will speak to a wide audience of students and teachers, fostering curiosity about how politics-as-usual, like business-as-usual, does so much damage-as-usual – legitimately.

The content of this book largely derives from Laura Lyddon's graduate work and PhD thesis on gender and the arms trade that was co-supervised by Paul Higate and Terrell Carver and awarded in 2016. In addition, much of Chapter 2 originates from the paper, 'Strange Bedfellows, Marriages of Convenience and Military Eunuchs: When States are Queered', which Laura wrote and presented at the International Feminist Journal of Politics annual conference in 2013, and later developed further.

Laura's PhD thesis spoke directly to the literatures and communities in International Relations, security studies and gender studies, drawing on feminist scholars and activists in those areas, among others. She sought to address the loud silences in these literatures regarding gender and the legitimate arms trade, by exploring the role of gender in various sites where the arms trade is legitimated, including arms control discourses, narratives about why states buy or sell, arms industry videos and at arms fairs.

As explained above, this book speaks to broader audiences, including general readers, and indeed to anyone interested in world politics. Turning this body of work into a book has been an enjoyable and collaborative process over several years, initiated, orchestrated and edited by Terrell Carver, who was approached by Bristol University Press to write a book on masculinities and International Relations. But this effort derives from Laura's original research question – how does gender legitimize the arms trade? And without that, this project could never have arisen.

1

Wasn't It Always Just About Men Anyway?

What has masculinity got to do with International Relations? And what does the study of masculinities have to do with politics at whatever level? And how does gender fit into the answers? These are the opening questions for this introductory chapter.

To get us started with answering these questions this chapter will review and critique some familiar presumptions about men – about men in relation to humanity, men in relation to women, men in relation to state- and non-state-actors, and men in relation to what's public and what's merely – and supposedly – private. Crucially this book is concerned with men in the hierarchies through which they position themselves in relation to each other. This view of masculinity as a set of nested hierarchies is the intended 'take-away' from this study.

In political studies and International Relations 'the week on feminism and gender' appears increasingly on the curriculum at undergraduate and postgraduate levels. In that context the term 'gender' highlights the presence and importance of women. Alternatively, for most male-centric audiences, 'the week on feminism' puts gender-and-women into a niche. That niche is somewhere you *might* visit, once you've learned the supposedly ungendered or gender-neutral, generically 'human' basics of the discipline.[1]

This book reverses that familiar pedagogy,[2] arguing that gender comes first, because where there are humans, there is gender. Gender is not just a binary of men and women, but also a hierarchy of masculinities over femininities.[3] This is a hierarchy of value and power that applies not just across the gender binary, but also within it. The nested hierarchies within masculinizing power structures explain why there is feminism in the first place.[4]

The notice accorded to masculinities within the gender-and-women framework is oftentimes very limited and, for various reasons, quite marginalized. If masculinity is mentioned in that context at all, a brief notice often reproduces what we think we already know. We think we know a lot about men, because they are everywhere. Their masculine selves are on display in national and international leadership circles and action zones, such as sports and militaries. As icons they present themselves as role models for men. In doing that, they foreclose the idea that there is very much to question.

Even when masculinity is seen as a problem, which it is in relation to violence, sexual and otherwise, it is generally displaced onto the study of criminality. In that dark and 'toxic' zone it is kept physically and conceptually quite separate from the everyday masculinities, and from the nested hierarchies through which they function. Those everyday masculinities generally pass without much use of the gender lens.[5] They are simply how men are, because that is how sports are, how militaries are, how businesses are, how politics is. Gendered activism related to masculinity has indeed revealed how all kinds of men suffer in all kinds of ways from the nested hierarchies of domination and subordination that this book charts as constituent of the gender order.[6]

In point of fact, men control – to an overwhelming degree – public space, political space, academic space, discursive space, media space, physical space, outer space and inner space. This book will investigate how masculinity actually works such that some men obtain all this power and control. Exclusions and oppressions are then knock-on discriminatory effects of this power structure, often referred to as 'patriarchy'. And, of course, there are many forms of resistance and subversion.[7]

Masculinity is understood here as competitive relations among men that generate successive levels of inferiority 'man to man', and that persistently exclude and inferiorize women.

In our analysis the notion of fairness in any of these self-styled competitions is itself an artefact of masculine power relations. In that way competition is a movable rule of the game. Moreover, when masculinity is the game, male players have an automatic advantage, although hardly an equal one. That is the point of the nested hierarchies.

To look into this we need to lose sight of men as simply 'the other half' of the gender binary. That binary is commonly presented as M or F, male or female, man or woman,[8] as if the two 'halves' were symmetrical. However, it can't be true that masculinity and femininity are mirrors to each other, because the power differential is so stark. There must be some difference that accounts for this.

The sharp point of the power pyramid is the subject of the chapters that follow in this book. The study of men and masculinities from that perspective reveals the mechanisms through which an ever greater amount of the world's productive resources, as well as destructive capabilities, relentlessly accrue to a very few men. Those resources do not accrue to humanity in some generic and gender-neutral sense. As the pyramid of power sharpens, so the gender-order dominance of some men over others increases, and over everyone else.[9] How does this happen?

Gender asymmetry

Masculinity works differently from femininity. First, men can present themselves as 'apparently de-gendered', thus representing 'the human'. Indeed, the default generic human isn't 'woman-shaped', as feminists have amply demonstrated.[10] Second, men *also* present themselves as 'overtly gendered' male exemplars – good husbands, brothers, fathers, uncles, nephews, and so forth. This representation then brackets off the less savoury aspects of male behaviour.

That conflation – between males gendered as 'good' and males as quintessentially 'human' is crucial to understanding how masculinities work. Femininities don't work that way, because the terrain of 'the human' is already occupied.[11] Instead, women fit into humanity as always already 'gendered', whereas men have another option. They can present themselves as generically human – a being that could be a man or a woman, indifferently. The gendered male, however, is still *covertly* present, and gives the lie to an indifferent equality.[12] Men can switch – even in the same sentence – from one subject position to the other. Indeed, their discourse is often a conflated ambiguity.

Following the influential theorizing of gender inaugurated by Butler,[13] we understand masculinity and femininity as arbitrary codes projected onto bodies. Those bodies are then binarized into males and females according to criteria that are thoroughly historical and subject to change.[14] And in turn, the ways that males and females deploy and interpret those codes reflect what bodily males and females are supposed to be like.[15]

Moreover, the binary codes are already in a value hierarchy through which masculinity/maleness is more highly valued, and thus accrues more power, than femininity/femaleness. Unsurprisingly, then, masculinity and men, as self-referentially valued, come to represent a generic humanness. They are therefore mirrored as human exemplars, yet covertly understood as masculine. And in gendered-male terms, they are moral exemplars for their sex.[16] For men, then, this is a win-win.

However, there is a twist in this tale. It comes when 'bad men' are described in ungendered terms that seem to refer to a generic human nature. 'Bad men' exist descriptively in ungendered terms, such as criminal, gangster, rapist, abuser and so forth. Marking those categories as male is apparently redundant, for example male criminal, since no one can miss the fact that overwhelmingly the world's suspected, convicted and incarcerated criminals are male. So ungendered terms invite notions of female participation, in principle at least, since the criminal terms reference a generic humanity, of which women are – for these purposes – surely a part. Those masculinizing processes – the ones that produce criminality and violence – thus disappear into human nature, generic humanity, the problem of evil, and such like.

So what do masculinities actually *do*? Those are the puzzles that this book will address. However, there is a further puzzle. The power that men accrue and hold is immense. So why is the study of masculinities not a mainstream subject and an essential element of methodological training? Or, to put the question another way, why and how did the present study emerge? Evidently something was hiding in plain sight.

Founding fathers

Masculinity studies has its roots in the sociology of men. Studies of men, as men, doing manly things – but *not* historically important manly things – originated in the 1940s and 1950s. This development occurred in the sociology of the working class, and in particular, studies of working-class men.[17] That conjunction of terms already tells us something: studying a class, or indeed ordinary people, in the 1940s and 1950s, meant studying men. That is because men occupied almost all the senior university positions, and indeed, almost all the training and selection routes to those positions. Thus men defined what was important enough to know about; hence they controlled what new studies would be worthwhile. In order to study people of any importance, they studied men, since by definition and by judgement, men were the important people, and women were not.

Moreover, that interest in working-class men, as men, represented a class curiosity, since the men doing the research and writing were investigating an 'other' to themselves. That 'other' was a puzzling world of working-class masculinity. Middle-class sociological researchers, securing their own class position against a devalued but intriguing 'other', presumed that they, as researchers, had little intuitive knowledge of such an unknown world. Masculinity studies was thus marginalized and moved safely away from the researchers themselves, and from the 'normal' masculinity through which their world operated.

If we go back to the founding days of International Relations in the 1930s, the defining characteristics of the field – in relation to men and masculinity – would have been clear: International Relations considers politics that is specifically international, sex is personal and certainly not political (except when criminalized), and masculinity is not really of interest, because men already make the world go round. What you see is what you get, and what you get is what there is.[18] And in the founding days there were only 'fathers' and 'sons', some of whom would ascend within the nested hierarchies of the discipline to superior positions, and others would consent to their hegemony. In Gramsci's classic definition, hegemony is domination *by consent*.[19]

But then no one in the 1930s would have asked all those questions posed above about politics and masculinity/ies anyway, and the term 'gender' hadn't yet emerged in anything like its present-day definitions and conflations. Moreover, sex wasn't a subject for polite conversation in academic settings in any case – or only after dinner, with port and cigars. However, those views, and those masculine-centric and masculinizing practices, are not wholly long ago or far away.

In fact, masculine-centric and masculinizing processes aren't over and done with, and they are – as some scholars have shown – actually quite noteworthy.[20] After all, how many of the world's heads of state or government, top military brass or corporate CEOs, national treasurers and bankers, legislators and judges, highest paid celebrities and influential pundits, professional athletes and celebrated broadcasters, university presidents and top-ranked professors, Nobel prize winners and leading scientists, and similarly powerful people – including mega-billionaires, high-net worth individuals, criminals and gangsters – *are women?*

Or rather, why isn't the question, how many are men? The question isn't really worth asking, and indeed, simply counting women as a minority percentage in among the men doesn't actually pose this question. Why are all those positions of wealth, power and influence 'still' so male-dominated? And why is masculinity – and in almost all its forms – such a focus of *in*curiosity? And if anyone is actually curious, how is it that male-dominated normality is so easily referenced, and often so glibly accepted, as legitimate?

The 'm-word'

Posing that kind of question about the gender-order hierarchy, even to students of politics, International Relations and other social studies and sciences, often elicits a characteristic mode of reply. Replies usually reference abstractions, such as history, tradition, values, structures, religion, society, norms and the like. Rarely, if ever, does anyone mention the single word 'men'. Of course, the rare answer 'men' usually and rather naturally comes from a male-identified person. But it doesn't come, as a rule, with anything other than unproblematic descriptive self-reference and mirrored self-recognition, plus a dose of idealization. That easy mirroring of gender privilege isn't available to women, because that is what the gender-order hierarchy of masculinity over femininity says and does.[21]

For some 250 years or so there have been notable, hard-fought – and violently resisted – breakthroughs by women to get into these hierarchies of wealth, power and esteem *at all*. Those women's movements were very widespread, and quite variously diverse.[22] They were generally riding on, and pushing with, rising waves of democratization. Or more accurately, they were navigating the eddies and ripples in those highly masculinized processes of men's nested hierarchies. Even getting into public meetings, never mind speaking, and certainly not voting – indeed entering onto the actual floor of a parliament or congress or legislature – were made by some men, with others' complicity, into trials by fire. The outcomes were often two steps forward, one step back, and taking considerable time to get much of anywhere. That pattern continues, with rather a lot of backlash to masculinized authoritarianism, in various modes.[23] While at many levels there are exceptions, and indeed, cited evidence of changes in men's views and behaviour, on a global scale across the world's nation-states, it's hard to say that there is a significant trend.[24]

What is going on here? Is it physical or psychological? Biological or cultural? Ideological or educational? Rational or hysterical? How do men perform these exclusions and yet celebrate their magnanimity? How do they marginalize contrary views so effectively and thus exercise such hegemony? How does this pattern of consent and complicity convey such legitimacy?

Legitimacy as a noun/legitimizing as a verb

Legitimacy is a key concept in studying the sexed-gendered power structures through which masculinity operates. Indeed, power and legitimacy are man-shaped, and thus, masculinity, power and legitimacy are a conflation. The conjunction of legitimacy claims with power claims is well known in international politics, but the imbrication of those two familiar terms occludes the role that masculinities – as nested hierarchies of some men over others – play in the ways, often implicit, that claims to power and legitimacy are made and gain traction.

The concept of legitimacy holds an important place in international politics, not least because of its fundamental role in most (if not all) theories of the state as the central unit of investigation and concern. As the study of International Relations has evolved, the concept of legitimacy is also of increasing importance in arenas outside the state. These include global governance, international law and the array of governmental and non-governmental institutions that go with them. Those structures are still linked to, or dependent on, the legitimacy of the state system, and particularly the auto-legitimacy of the dominant states within them.

Hurd argues that legitimacy is a 'shifty, intersubjective quality which is only indirectly available for empirical study'. Yet, to 'read international politics without paying attention to the competition over legitimacy would leave one with no way to understand such common acts as saving face, offering justifications, using symbols, and being in a position of authority'.[25] Legitimacy is thus a complex web of claims negotiated in daily practice between states, including behind-the-scenes diplomacy and commercial deal-making. Legitimization is a practice that makes some things legal or official, acceptable rather than questionable.

A state achieves legitimacy through recognition as such by states, of greater or lesser power, within the international community. In that setting great-power politics – the G7/ G20, United Nations (UN) Security Council, North Atlantic Treaty Organization (NATO), the 'nuclear club', World Trade Organization (WTO), Davos, International Monetary Fund (IMF), in various alignments – sets the terms and rules. And rather similarly states can be delegitimized as rogue or failed, again within the great power setting. Legitimacy is therefore closely related to power and authority. Hurd summarizes: 'An institution that exercises legitimated power is in a position of authority.'[26] And reciprocally, authority is the legitimate exercise of power, so an institution or person with authority is considered to hold and exercise power legitimately. What, then, does masculinity do for this process, and what does the process do for it?

Hegemony and masculinities: power and domination

Hegemony, as theorized by Gramsci, is domination by consent. And hegemonic masculinity, as theorized by Connell, is the answer to a *question*. The question is: how is the gender order – a hierarchy of masculinity over femininity, *and* some men over others – legitimated?[27] As we know from theories and practices dating from the mid-17th century, legitimacy for one person's right to exercise power over another comes *only* by consent. Claims to 'having power over' arising on some other basis, such as religious or patriarchal authority, or simply might-being-right, are thereby *illegitimate*.[28]

Hegemonic masculinity, as Connell puts it, is the current form of masculinity that could plausibly be said to legitimate, or to help to legitimate, the gender-order hierarchy. From that perspective, gender represents *hierarchy*, not just difference. In any case, gender difference has never been a simple or supposedly biological binary. Cytology, sexology, genetics, endocrinology, psychology and any number of queer, intersex or trans persons in any number of ways can testify, empirically, to that.[29]

Moreover, and continuing with Connell's analysis, the hierarchy – put as a sweeping but truthful generality – of masculinity over femininity, and some men over others, is a potent way of conceptualizing both intersectional marginalizations *and* gender-specific oppressions. It is through those subordinations that masculinized competitions reward some men with wealth and power, and not others. In that way nested hierarchies control access to wealth and power generally for women. Successive chapters in this book show how this also works in relation to race, class, sexualities and further marginalizations and oppressions. Intersectionality is a way of demonstrating that, in the experience of individuals, oppressions are not experienced separately but rather in inextricable conjunctions, and indeed, rather similarly with accumulations of privilege.[30]

It follows that hegemonic masculinity is not a 'thing' that you can point to because it displays masculine dominance. Most often the thing that is pointed to − or, in some cases, exhibited to be pointed at − is a male body. Or rather that dominance − symbolized most usually in a male body − is something that you would point to as the answer to Connell's *question* about validation and legitimacy.[31] Indeed, understanding hegemonic masculinity simply as 'something you can point to' reinscribes the singularity of masculinity that Connell worked hard to pluralize.

For our purposes this legitimation process shows up importantly in the consideration of nested hierarchies of some men over others. Those hierarchies can be understood as the domination of some masculinities over others, offering discourses and practices through which men may come to understand themselves as subordinated − or alternatively dominating − masculine types. In this text we use the singular 'masculinity' to connote the plural 'masculinities', and thus we move between the two.[32]

Connell's question presumes that the masculine-dominant and masculinizing gender-order hierarchy is a political phenomenon. Generally these masculine hierarchies are conflated with the social, political and moral orders as such. Activists who are working for liberatory and democratizing struggles − deriving from concepts of class, sex, race/ethnicity, sexuality, (dis)ability and the like − have struggled, sometimes to the death, in order to gain ground. Those struggles argue the *illegitimacy* − in some ways and to some degree − of hierarchies and exclusions already in place.

Connell's *question* in itself makes the legitimacy of the gender order problematic. An answer to Connell's question, therefore − if accepted as a valid one − shows how this legitimacy is secured by some masculinities, and therefore by some masculinized people, and indeed by some agencies personified as masculine. This gets us closer to seeing what masculinity actually *does*.

Looked at that way, the answer to Connell's question − about how gender as an ordered and ordering hierarchy attains its legitimacy − must be a *process*, not a thing. To conceptualize a process requires thoughtful investigation, not hackneyed gestures to a masculinized body. It also requires a will to make 'what everybody knows' questionable and therefore problematic. Doing that makes a conflict-creating political issue.

Domination by consent

Domination is one thing; consent is another. And consent, remember, is the *only* mode through which legitimacy can be secured. Legitimacy, in turn, implies consent, that is, a presumption that consent *has been given*. Or rather, claims of legitimacy put critique on the back foot: critics must validate their own claim that the current orders of hierarchy are in and of themselves illegitimate.[33]

Even in the classical theorizations, more or less silently incorporated into the Anglophone language of constitutionalism, writers were nervously vague on what it takes to *unconsent* to a hierarchical order of power. Legitimacy and consent are both, more often than not, claims rather than facts. Or more perspicuously, they are claims couched as facts, so consequently formulated with rhetorically powerful, rather than merely descriptive, intent.[34]

That sort of understanding – of consent, legitimacy and hegemony – was described by Gramsci as the 'common sense' that he was battling to dislodge in early 20th-century Italy. His own activism was grounded in a conceptualization of social class, so it was not the feminist battle, or one located in race/ethnicity or similar ascriptions. Nonetheless his theorization underpins Connell's strategy of destabilizing the gender-order hierarchy of masculinity over femininity, and it is regrettable that so many readers have missed this crucial move. 'Hegemonic' is not an adjective applicable to 'a masculinity': it is an *outcome* of the ordering processes through which masculinity operates to legitimize the gender-order hierarchy.

Moving on and reaching out

With all this in mind we can now proceed to the further chapters in this book through which the analytical 'gender lens' crafted above will be deployed. These chapters will also show how this theorization of the gender-order hierarchy provides crucial insights into understanding the intersectionality of power relations. Those exclusions and oppressions are expressed and experienced in terms of race, class, sexuality, (dis)ability and similar configurations of disadvantage. Moreover, these illustrative accounts will be articulated within overarching interpretive frameworks derived from queer theory and decolonizing perspectives, as well as the critique of ableism. So in that way the study of masculinities should operate inclusively, rather than – as could easily happen – by marginalizing everything else.

In the following chapters we do more than classify and map what can be observed typologically. We show how male dominance derives relationally among men as nested hierarchies by consent. Since hegemony is domination by consent, the way that we trace out symbolic constructions, and patterned flows of political power, will also help to answer the really interesting question: how do they get away with it? It is crucial here to focus on causes, rather than just on effects, although without overlooking or forgetting what those effects actually are – on women, on subordinated men, and on an array of related exclusions and oppressions.

Famously consent is manufactured,[35] and once manufactured, that legitimacy is easily taken for granted. The overwhelmingly white and industrialized male power elite of great-power politics, great-power military might and great-power economic domination is the focus of media attention, although almost always in apparently de-gendered, generically 'human' terms. Moreover, in that coverage these men are framed in public as moral exemplars, because they are heterosexually partnered – whatever the supposedly 'private' realities.[36] As such this familiar hegemony becomes auto-legitimated and dangerous to question. Practices of journalistic critique, and holding the powerful to account, cannot be taken for granted. That is because constitutional guarantees of free speech and information transparency are antipathetical, or at least highly inconvenient, to those in power. Their own legitimacy, supposedly by consent, derives from the apparent absence of dissent, since consent need only be tacit. And these elites have many in the world's media helping them in this self-validating project. At the top end of the political scale, obligations to disclose the workings of power are constantly evaded; at the bottom end, journalists and investigators are simply murdered.

Hence, in succeeding chapters we focus on the top tiers of the political world, the military world and the commercial world, otherwise known as the 'global north' and 'the west', because that is where male hierarchies are consolidated, such that marginalization and exclusion, including disadvantage and destruction, are the global result. Those results are produced in predictable patterns of discrimination, exploitation, victimization and exculpation, as experienced over the years through capitalism, colonialism and imperialism. The object here is to see how they get away with it, pursuant to protests directed at what they are doing and to whom they have done it.

This analytical study matters because it exposes the nested hierarchies of domination and subordination among men – and these hierarchies are overwhelmingly male – through which the gender-order hierarchy normalizes violence against women and others deemed deviant from the heterosexual norm. The 'orderliness' of the hierarchy thrives on militarism as the exemplary masculine mode and reservoir of male-directed power. In very practical terms this set of hierarchies underwrites capitalism as an exploitative and extractive process through which everyone suffers, some much more than others. It enforces itself as modernity with few other options, if any, to the detriment of many cultures, communities and sexualities. And it displaces funding and activity that could otherwise generate equalities of wellbeing, technologies of environmental sustainability, and reparative relationships, international and personal.

Chapter 2 **Sovereign States, Warring States, Queer States** investigates how complex codings of sex, gender and sexuality are crucial to the ways that sovereign states and commercial powers operate. These same codings also apply to the human individuals – almost always men who enact international politics in their messages and meetings. Sovereignty is thus both abstract and disembodied, and also very physical in visible bodies. These are overwhelmingly coded male through deportment and dress sense. Such parades of normality, whether of bodily leaders or disembodied states, can be queered in theory and even in practice, as we will see. Indeed, they are necessarily queered already because they depend on the non-representation of disavowed 'others'. This chapter contains descriptive accounts of torture and rape that some readers may find disturbing.

Chapter 3 **Arms and the Men** introduces and contextualizes the arms trade, that is, the manufacture, sales and purchase of weaponry. It explores the links between 'boys and toys' allusions to the activities of state and corporate elites by adopting warrior-protector and bourgeois-rational models of masculinity. Thus we consider the legal framework and international discourse of arms control through which the legitimate arms trade is defined and monitored, over and against illegitimate trading as criminal activity. Taking the UK as a particular state agent, the chapter shows how legitimating strategies – grounded in the nested hierarchies of auto-coordinating masculinities – invisibilize policy contradictions and sanitize human rights violations.

Chapter 4 **Gender at Work! 'Get Pissed and Buy Guns'** visits the very pinnacle of global power where competitive nation-states, competitive military establishments and competitive commercial interests come together regularly in festivals of might and money. It isn't easy getting access to top-level 'arms fairs', because they are closed to the public. However, we take you right inside, as an observer. Arms traders and weapons manufacturers have a legitimation deficit that they address at arms fairs through strategies of sanitization. These are stabilized by reinscribing the heterosexual certainties of the gender-order hierarchy of masculinity over femininity. In turn, company promotional videos do this similarly with the race-class order to stabilize themselves politically. Their legitimacy deficit arises within an economic environment dominated by American 'defence' spending and thus by 'western-liberal' norms of legitimacy. Legitimacy then erases any idea of hypocrisy and subterfuge.

Chapter 5 **Looking Back/Pushing Ahead** takes us to the anti-militarism activisms that confront the imbrication of weaponry and masculinity that the preceding chapters have outlined. Those activisms include both men and women, although they have a particular and often problematic relationship with feminisms and feminist activists. Moreover, those groups and movements include a variety of understandings of, and internal conflicts about, critical approaches to masculinity. Rather than typologizing any masculinities as somehow 'alternative' in varying senses, we focus here on courageous grassroots efforts to delegitimize weaponry and militarism by destabilizing the gender-order hierarchy. In that way this book relates descriptively and normatively to power.

Further reading

Caroline Criado-Perez (2019) *Invisible Women: Exposing Data Bias in a World Designed for Men*, London: Chatto & Windus.

Cynthia Enloe (2016) *Globalization and Militarism: Feminists Make the Link* (2nd edn), Lanham, MD: Rowman & Littlefield.

Lukas Gottzén, Ulff Mellström and Tamara Shefer (eds) (2019) *Routledge International Handbook of Masculinity Studies*, Abingdon: Routledge.

Laura J. Shepherd (ed) (2014) *Gender Matters in Global Politics: A Feminist Introduction to International Relations*, Abingdon: Routledge.

2

Sovereign States, Warring States, Queer States

Let's take masculinity, gender and International Relations from the top.

Great-power politics exists in and through the peacetime/ wartime dichotomy that defines the national security dilemma. That dilemma is one of strategic interaction and game playing within a competitive struggle for dominance that threatens, and sometimes uses, armed force and organized violence. The dominance of one state over another can, however, arrive by consent from other states, even if cowed and bullied, grudging and conditional. That global competitive structure is mirrored in the commercial exchanges through which some national economies accumulate and maintain more wealth than others. That wealth, however, doesn't look violent in itself. Indeed, world trade is often defined as the antithesis to armed conflict, which is said to disrupt it. That view of trade as inherently peaceful, and as oppositional to war-making, has been a proselytizing orthodoxy in and of western and southern Europe since the early 16th century. Thus it is coincident with the rise there of aggressive, exploratory commercialisms.[1]

The connections between wealth as an outcome of competitive commercial hierarchies and armed conflict between and among states and would-be states are not made quite so obvious and explicit in theorizations of the international system, international community, international political economy and great-power politics. Wealthy states are consumers of armed weaponry, and the wealth has to come from somewhere, namely taxpayers, individual and corporate. But wealthy states are also producers of weaponry, which is itself locked into competitive commercial hierarchies. These are often bracketed off as 'private', 'public–private', 'security-related' and the like. This chapter, and the two that follow, makes visible what is sometimes kept rather out of sight. Or alternatively, it is put on display sometimes, but in ways that keep out of sight what really happens. The politics–economics distinction functions as a deflection and a disavowal, as does the state–public vs private enterprise distinctions deployed rhetorically. Here we make sure that those strategies of semi-visibility and legitimated normality get derailed.

Dominance in great-power politics arises through the threat and actuality of physical force, ranging from highly organized and hi-tech militaries to political violence undertaken by non-state or proto-state groups. These latter groups are clandestinely organized as networks and are rather low-tech and unshowingly masculinized by comparison. The peacetime/wartime binary is universally moralized to justify war so as to secure peace. It is reflective of the gender-order hierarchy, and constitutive of warrior-protector masculinity by definition.[2]

The categories of terror and terrorist, derived from responses to 19th-century colonial aggressions, are now hypermoralized over and beyond the peacetime/wartime binary. Terror and terrorist are a constitutive 'outside' to the security dilemma through which sovereign states define themselves as such. And since the foundation of the United Nations (UN) in 1945, they project themselves as a moral and moralizing community. Terrorists are not, or not yet, state-actors with state sovereignty. Sovereign states facilitating terrorism are at risk of demotion and exclusion to rogue status, stringent sanctions and violent intervention, especially since the American-led reaction to the events of 11 September 2001.[3] During the later 20th century and into the next, the international system has self-defined in this way, and been understood in those terms, by leading scholars of International Relations.[4]

The security dilemma is a spiralling regress from merely competitive rivalry to mutually assured destruction: states that arm themselves for self-protection generate suspicion in other states that such actions portend acts of aggression. Hence they arm themselves against such actions in self-defence. As trust and thus cooperation recede in inter-state relations, and as paranoia increases in response to heightened suspicions, so the likelihood of armed conflict – through whatever means – increases to certainty. Even trivial or suspected slights then confirm suspicions and also offer pretexts for pre-emptive attacks.[5]

It follows that the peace/war binary doesn't describe periods of time when armed conflict is present or absent, but rather disguises the way the security dilemma operates. Within that dilemma the defender/aggressor binary isn't temporal, either, but rather perspectival: it is constitutive of the international system through which states are going to be both defender and aggressor, each applying one term of the binary to an 'other'.

The logic of commercial rivalry mirrors the same dilemma. In both cases that logic is the gender logic of masculinity, by which some men dominate others in nested hierarchies. The tactics through which those subordinations operate will then differ according to circumstances. In that way the spheres of great-power politics, commercial rivalries and hierarchies of masculinized subordination are made to appear quite different. But the strategies of the competitors, and the logics of the competitions, are really the same. And so are the players, who are overwhelmingly men, visibly masculinized in quite uniform ways, so that they also and importantly confirm the validity of the gender-order hierarchy. Those practices of visual and textual representation are crucial to the repetitive processes through which masculinity is legitimated, even if only a tiny minority ascend to the highest ranks of power and visibility. And in great-power politics, globally celebrated and symbolically potent, they become warrior-protectors.[6]

This chapter focuses on the activities characteristic of great-power politics and the ways that it works in and through the international rivalry of sovereign states and competitor economies. To do that, we consider militarism as a gendering process, and crucially a state-forming process, which is always already ongoing. This is because it is constitutive of sovereign states and of the masculinized individuals – overwhelmingly men – who constitute the leaders and cadres of the state-actors. These are the players – major and minor, winners and losers, rivals and upstarts – in great-power politics. Using the perspective adopted here, it is evident that the familiar political-military hierarchies are necessarily imbricated with global commercial hierarchies, and that both operate together conjunctively with threats and sanctions, including force. Those hierarchies, normally separated for political purposes, and rather unfortunately invoked in familiar commentaries, are treated here as an analytical conflation. Indeed, those who are in these positions of power – who are overwhelmingly male – are well known to shift easily from one hierarchy to another, 'in-and-outers' in the phraseology of global commercial and military dominance.

That framing of human activity is already a global hierarchy: states over non-governmental organizations (NGOs), NGOs over individuals, and thus organized over unorganized activities. It values hi-tech military and commercial agencies over low-tech criminals, irregulars, guerrillas and self-styled or demonized terrorists. Along with that moralized hierarchy of esteem – the defining pinnacle of which is UN membership as a sovereign state – goes a monetarized hierarchy of moral, not just commercial, importance. Poorer nations struggle to gain the moral high ground that richer nations presume is necessarily theirs.[7] Hence we see a rank ordering of greater and lesser powers mirrored in the IMF, G7/G20, WTO, Davos summits and similar commercially oriented international networking structures. While militarism is apparently excluded from these civilianized rivalries, it is importantly present – as we will see – in relations of production and distribution, in payments systems and capital flows, and in presumed geopolitical clout in securing national-corporate interests. Those interests are, of course, defined competitively, not cooperatively – other than in cartels of overlapping, 'log-rolling' trade-offs. Strategies to maximize advantage aren't bounded by the analytical distinctions through which they are discussed and publicized. Indeed, this book explains how great power politics melds these distinctions into the practicalities and representations of the legitimate arms trade. Without that trade the firepower of armed struggles would not exist.

Hence, to consider masculinity and masculinization we must consider the agencies and industries that track the security dilemma 24/7, taking militarism as a general heading, but foregrounding ongoing competitive commercialism as 'preparation for war'. In Steans' definition, militarism is 'an ideology which values war highly, and in so doing, serves to legitimise state violence ... but also a set of social relationships organised around war and preparation for war, and so occurs during periods of both war and peace'.[8]

War and peace, arms and the man

Sovereignty is co-constitutive with militarism, not simply because states generally arm themselves as agents within the security dilemma, but because struggles to obtain sovereignty – through secession, annexation or civil war – seldom take place without armed struggle, or at least some credible threat of a fight. Armed force is thus generated in order to proclaim and defend the national interest, to generate sovereignty, and thus to secure agency status in the international system. In that system political, economic, cultural and weaponized rivalries seamlessly come together, although this is not always made visible and perspicuous to the public eye. Suggesting that this system is merely 'competitive' rather understates and mischaracterizes the struggles involved. Competitions exist within rules, sanctions and ordering mechanisms that distinguish them from 'free-for-alls'. The 'competitive' international system is supposedly self-regulating within the hierarchical structures of advantage and disadvantage that make it what it is. Or, in other words, those in charge of any supposed rules are already legitimated within the 'free-for-all' structure. They are then empowered to alter and break rules as they make strategic judgements of aggrandisement and risk, recrimination and mistrust.

Cohn and Ruddick comment that an essential component of militarism is the 'cultural glorification of the power of armed force',[9] almost always hypervisible on state occasions such as national days, whether of celebration, commemoration or mourning. Through those repetitive displays states gain the consent, whether enthusiastic or grudging, through which their domestic legitimacy arises and without which their international legitimacy would be threatened.

Moreover, commonplace celebrations of national heroes – overwhelmingly male – are repetitive and didactic lessons taught by war films, video games, public pageantry, media reportage, school curricula and clichéd imagery. While the hypervisibility of men defines all these genres, masculinity-centred gender analysis adds considerably to what might otherwise be a banal spectacle or commonplace moral debate. Hopton argues that '[m]ilitarism is the major means by which the values and beliefs associated with ideologies of hegemonic masculinity are eroticized and institutionalized'.[10] Thus militarism makes both the gender-order hierarchy of masculinity over femininity, and some men over others, even more visible and more valued than it is elsewhere.

Personifying the state-as-warrior-protector, then, 'he' (the state) requires an army and arms, which historically and fundamentally define militarism. Within that definition Cohn and Ruddick highlight 'the research, development and deployment of weapons', or the acquisition thereof, thus referencing the commercialisms through which the physicality and materiality of militarism can be secured competitively. Militarism is the dynamic that drives the manufacture of, and international trade in, militarized and militarizing technologies and services.[11] Despite the apparently feminine, humanitarian, peace-building concerns espoused by many wealthy states (when it suits them), that tactically female-gendered message arises within the paternal and patriarchal framing of the masculinized gender-order hierarchy.[12] Through that hierarchy sovereignty itself arises as a state-building and thus state-defining project requiring masculine domination and control.

Nearly all states strive to maintain masculine credentials, such as a very visible military establishment and concomitant weaponry-on-parade, in order to project themselves domestically and internationally as viable competitive agents within the commercial/military struggles described above. As Enloe explains, 'national security and the globalisation of militarisation need to be considered together',[13] rather than separately and abstractly. As argued here, these are instances of the nested hierarchy of domination – some men/states/economies over others. But in this use of the gender lens, perhaps there is yet more to reveal than usually meets the eye.

How does the queer contain the normal?

In the theory of International Relations and practice of international politics the state is doubly sexed and gendered.[14] It can be understood as female and feminine domestically in relating to what happens within its own boundaries, but as male and masculine internationally in relating to other states and agencies beyond its borders. Thus the state is the heterosexual projection of masculine aggression towards the internal/female/feminine affairs of other states or territories. It is also a heterosexual projection of masculine competition with other states in the realm of international politics. This is famously the war-of-all-against-all in the 'realist' anarchy of states studied within International Relations.[15] In this way we are looking at a sex-gender-sexuality coding through which oppositional masculinity–femininity tells us how to understand states in sovereign relation to each other as masculine agents. States are both competitors within the international order, and, as sovereign enforcers of that order, they operate through masculine incursions over borders into the feminine realm of other states.

As sketched above, that analytical intrusion of sex, gender and sexuality into the realm of great-power politics seems an oddly discordant and even trivializing transgression into the supposedly de-gendered world of generic humanity. But, as argued in Chapter 1, that world of generic humanity is covertly gendered masculine, and with that insight, then, the relevance of bodily sex and heteronormativity should no longer be disavowed.

The performative reading of sex, gender and sexuality, as developed in this book, sharply resists the binary simplicity and presumed stability of the masculine/feminine coding previously mentioned. Butler reversed the sex–gender relationship, such that two 'opposite' sexes arise when and because gender binaries are projected onto disparate bodies. Similarly the nation-state as performative opens up an informative realm of complexity. Those complexities – rather than reductive simplifications –

then become very revealing objects of knowledge, provided that 'knowers' are liberated from incuriosity and unafraid of real life. Thus the familiar internal/external, female/male, feminine/masculine codings, through which state sovereignty is expressed and performed, are made problematic.

In this chapter we begin to investigate how quite various, very particular, and politically complex codings of sex, gender and sexuality are crucial to the ways that sovereign states and commercial powers operate. Moreover the same applies to the embodiment of those concepts in the human individuals – almost always men – who enact what we understand as international politics. In that context bodily sex operates as a stable presumption, for which gender, performed as masculinity, functions as a readily intelligible marker.

Furthermore, masculinity in that public mode marks not just maleness, but also heterosexuality. International summits nearly always include group portraits of wives/spouses/partners, signifying conventional 'opposite sex' marital relationships regulated as visible monogamy. Those photographs invoke a supposedly natural, universal factuality from which to understand world leaders and world systems as morally good. Those individuals, of either sex or whatever sexuality (or asexuality), who do not immediately conform to this expectation, are either marginalized or excluded. For example, a 'first bloke' doesn't usually appear with the 'wives' of great power males. Such marginal individuals are included via a formalized 'coupledom' that mimics the heterosexual ideal. That might conceivably happen with a 'partner' to a 'gay prime minister', whether male or female, or non-binary in some way. None of that has yet, in fact, occurred at the highest international levels. The whole picture signifies an idealized normality by performing ritually as an obviously visible factuality.

That factual stability afforded to normality, however, is secured by an *unthinkable* queer antithesis, for example, a world in which the leaders of sovereign states were overwhelmingly, even exclusively, female, backed up photographically by a rainbow of partners in some not necessarily monogamous sense or other, who were overwhelmingly male, or perhaps overwhelmingly female, or even some mixture of indeterminacies.

However, as this chapter progresses, the comfortable realms of stability and zones of thinkable certainty will begin to crumble. Heteronormative masculinity already contains its 'others', the queer thoughts and practices that normalizing representations, such as the 'marital' photos mentioned above, work hard to forestall and suppress.[16] Rather, homosexual and/or queer practices participate in the constitution of the presumptively heterosexual context of international politics in crucial ways. That disavowed queerness operates from the high politics of great-power conflicts and interventions to the low politics of one-up-*man*ship, dirty tricks, hypocritical trolling, media bombs and cybercrimes.[17]

Rather than define all those phenomena as unthinkable, or if thinkable, as unserious, this chapter will develop the queer aspect of the 'gender lens' that feminisms and queer theorists have afforded. Or, in other words, if all that queerness wasn't important, it wouldn't be there in the first place, cowering in our closets.

States and nations

As defined by Wendt, the nation-state is conceptualized as an actor or person: 'it is a "someone" or a "subject"' to whom 'intentions, memories, rights and obligations are attached'.[18] This understanding of an entity is quite abstract, yet very knowable. It is knowable through its self-manifestations and experiential effects, which is how we make sense of it as an actor in International Relations. The state as actor does not exist for us in some material sense outside the repeated practices of textual and visual citation that create and sustain it.[19] The performative reality of the state as a personified actor is so strong that it is nearly impossible to think of it in any other way. Even writers who accept that '[s]tates are not *really* persons, only "*as if*" ones',[20] still rely on the personified state 'as one of the most fundamental – and in practice irreplaceable – assumptions of their research'.[21]

The state as person is merely a 'useful fiction', as Wendt concurs.[22] However, we argue here that it is actually a *crucial* fiction for the way that international politics is practised and understood. It is impossible to drop the anthropomorphic personification, precisely because we cannot think about the state without it, and because that personification is so readily and universally understood. The state and the physical body of the ruler as 'head of state' – almost always male – is a very ancient visual trope, as well as a textual double synecdoche. The world of the state and the world of commercialism have also long been visibly imbricated in king's head coinage since the 1st millennium BCE.

Moreover, within the imagery of the state-as-person there is a further trope of embodiment. A head of state becomes the human face for the state-as-person. And the human body becomes a physical presence for the personified state, adding visual reference to the otherwise textual allusions. Giving the abstract state, a human head is where metaphor merges with physicality, and textuality with visuality. In the same way the human bodies and character personalities of world leaders together make media visuality performative. With repetition comes recognizable reality. This happens over and beyond the static photographs and stylized iconic representations that preceded technologies of the moving image. Thus the state comes to life as a human creation in a bodily image, where the part is physical but the whole is an abstraction, displaying the individual features and foibles of a single person. Overwhelmingly those people are male.

Working again from the individual part to the political whole, and thus from the state as international actor up to the international system, the state becomes synonymous with its people and its territory. In Lakoff's scheme of basic metaphors, said to be foundational to modern common sense, the state as 'container' figures large.[23] Even if Lakoff's extravagant claim to foundational universality is rejected, nonetheless the container-state is readily familiar as a basic trope in the great-power politics of the international system. Like containers, state borders are boundaries, supposedly securable and secure, between inside and outside, just as physical bodies are understood to be an idealization. However, territorial borders provide security that is more cartographic than physical, as a rule. But then securitizing politics proceeds from defensive claims to physical actions, and on to further paranoias.[24] Thus we arrive at the commonplace discourse through which all these presumptions arise – as in, for example, this sentence from *The Economist*: 'Israel feels resentful towards Britain.'[25]

Because states are personified in human terms, they are necessarily conceived in gendered terms.[26] Within International Relations the state is clearly marked by a domestic/international, inside/outside binary. This means that most scholars in the discipline avoid transgressing into the domestic arena, or do so only to bring it in for some special reason. As Weber explains: '"Domestic" refers to the private sphere of state relations that gives a particular state a unique character. "International" refers to the projection of this domestic identity into the public sphere of relations among states.'[27] The domestic/international binary is the principle on which the discipline is founded. Without it International Relations is merely the study of politics or a political science, applicable at any level, which is very largely what the situation was before the mid-20th century.

'Domestic' refers to the national frame as opposed to the international, signifying the home, the household or family. Commonly this domain is understood as woman-centred, and so inherently gendered as feminine, and thus sexualized as an object within the male gaze.[28] Moreover, it is the male-centric perspective that guides knowledge production, validating some as knowers and demarcating what is worth knowing. Using the word 'domestic' in relation to national politics invokes the national/international binary divide, and thus further forecloses any view of the state as a non-gendered abstraction. The domestic is therefore contra-positional to the public realm, outside the home, most often normalized and disciplined as a male preserve, yet managed through the apparently de-gendered state. The nation-state as a personified and gendered international agent relies on this heterosexual pairing of the domestic and the international, thus positioning the latter as masculine in the gender-order hierarchy.[29]

Because gender is a system of power through which 'actors are constituted and positioned relative to each other',[30] in Wadley's words, so constructions that depict the state as a masculine actor are avatars of human individuals. These are the individuals, overwhelmingly male, at the top of the power structures through which 'the international' is constituted as a substantive abstraction. Any contrary referential tropes that depict a state as feminine, and thus emasculated, then devalorize and discredit it, exactly reflecting the competitive hierarchies through which some men and states dominate other men and states. Even *faux*-respectful and complimentary symbolizations of states as female merely confirm the power of masculinized and masculinizing great power politics.[31]

The state as masculine is sometimes distinguished from the nation as feminine, and therefore the former is rational, dominating and sovereign, whereas the latter is emotional, passive and subordinated. The state as an international actor is masculinized because it represents male power as international, and thus universal, hence controlling the feminine as merely national and domestic: 'The body of the body politic is taken to have a "female" identity to which the head (the "male" ruler) is married', in Campbell's alternative analysis.[32] The international/domestic heterosexual pairing underpins the dichotomy of the masculine state vs feminine nation, the latter referring to the inhabitants, the land, and through that signification, common cultures and legitimating histories. Sovereignty and legitimacy are the twin concepts through which states are constituted and contested, and nations are contained and controlled.

In contrast to the state, the nation is feminine, necessarily subject to masculinized control and restraint. Cohn argues that '[n]ationalist ideology frequently symbolises the nation, the homeland, as a woman; it is the (symbolic) body of the woman/mother/land that the male citizen soldier must protect against violation, penetration, conquest'.[33] Because the state is masculine, it is the protector of its inhabitants and thus the nation. This warrior-protector trope underpins the state's definitional claim of a monopoly on the legitimate means of violence, since, in Pettman's words, 'the outside is seen as beyond community, a place of anarchy, danger and foreigners'.[34] The people within the nation are thus feminized as passive subjects 'in the patriarchal household', headed by the state as masculinized actor.[35] The state, as protector of those within, serves an important function in legitimating the foreign policy of its government. As Young argues, '[s]ecurity states do not justify their wars by appealing to sentiments of greed or desire for conquest; they appeal to their role as protectors'.[36]

Thus states are men acting in a world of other men, taking care of their 'womenandchildren',[37] domestic households feminized as nations. As warrior-protectors, states are heterosexual, as seems obvious, given the patriarchal framing of sex/gender/marital relations. However, on closer inspection these things are not always quite so straightforward – and straight – as they seem.

How sexuality queers gender

Historians and other scholars of sexuality have pointed out that where the masculine norm is assumed, there is a heteronormative assumption already built in. That assumption tells us that heterosexuality is *the* natural and therefore legitimate way of living and being. The heterosexual norm is therefore the standard by which everything else relationally becomes queer.[38] As it is the triad of gender, sex and sexuality that secures heteronormativity, and thus the gender hierarchy or patriarchal order,[39] studies of gender that do not include sexuality, or which take it for granted, fail to capture the real-life workings of power through which oppressions are constituted and experienced.[40]

Because states are understood as masculine actors, for that reason they demand a thorough consideration of sexuality, and of heterosexuality in particular.[41] In that way the gender lens invites us to examine masculinized state actors for queerness of any kind. Because dominating masculinities are built on heterosexist premises,[42] they are always and already constituted by homosexuality as a defining 'outside' and 'other' against which the concept makes sense.[43] Because of this co-constitution, and the fragility of performative practices, the 'other' is itself always desired. But it is also then disavowed, so that unruffled straightness is restored. With that understanding, then, queer and homoerotic practices are unsurprisingly rife in the overtly masculine, misogynistic and homophobic institutions of male domination.[44] They are the disavowed 'outside' that never goes away, as otherwise the 'inside' won't still be there.

Thus queer practices are actually *required* in order to constitute idealized masculinity as heterosexual and therefore dominant in the gender-order hierarchy. The relationality isn't purely conceptual or simply implicit. It is embodied in human subjects and their quite real desires, aversions, repressions, emotions and memories. As Belkin explains, masculinizing institutions, such as militarized armed forces, are repetitively recoded as masculine and heterosexual when servicemen are *required* – albeit in informal, off-the-record ways – to 'enter into intimate relationships with femininity, queerness and other unmasculine foils, not just to disavow them'.[45] Or to put the matter very simply, masculine and masculinizing institutions produce both straightness and queerness at the same time, denials and disavowals notwithstanding.

What is so hypocritical and dangerous about this defining contradiction is that the construction of dominating masculinities depends on the defining imaginary – and very often the real – bodies of the homosexual/feminine 'other'. And more often than not, those practices arise in and through intimidation, force and violence. So how does this work in the constitution of states as masculine/heterosexual agents within the international system of great-power politics?

Queering penetration and state rape

War and conflict are easily presented as sexual penetration and heterosexual conquest, given securitized borders and allegations of violation. In Weber's words, intervention is defined within International Relations as 'the violation of one state's sovereignty by an uninvited intruder. It is rape on an international scale.'[46] To penetrate is to be masculine, and quintessentially so; to be penetrated is to be feminine and perforce, feminized. Famously Machiavelli advised princes that Fortuna is a woman to be overpowered by the adventurous in pursuit of territorial conquest. But woman is also to be feared by men as 'other', hence unreliable because unknowable.[47] Exemplars of warrior-protector masculinity, and militarized patriarchal states, are presumed, by contrast, to be resolutely steadfast, masterfully violent and impenetrable.

Puar argues that much gendered theorizing of war and conquest is dominated by heteronormative penetration paradigms, where invasions are seen as male heterosexual rape of the female land.[48] Seeing invasions as male state rape of the female nation also reproduces the heterosexual pairing of the feminine nation and thus domestic spaces within the masculinized state and its international interactions. Yet, Weber writes, 'actually it is perhaps more useful to combine them' analytically,[49] that is, to consider the binary of feminized nation and masculinized state as a unity or conflation, so as to follow how this relationality is made visible.

By pursuing our analysis to this point we can see that it is not just the invader's warrior-protector masculinity that is being guaranteed here, but also its heterosexuality. This is rather in defiance of a clearly homosexual act, that is, male penetration of a rival state, a rival male warrior-protector. Puar argues that constructing invasions as heterosexual rape of the female nation also functions to displace the 'fear – and fantasy – of the penetrated male' onto the 'safer figure of the raped female'. This displacement ultimately reinforces heteronormativity and patriarchal protectiveness.[50]

Despite the focus on heterosexual rape of the nation as a commonplace trope relating to conflict and war, Belkin actually found within the US military 'an obsession with anal penetration as a metaphor for national and corporeal violation', that is, victimized by a homosexual act. That metaphor is particularly potent for warrior-protector men whose occupation is to defend and represent their nation: 'Service members have been taught to believe that to be anally penetrated and to fail to fight back signifies that one is neither a man, nor a warrior, nor a heterosexual.'[51]

Furthermore, Belkin also found that the fear and fantasy of the raped male is central to US military culture,[52] as opposed to being displaced onto the 'safer figure of the raped female', in opposition to re-masculinizing strategies of displacement.[53] Within initiation or 'hazing' rituals there are a host of different meanings for being penetrated: sometimes it is a mark of weakness, femininity and excommunication, and at other times a marker of strength in the ability to 'take it like a man'. Hazing victims were penetrated and also sometimes forced to penetrate the penetrator in turn.[54] Often the ritualized experiences combined all these things. But despite the studied confusions and evident contradictions, the perpetrator's masculinity and heterosexuality is not in question. This is because it is guaranteed by the militarism through which the sovereign state is constituted.

GWOT – a 'probable queer' war[55]

The Global War on Terror (GWOT) was declared as a political reaction to the destruction that the United States suffered from the terrorist crimes of 11 September 2001, and subsequent acts in London and Madrid. As a supposedly defensive, yet violent and incursionary set of militarized activities, GWOT was certainly associated – as is always the case in such interventions by one state into another's territory – with ancillary geopolitical and commercial-economic motivations and interests. Whether such a campaign was appropriate or proportional as a response to a terrorist crime is one question, but whether terrorists in a network or similar clandestine organization can be the object of warfare is another. GWOT represents a metaphorical extension of the strictly inter-state conflicts envisaged by the international laws of war, where state engages with state. In that way the GWOT was conceptually abstract as a war, but fully physical in terms of what happened in the air, on the ground, at sea and in the news media.[56]

Rather similarly the notions of terror and terrorist were used to erase the internationally agreed procedures through which crimes, such as murder and property damage, are routinely policed by and through inter-state agencies. Those notions were also used to erase any more general charge of crimes against humanity, along with the international procedures through which that judicial apparatus normally operates. The GWOT formula was deployed in order to legitimate violations of state sovereignty and tactics of political assassination that defied the laws of war. These have emerged from the international system since the 16th century, yet non-observance and outright defiance have clocked up a large number of deaths and injuries.[57]

Many of these assaults and murders have been dismissed as collateral damage suffered when people are in what is termed 'the wrong place at the wrong time'. Moreover, in intention and execution GWOT was very arguably disproportionate to any actions for which a justification in international law could possibly have been framed.

As a war GWOT was a phenomenon of extremes and dichotomies: good vs bad, right vs wrong, us vs them. Binary opposites in discourses, such as these, frame an understanding of what is happening. Thus dichotomous gendered stereotypes, which are central to intelligibility, are easily mapped onto any number of political and moral dichotomies in order to amplify the stated oppositions. Through repetition and global media circulation the masculine warrior-protector ideal is understood to be rational, strong, powerful, brave and protective, while womanhood and femininity are, by contrast, irrational, weak, passive, emotional and protected. Moreover, in this stereotypical construction womenandchildren are paradigmatically lumped together, infantilizing them variously and denying them agency. That move in turn re-legitimates the warrior-protector ideal, of which the stereotypical exemplar is always male, even if very occasionally females are masculinized in this way. That gender performativity is effected through an uneasy process of metaphorical extension, which is then physically performed, albeit awkwardly.[58]

Given that national sovereignty in the international order defines and legitimates a state as an actor–agent, and that agency in this capacity requires armed forces and technologized weaponry, it follows that warrior-protector masculinity as a readily intelligible ideal applies to both the state and to its forces. The personnel in both instances are visible as overwhelmingly male, thus mirroring the concept performatively with physical realities and public displays. Both conceptual imagery and physical reality are inscribed within a competitive man vs man nested hierarchy.

Moreover, taking this warrior-protector masculinity within its heteronormative framing, heterosexuality figures in the GWOT as a renewal of virility and potency after a castrating and therefore feminizing attack. Puar and Rai characterize the 9/11 terrorist

33

crimes as 'the castration and penetration of white western phallic power by bad brown dick'. A wide range of media, including website postings, magazines and television programmes, are cited by Puar and Rai, who argue that they reveal the 'racial and sexual genealogies that imbricate the production of the radical other, as monster'. Images depicting Osama bin Laden being sodomized by white agents and technologized weapons thus feminizes and negates the masculinity of the enemy, and in so doing, reclaims its own heterosexual role as progenitor, as well as protector, in relation to womenandchildren.[59]

The heterosexuality/homosexuality binary, once again, is a hierarchy of esteem, easily deployed within processes of masculinization and re-masculinization, in order to 'other' another man, state or pseudo-state, as Al-Qaida was understood to be. Moreover, homophobia was deployed in order to legitimate, repetitively, the heterosexual reproductive family norm. Osama bin Laden was conveniently male, although if he had been female, a similar dynamic of pariah femininity would have been invoked.[60] But as a man he was also a synecdoche for his associates and networks, which were presumed to be overwhelmingly male, even though shadowy and unknowable. As a feminized monster-man he was a metaphor as well for an unknowable vortex of inhuman and unhuman evil.

Homophobic depictions that queered the Muslim 'other' were happening alongside other discourses that constituted the Muslim 'other' as homophobic, misogynistic and backward, in contrast to the progressive American self as tolerant of homosexuality, 'but sexually, racially, and gendered normal'.[61] This figuration was identified by Puar as 'homonationalism', functioning within a homonormative nationalism. In certain contexts gay identities were embraced nationalistically at the same time as gays embraced national identities.[62]

It has been said in speech and text, and depicted in cartoons and memes, that the US was feminized by the 9/11 attacks. And as many scholars have noted, GWOT served to re-masculinize it. US borders had not been so obviously penetrated by intruders since the Pearl Harbor attacks of 7 December 1941, which were much cited after 9/11 as analogies and justifications unfolded. Was the American state feminized because it had failed as warrior-protector to safeguard its feminized nation from rapist penetration? Or was it feminized because the male-personified warrior-state had itself been penetrated and thus subordinated by a rival dominating male? Or both?

The American nation was certainly penetrated by the 9/11 terrorist attacks, because the hijackings took the warrior-protector border defences completely by surprise, undermining the control and strength of the masculine security state. Ultimately the hijackers reduced two major phallic symbols, the twin towers in New York City, to 'a couple of holes', and penetrated the visible 'opening' to US military might at the Pentagon. Indeed the official 9/11 report detailed the shocking extent to which the US military establishment couldn't even get rapid-response fighter planes going in the right direction, mimicking rather precisely commonplace misogynist claims of female incompetence. In the America-centric media, however, that analogy was unsayable because it was doubly taboo: penetration and femininity. Post-9/11 the foreign and domestic security policies of the US were intentionally hypermasculinized in response.

Those theatrical actions of counter-terrorism and invasion, up to and including hi-tech assassination squads, were incessantly cited in media commentary and images, projecting the symbolic integrity of the US as international warrior-commander. The state as patriarchal protector of its citizens domestically was used to legitimize the PATRIOT Act in the US, thus increasing the state's control over its citizens, resident aliens and 'green card' non-citizens. It was also used to justify full-scale wars in Afghanistan and Iraq.

When the US invaded Iraq in 2003, its president, Saddam Hussein, was personally targeted as the enemy. He was thus hypermasculinized into an opponent somehow comparable to, and worthy of, the world's greatest military power. As ruler-dictator he was discursively separated from the people of Iraq, who made up the feminized, victimized nation, as figured in American presidential tropes. Those discursive constructions separate the people and the nation from the state and its leaders. That move guarantees the construction of the American invader as masculine in warrior-protector mode, and the leader's embodiment of the rogue state as feminine, thus subordinated through penetration/invasion.

As well as warrior state and militarized war-making, the patriarchal–paternal element of warrior-protector masculinity was also deployed. Doing that required the enemy to be misogynistic, a characterization easily portrayed through Euro-American eyes as images of burqa-clad women. In that gaze they are assumed to have been denied education, and to be subject to being whipped or stoned to death for breaking sex-specific rules. Female oppression to that degree is a very real and pressing issue, of course, whereas weaponizing that idea to support GWOT is a very different matter. Moreover, following the same popularized assumptions circulated to support 'western' interventions, Islamic men were exoticized in a hypersexualized way as polygamous. Polygamy is an unthinkable concept within Christian heteronormativity, and also illegal in most 'developed' states. Islamic and other exceptions to this imperial norm were thus doubly marginalized and immoralized.

The George W. Bush administration, in messages notably articulated by the First Lady, narrated a feminized humanitarian justification for the violent invasions of sovereignty through which GWOT operated. Hunt and Rygiel summarize: 'This engendering of the war not only constructs the "victimized women to be rescued", but also their "hyper-masculine rescuers" and "cowardly oppressors".'[63] The enemy had to be imaginatively portrayed as threatening enough to justify the technologized warfare undertaken by the 'coalition of the willing'. In turn, the GWOT had to be constructed as moral enough to warrant the deaths and injuries of American and European soldiers, along with the numerous deaths and injuries suffered by supposed terrorist associates, including many women and children.

Of course GWOT was also fought on the home front. Repetitive militarism affirms the state as protector of the nation, understood as its own people. It also empowers the state to recruit and conscript some of its own people, overwhelmingly male, to function as warriors. States thus provide real individuals to enact the otherwise rather abstract understanding of itself as sovereign-with-arms. At that point the competitive masculine hierarchies, through which subordination ensures domination, visibly merge: inter-state dynamics with intra-troop dynamics. Whether the scene was the immediate aftermath of the 9/11 twin towers collapses, involving firefighters and police personnel, or the overseas deployment of weaponized military forces, the political imagery and media images repetitively foregrounded males and largely excluded or marginalized women. That masculinist pattern follows the easy intelligibility of the warrior-protector ideal. However, those same firefighters and policemen were also shown crying in public, yet still exerting strength and bravery. In that way they were tough yet tender heroes.[64] Characteristically this move resolves an apparent gender contradiction through a masculinizing redescription. Thus it recovers the heroic warrior and validates the patriarchal protector.

Thus GWOT legitimated the tough yet tender male hero in order to reproduce patriarchy at home as inherently benevolent. Firepower as penis power was directed elsewhere in order to generate the presumed security of the feminized, infantilized domestic spaces of nation. Concurrently, American and allied European foreign policies deployed 'hard' military initiatives that were mirrored through the media as warrior masculinity.[65] In protecting the nested states in the rank-ordered 'coalition of the willing' it was also their job to enforce heteronormative purity by assassinating and obliterating a monstrous evil-'other' male rival, personified as Osama bin Laden.[66]

Torture and taboo

In April 2004 something unusual happened that disrupted the narration of warrior-protector masculinity undertaken by the US and its coalitional partners. The global media published photographs of the racialized and sexualized torture of Iraqi males at the Abu Ghraib prison in Baghdad, established after the US invasion in 2003.[67] Those shocking images damaged the moral and heterosexual, perforce male-centric purity of the masculinizing narratives through which the GWOT was generally reported. Even in reportage that was critical on various grounds, the media seldom traced out the processes through which gender-stereotyping was deployed in order to legitimate the overall enterprise, not least because it was difficult to imagine masculinity in the circumstances as other than warrior-protector.

The photographs were meaningful precisely because they contradicted male-centric warrior-protector masculinity. This is because they portrayed warrior-protectors who were not just using, but evidently enjoying, activities that were far outside the norms of heterosexual purity.[68] Male prisoners of war, understood as such within GWOT's framing of the American invasion, were stripped naked and forced to masturbate. Some were sodomized with implements. Others had what was said to be menstrual blood smeared on their bodies by female soldiers.[69] As Eisenstein puts it: 'men who are raped ... are "humiliated" because they are treated like women. ... Men who are naked and exposed remind us of the vulnerability usually associated with being a woman.'[70] The fact that there were women witnesses to, and women taking part in, the torture of men – and in male-exclusive settings and tableaux – doubled the feminization by upending the gender hierarchy. The actions of those women contradicted the dominant and dominating maleness of the warrior-protector masculine ideal.

Moreover, the warrior-protector masculine ideal is very white and very imperial, as the stagings within the photographs reveal, once that postcolonial interpretive lens is applied. Mirzoeff argues that in the Abu Ghraib ritual tortures, 'sodomy denotes and connotes a hegemonic power relation that classifies certain practices and bodies as deviant. ... A sodomite is, then, what the imperial subject is not.' What we see is not a representation of deviance, as the prisoners were made to simulate sodomizing acts. Rather, we see the 'assertion of the imperial body, necessarily straight and white, over the confused sodomizing mass of the embodied spectacle that is the object of empire'.[71]

This incident was a disruptive moment in an otherwise predictable representation of events and political process of repetitive political justification. Warrior-protector masculinity, as an activity of gender heterosexuality, does not include or countenance sexual activity – even heterosexual activity – as consistent within warrior-like behaviour. Or rather, any sexual aspect of heroic warriordom is marginalized to the private 'family' sphere, to the exceptional, to the excusable, to the recreational. So in whatever way sexual activity takes place it is a visible lapse in 'doing the business' as warrior-ideal, and thus an intrusion to be smoothed over.

In the GWOT hard interrogation and allegations of torture were acknowledged in and through official processes and press releases. Female soldiers were sometimes mentioned and featured as advertisements for gender equality, understood, of course, on militarized and thus masculinizing terms. However, the photographs portrayed male and female military personnel together mimicking pornographic humiliations in disturbing ways involving criminal assaults and graphic tortures. In no way did these activities conform to conventional notions of serious-minded, asexual interrogations, or even to punishments that might be meted out to combatants who had threatened the innocent, whether people or states. Thus the photographs portrayed the deliberate destruction of the foundational binaries through which morality, gender, sexuality, sovereignty and warrior-protector masculinity had repetitively made sense. Those binaries were: heterosexuality vs sexual perversion, militarized disciplinary pain vs pleasure-seeking indiscipline, male domination vs female passivity, militarized hierarchy vs unauthorised actions, and doubtless many other binary oppositions through which the commonplace intelligibility of 'proper' military activities is constructed.

Contrary efforts to explain away the shock, and to marginalize the perpetrators as exceptions, were swiftly deployed, but were never wholly successful. Those efforts could never fully succeed because the obscene images and shocking reportage remain in the public domain, and their character speaks for itself. The photographs do this because they portray what repetitive purity represses. Soldier Lynndie England and the other military women involved became 'gender decoys' who diverted attention from the homosexual and homoerotic nature of the acts committed by male soldiers. Thus they recovered the heteronormativity of the American military. That move ensured that the masculine exemplar was reinscribed as moral, both as warrior and as protector.[72] The decoys also gave viewers an object on which to shift, as Brittain states, the 'revulsion they might feel at their own enjoyment' of these racialized and sexualized fantasies.[73]

Any breach of normative purity can be constructed as queer, one way or another, so that is not the point here. Nor is it the point that mergers of sexuality and warfare are known to be ubiquitous, at least among those with first-hand experience. Otherwise we would not have the repetitive instantiations and defences of warrior-protector masculinity as pure, together with the familiar demonization of deviant females as a diversionary feint. The point here is not that the normal marginalizes the queer, but that the normal – despite its ready intelligibility – makes no sense *without* the queer. Normalization is a process that repetitively marginalizes the queerness that inevitably appears, despite all such melancholic efforts. Abu Ghraib was the norm without which purity cannot be understood. And if purity is not understood over and against an evil 'other', then neither GWOT nor warrior-protector masculinity makes sense either.

Visibly queered heterosexual masculinity

Representations of heterosexual masculinity combined with queer masculinities, notably homosexual penetration – appearing together as the state – are actually well established in mainstream media discourse. That imagery and those images often function as hermeneutic hooks to get the attention of readers and viewers. Having done its job, the queerness disappears, so that normal 'surface' meanings reinforce the political message in familiar terms. Hence queerness appears briefly in the foreground but then rapidly recedes, almost forever, into the background, there to be forgotten.

The commonplace term 'couple', as understood in heteronormative parlance, refers to a man and woman in a romantic and sexualized relationship. That language is also commonly used to describe a relationship between two states, such as the US and China, for example. A cartoon, heading an article in *The Economist* titled 'The odd couple', represented Uncle Sam (standing in for President Obama, so as not to distract from the US as racially white), and President Hu Jintao ('Asianized' and in a Mao jacket), as a heteronormal couple in a marital bed. A red rose has been laid carefully on the coverlet, and the man-state duo is framed with visible phallic weaponry on each side – a baseball bat and a Kalashnikov.[74] The title, however, points out the same-sex oddity.[75] The realm of media representation thrives on queerness as both hermeneutic 'hook' and as tabloid content, making it difficult for the viewer to miss the message. Gender and sexuality are, of course, not the whole story here, given the imperial whiteness of the relationship in question.

If the characters were naked and crudely sexual they would be less easily characterized than they are in their iconic costumes as male-embodied states. 'The odd couple' title refers some readers, at least, to the 1968 movie-classic based on a highly successful Broadway play of three years earlier. The (then) frisson of two married men moving in together to 'keep house' and develop their odd 'marital' relationship clearly represented fantasies and desires that could not appear other than as comedic parody. That kind of cinematic representation is now understood as making queerness visible on the screen, yet disavowing it then as even possible, or even sayable, within the dramatic narrative. Such things are so strange as to be at the outer edge of truthful speech, at least in movie dialogue, even as visuality presents a clear depiction.

As re-represented over the years this use of 'odd couple' queerness as hermeneutic hook becomes quickly intelligible. Perhaps the initial idea was to shock, but the tactic has settled in to being a commonplace trope, 'in bed together' in textual terms. The trope guarantees that any queer relationship attributed to the masculinized heterosexual state will be just as quickly backgrounded. This happens not merely to restore heteronormativity unthreatened, but also to work a similar effect on great power relations among masculine state-actors. The sexualized, gendered and raced legitimacy, through which International Relations and state-centric international politics operate, thus draws strength from the tenacity of heteronormatively competitive male male relationships, precisely when seeing is not meant to be believing.

In covering international politics, using text placed just below the queer cartoon, *The Economist* readily adopts the straight mode of political and sexual normality. It uses commonplace and easily intelligible metaphors of romance and sex: 'The heart of the problem is a profound uncertainty in both countries about where the relationship may lead. In many respects the two countries are in the same bed.' The uncertainty, mentioned by *The Economist*, however, takes us back to the queer anxieties embedded in heterosexual masculinity itself. The rather anxious-looking Uncle Sam, foil to the strong and smug-looking Hu Jintao, is safely re-masculinized at the end of the actual article. There China is portrayed textually as a female host for the great power talks, feminized as misguided, emotional, irrational, needing firm masculine control: 'Locking up activists, as China has been wont to do recently, is not a lasting solution. Mr Obama should meet some of them in Beijing to find out for himself. If his hosts have a hissy fit, let them.' Textual mention of Mr Obama here, rather than visual representation of a black man as US president, lands us in a reliably abstracted, disembodied and de-racialized white heterosexual normality.

There are numerous similar textual and visual imageries through which international politics is constructed, all typically used with the same logic: 'hooking' viewers and readers with queerness, then backgrounding it, and thus restoring the political/heterosexual norms. Viewers and readers are thus returned to the security of states as safely gendered masculine actors. One of these tropes is 'bedfellow', as in 'strange bedfellows'. That word in a literal mode refers to a person with whom one shares a bed, something in Anglophone and similar cultures that has a distinctly sexual implication. Thus the 'hook' is that we can see these nation-states as gay male lovers, the quintessential object and subject of queerness as it has emerged historically.

However, using the term 'bedfellow' in this sexualized way, instead of using the term 'lovers' to mark full sexualization, makes a further mockery out of the state-to-state relationship. The implication is that the two are just using each other as transactional competitive masculinity directs, whether the activity is commercial or sexual, in contrast to engaging in acts of love and building up trust. That kind of uncompetitive relationship is thus taken to be feminine. Queer innuendo positions sex as a transaction among competitive males in relation to each other. Same-sex competition in that way is normalized in relation to masculinity and thus rescued from queerness and femininity. That same male–male competition then drives heterosexuality as the exchange of women into or out of marriage by men as nested hierarchical indices of masculinity. Those female tokens thus enable and index the hierarchies of power that men exercise over each other, and through that means, secure the gender-order hierarchy.[76]

The same can be said about the term 'marriage of convenience'. *The Economist* refers to 'crude oil's marriage of convenience' in order to introduce readers to a factual discussion of oil flows from Russia to China, set in contextual contrast to previous inter-state hostilities. That marriage is not something they really want to do, but they will do 'whatever it takes' in the cut-throat masculine worlds of geopolitical and economic competition. These discursive manoeuvres in textual and visual imagery 'notice' both queerness within heterosexuality, and feminine positioning within masculinity. But that discursive manoeuvre then backgrounds both, and thus re-legitimates both, within the gender order of male domination.[77] That gender order, as Butler explains, is an effect of the sexual order in and through the marital and kinship ordering of binary-sexed individuals.[78]

Overt queerness and hypervisible masculinity

On Valentine's Day in 2003, the front page of the *Daily Mirror* featured an image of President George W. Bush and Prime Minister Tony Blair kissing, surrounded by a heart-shape with the headline, 'Make love not war'. This went beyond innuendo, because it used an overt homosexual imaginary to delegitimize the UK–US 'special relationship' in the context of the Iraq War. To destabilize this political relationship, by making it about love and romance, renders it effeminate and thus queer in relation to both the competitive order of man-to-man heterosexual relations and state-to-state relations through which the international system arises. To this feminization can be added explicit homosexuality as hyperbole.

43

More recently, the US media attempted to delegitimize President Trump by portraying his relationship with President Putin as one of gay male lovers. This explicit depiction was in a cartoon, published in *The New York Times*.[79] Even though in the article this figuration turns out to be only a fantasy in Trump's mind, 'the implication is very much a reality', as detailed by comment in the *Independent*: '*The New York Times* wants you to think that Trump is gay. Not only is Trump gay, but Trump is gay for Putin. Trump wants to have gay sex with Putin. Trump possibly even wants to be in a gay relationship with Putin.'[80]

The point here is that this political dialogue about sexuality was playing out in media outlets that are usually considered liberal and therefore sympathetic to gay rights and equal respect. While being used to invoke humour, 'the whole thing is deeply, deeply homophobic', as the *Independent* concluded.[81] Trump was being feminized by homosexuality, a tropological tactic still being used by supposedly progressive media outlets. The effect-by-juxtaposition is to discipline masculinity and to reconstitute its heterosexual normality.[82] The irony and double power of this imagery is that both Trump and Putin are self-portrayed hypermasculine political figures who are also sometimes accused of being homophobic.

Concurrently, that which is obviously homoerotic can be recoded as hypermasculine. This works both ways. President Johnson was reputed to get his penis out in conversations at the White House, thus producing the classic example of this from the heterosexual perspective. But this recoding also works from 'the other side'.

Mackintosh has developed a very useful distinction between homosexuality as desire and practice, and manliness as object of identification between 'self' and 'other', often enacted in pseudo-military body-building activities. He notes that the experts on the latter are really the former, as homosexual men are really the men most crucially interested in manliness. However, this is not to say that heterosexual men are unaware that they are in a zone where the hetero/homo binary distinction begins to look and feel quite fragile.[83]

There is a fine line, Mackintosh argues, between being self-interested in bodily manliness, and being sexually interested in the men who embody it. The notion that displays of manliness are for the benefit of heterosexual women, rather than an activity within competitive masculine hierarchies, falls quite flat. Within those hierarchies women are tokens of value, not human beings entitled to their own desires. The masculine/heterosexual apparatus does not permit an independent female gaze, because being looked at sexually puts men in the quintessentially feminized position of being a sexual object.[84]

As a personified male, the state is fraternal and encourages men's homosocial bonding as a way of discouraging homosexuality. Most commonly this occurs in military ranks, sports of all kinds, men's clubs, and politics itself. Puar sums this up: 'Heterosexuality works to secure the uninterrogated, unremarked upon access to homosocial spaces; through its prohibition of homosexuality, heterosexuality sanctions homosociability while naming and producing the disallowed homosexuality. Thus the homosexual–heterosexual binary is a primary rather than secondary facet of the project of nationalism.'[85] Homosexuality and its association with feminization can be seen as a means of disciplining both masculinity and militarism, making both heteronormative. In sum, states are 'heteronormative because of, rather than despite, homosexuality'.[86]

Thus the homosexual imaginary supports, rather than contradicts, the imaginary of the straight, impenetrable, hypermasculine soldier. Servicemen participating in homoerotic and other norm-transgressing rituals have something onto which to displace their own anxieties about what they are doing and what is happening to them. It is these inherent, constitutive and defining contradictions that make up masculinity. As Belkin concludes, 'being penetrated embodies all of these notions simultaneously: strength/dominance/control on the one hand and weakness/subordination/powerlessness on the other'. Those confusions, however, 'have helped to structure military masculinity as an archetypal ideal and to sustain the production of compliant, obedient warriors'. Thus the contradictions surrounding penetration are – like many other contradictions – inherent in masculinity. Those contradictions are made to seem natural, 'almost as if there were no contradictions at all', in Belkin's summary words.[87]

Queerness is subject to concealment within heteronormative warrior-protector masculinity. But those queer practices necessarily leak out because they are so pervasive, after which they are disavowed. Masculinity itself is disciplined by the homosexual imaginary, and by any number of other queer transgressions. These transgressions tell us what masculinity 'really' is, by showing us what it supposedly 'isn't'.

Therefore it is no surprise to find that states as masculine actors rely on feminine or homosexual 'otherness' exemplified by, or projected onto, rival states in the international system. For the masculinized people who embody the masculine state actor, the public performance of the panoply of formalized ritual meetings keeps their own physicality safely and correctly coded as masculine and heterosexual, with few, if any, exceptions. These performances are constitutive of the normalization that secures both the personal and institutional ideal of heterosexual masculinity, even when, on occasion, the personal side is embodied in females. Representing the institutional side of the state as ordered ranks of embodied females isn't an option that is available at present.

The masculinity of the state-actor transcends queer contradictions, hence the official photoshoots of in-office female leaders display carefully costumed 'transitions' to masculine, *faux*-military attire and demeanour. While she was female defence minister in Spain, the visibly pregnant Carme Chacón changed her attire to *faux*-military black-and-white in uniform-style tailoring that trimmed out the bump line.

Although failed, fragile or weak states are feminized in relation to successful states, understood as such within the competitive hierarchies of great power politics, they are also by implication emasculated in relation to themselves. Weak or failed states once were, or were attempting to be, strong successful states. In that way they would become fully masculinized, heteronormative state-actors in the international system. Failing or otherwise weak and fragile states are by definition in need of protection and rescue by more masculine warrior-protector powers. And within that logic, it is not just states that need rescuing, but also the inhabitants within them.

When a state is labelled failed, fragile or weak, it is therefore emasculated. It is further feminized when other states move in as rescuers.[88] The political use of those terms indicates, as Duffield says, 'a new willingness by the west to engage weak or defunct state entities developmentally'.[89] In state-building practices then, fragile states are being taught by rescuer-states to be proper men, thus performing heterosexual masculinity through diligent pupil-hood. They are then tested, by the rescuers, on how well the trainee masculine state-actor performs in protecting 'his own' womenandchildren.

As has been shown, states are feminized through pejorative terms and allusions. They can be re-masculinized at the same time in order to demonstrate their potential power. This can be either as a threat to other states, or as homosocial big brotherly respect mirrored in juvenile hero worship. Moreover, by feminizing and thus discrediting another state or states, the self-styled strong, masculinized great power states are legitimated, as are the masculinized actors who embody them.

Costa Rica – a 'probable queer' state[90]

As Cohn and Enloe point out, ideas about masculinity are 'intricately and invisibly interwoven with ideas about national security'.[91] The personified state, with its masculinizing discourses of sovereignty, is necessarily imbued with militarism and war-making, even if these are denominated as purely defensive, as is usually the case. The military is one of the leading and most visible sites where dominating masculinity is eroticized and institutionalized, as Hopton argues, and also a site where heteronormative nationalism, along with its requisite homoeroticism, is produced.[92]

Against the gendered and therefore sexualized backdrop of states as masculine actors, we could ask a testing question, so as to develop a starkly defining contrast: what could a deviant, abnormal, 'probable queer' state look like? Can a state without an army, then, ever be masculine *and* straight, and thus a proper member of the competitive order of patriarchy in the international system?

When Costa Rica gave up its army in 1949, it metaphorically cut off its own phallus/penis, and thus became a eunuch. What then happens to the gender and sexual identity of Costa Rica?

As it castrated itself willingly, did it just emasculate itself and therefore uncode itself as a man? Or was it forced into doing this and thus feminized?

Given the clarity of the symbolic discourse and textual imagery through which states are understood as necessarily masculine and masculinizing, these are important questions to ask and not at all fanciful. Rather, the fact that they might strike most readers as fanciful tells us already that they are subjects we should be curious about.[93] Closures of that kind tell us how political forces work very hard to maintain and reinforce the repetitions that make the status quo unproblematic. In that way incuriosity secures traditional modes of knowledge as fully comprehensive.[94]

Sjoberg offers some helpful insights here. These include 'the assumption that clarity can come from understanding what [body] parts a person has – that person has a penis, therefore, that person is a man'. Hence we see the consequent 'intolerance for confusion and liminality in our understandings of trans-bodies'.[95] Applying that analysis to states, we can easily see that the military is the most obvious of its masculine credentials. A phallus/penis is a masculine credential for a man, so without one, Costa Rica cannot penetrate anyone, and, perforce, it is undefended against penetration. Therefore as a man, positioned within the patriarchal order, he/it cannot protect 'his' household of womenandchildren.

So did Costa Rica transition into being a woman? Or did Costa Rica then become asexual as a eunuch? After giving up its army, Costa Rica has projected – and has had projected onto it – the feminized image of a peaceful polity and an egalitarian society. Both of those are at odds with the dominating and competitive power structures of warrior-protector masculinity. Indeed, Costa Rica itself had a female president from 2010 to 2014, highly unusual in the international world of heads of state.

What is surprising is that Costa Rica appears to be treated as a man by other men in the order of manly states. As portrayed in the media, Costa Rica is masculinized in positive ways as an international economic performer and exemplary global citizen, even praised for the fatherly delivery of its domestic policies. It is celebrated for consistently being among the top Latin American countries in the Human Development Index, and it achieves good ratings on environmental sustainability. 'Costa Rica', *The Economist* writes, 'has been a small haven of egalitarian, democratic tranquillity since a 1948–1949 revolution which abolished the army, assigned the defence budget to education, and created a powerful, paternalist state.'[96]

So, then, is Costa Rica not completely and utterly queer, given that it used to have a phallus/penis but got rid of it? Yet it still presents itself as, and, more importantly, is treated as, a man? If Costa Rica can still be a man without a phallus/penis, what could that mean for the heterosexual masculinity of the state as such, because 'stateness' itself is constructed on that very basis?

The invocation of masculinity, and necessarily heterosexuality, in the comments above, can be explained by the subject that *The Economist* was dealing with, namely Central America, and the great-power political context. In that context Costa Rica is re-masculinized, and therefore heterosexualized, in relation to its feminized Central American counterparts, because it functions as a properly powerful state domestically.

Although some of the nearby states were military dictatorships during this period, and thus hypermasculine, the masculine traits that *The Economist* is keen to privilege are, as Hooper argues, 'bourgeois-rational ... rather than overtly military ones'. Or in other words, the masculinizing ranks of international business, particularly celebrated by *The Economist*, are modelled on the soldierly ranks of the military. Indeed the circulation of those elites across that supposed occupational divide is very well documented.[97]

However, Costa Rica's identity is also defined by *The Economist* in masculinizing terms in relation to the supposedly uncivilized 'others' surrounding it. Those 'others' are portrayed as disorderly zones of Central American criminals and terrorist radicals, inimical to the orderly flows of international business. Costa Rica's neighbour to the north is Nicaragua, whose domestic politics and international ambitions *The Economist* has regarded with no little suspicion. By contrast, as a re-masculinized, and so properly a manly state, Costa Rica represents for *The Economist*, and similar media outlets and academic commentators, a useful bulwark against further Central American unruliness. On the other border, as *The Economist* sees it, the well-pacified,

American colonial regime in Panama requires a buffer state to help protect its eponymous canal as a vital strategic pinch-point in world trade.[98] In geopolitical terms, then, Costa Rica's queerness arises and survives, but in a liminal fashion, as a buffer between colonization and confrontation.

Is Costa Rica actually faking it?

In considering the gendered and sexualized character of queer Costa Rica, the trans concepts of 'in-ness' and 'out-ness', derived from Sjoberg's work, also apply.[99] In international politics generally, and moving away from the great power commercialism that *The Economist* focuses on, we can see that Costa Rica, from the 'out' perspective, is a peaceful, pacifist, green, civilized, progressive country. It is considered a 'global good Samaritan' and builds its identity on its commitment to human rights.[100] It has a strong feminist movement, as well as woman-friendly and gay-friendly domestic policies, at least apparently and to some degree – it is marketed as a gay-friendly tourist destination and has featured as number one on a top ten gay destinations list on TripAdvisor. Lacking the masculine attributes of army and penis, it follows that the absence of war-making accoutrements makes Costa Rica a peaceful state. Because peace is associated with femininity, and therefore with women, we can safely presume that Costa Rica, from this 'out' perspective, could very well be feminized.

However, when looking 'in' at Costa Rica, it is not as queer or as feminine as it might first appear. From the 'in' perspective, officials do not make the claims that are ascribed to Costa Rica from the 'out' perspective. Rather than self-identifying as a womanly, motherly, altruistic state, promoting peaceful conflict resolution and human rights guarantees, Costa Rica frames these activities, as we look 'in', as ultimately in the national interest. Those activities are therefore a rational, calculating 'hard-minded' hence 'bourgeois-rational' masculine set of policy goals.[101]

Furthermore, while Costa Rica may appear peaceful and progressive from the 'out' perspective, the 'in' perspective shows us that its militaristic police force and secret army for drugs-busting operations are hypermasculinized on a familiar model.[102] Despite the active feminist movement, misogyny is rife in Costa Rica, and rates of violence against women do not differ much from those in other Central American countries, such as its neighbours Nicaragua and Panama.

Moreover, although Costa Rica does not have a military, it is able to define its masculinity and statehood through another, and perhaps more influential heterosexualizing, homophobic and misogynistic institution: football or soccer. Remarkably, Costa Ricans make the absence of an army into a masculinized plus point. Costa Rican football/soccer fans have carried banners reading: 'In Costa Rica we have no soldiers only soccer players.'[103] This appropriation of an absence not only makes up for the lack of an army, but also serves to *doubly* masculinize its football team. Somewhat similarly within Costa Rica's masculinizing institution of football, homosexual or queer practices are incorporated and recoded as masculine and heterosexual. When Costa Rica defeated the US at football/soccer, Costa Rican fans were reported to sing, 'we won, we conquered, we did them up the ass'.[104] In this instance 'them' refers both to the US players themselves and the US as a state-actor. 'We' is the nation-state of Costa Rica, celebrating success in the nested hierarchies of man–over–man domination and subordination.

Costa Rica thus redefines what it is to be masculine by channelling its representational efforts into one institution, instead of splitting those efforts between two. Does Costa Rica then become doubly masculine for not having an army? This was evident in coverage of its unexpected success during the 2014 World Cup: 'This soccer team is Costa Rica's army';[105] 'The small Central American nation may not have an army, but their players fought valiantly on the Salvador field of battle, holding the star-studded Dutch attack goalless for 120 minutes';[106] and again, 'La Sele [the name of the Costa Rican national soccer team] is the country's army, and the team is marching through Brazil'.[107]

However, the idealized masculinity attributed to Costa Rica during the World Cup was also tempered by some feminine/infantile discourse, such as: 'get back into the World Cup and root for an inspired Cinderella team',[108] and here we have 'the Costa Rican vision of their World Cup fairytale'.[109] But those attributions are rather more to do with the storytelling conventions of sports journalism, which understand defeat as feminization, than they are to do with Costa Rica's position in the international state system of competitive nested hierarchies of man-over-man/state-over-state.

Sports competitions are even more visible than armies. They are far more transparent in showing everyone how man-on-man competitiveness works. And through uniforms and rituals they are very successful in repetitively citing the hallmarks of militarization, albeit without the weaponry. Moreover, they are organizationally nationalized and nationalistically celebrated.

Costa Rica may be functioning, when we look 'in', as a strong masculine state, yet on an international level, when we place ourselves 'out' in the realm of global politics, it is still unarmed, vulnerable and thus feminine. '[I]t can't be denied that, devoid of a standing army, they [Costa Ricans] feel more vulnerable than ever', as the blog Foreign Policy in Focus puts it.[110] From that perspective Costa Rica's residual masculinity/ heterosexuality may be based on the fact that it has not been penetrated militarily with border incursions.[111]

But if Costa Rica were to be penetrated, would it then be represented as queer? When states penetrate other states, are they really penetrating that which is already deemed feminine, understood as the nation? Or are they penetrating the state itself, and thus feminizing/emasculating it? Should penetration by states, affected on other states, be conceptualized as male-on-male rape? Those activities are well documented in fraternity hazing and military rituals, and in the sheer male-dominated violence of conflict zones.[112] Elsewhere those activities are understood subliminally and, of course, unofficially, as they are well into the unsayable. But as we have seen here, they are certainly not unthinkable.

Conclusions

States as masculine actors are necessarily queer. Queer states, through the efforts of the international system, are still masculine, albeit in suitably subordinated or displaced ways. Although masculinity is co-constitutive with heterosexuality, and therefore with homoeroticsm, male rape and even homosexual liaisons, those contradictions of queerness can be reframed in a standardly masculine way. That tactic works because, in Donaldson's words, masculinity has 'the ability to impose a definition of the situation, to set the terms in which events are understood and issues discussed, to formulate ideas and define morality'.[113] That is how and why disavowal sticks.

Even peacefulness can be coded as strong, masculine and heterosexual. Despite the fact that Costa Rica may actually be more militarized than appears at first glance, the official line is that it isn't militarized but still has legitimacy and credibility in the international system. Other state-actors in the system concur, thus preserving the façade through which the required gendered and sexual uniformity of the international system is made to appear, and the military-economic competitions are legitimated.

What does Costa Rica tell us, then? It tells us about sovereignty, through which the state is legitimized, and through which it legitimizes itself, both domestically and internationally. Sovereignty, as Kantola states, 'refers to those social rules and practices that the state must follow to enact the characteristics of a state'. The state does this through warrior-protector masculinity that defines it in relation to its self-styled 'others' in global politics.[114] In GWOT, the American warrior-state constructed itself not only as the hypermasculine protector of its own inhabitants, but also as the paternalistic protectors of the Afghan nation's womenandchildren.[115]

Masculinity thus calls the shots, not least about itself. Crucial to its self-protection and self-validation is the invocation and disavowal of queerness, in whatever way or at whatever level. Missing that dynamic is to take masculinity at its own word, and to foster complicity with the powers-that-be. The next two chapters take us into the world of great-power politics through which the terms of trade are set so that sellers of firepower can meet buyers of weaponry, competitively and face to face.

Further reading

Raewyn W. Connell (2006) *Masculinities* (2nd edn), Cambridge: Polity.

Charlotte Hooper (1999) *Manly States: Masculinities, International Relations, and Gender Politics*, New York: Columbia University Press.

Stevi Jackson (1999) *Heterosexuality in Question*, London: Sage Publications.

Jasbir Puar (2007) *Terrorist Assemblages: Homonationalism in Queer Times. Next Wave*, Durham, NC: Duke University Press.

Cynthia Weber (2016) *Queer International Relations: Sovereignty, Sexuality and the Will to Knowledge*, Oxford: Oxford University Press.

3

Arms and the Men

Boys-and-toys masculinity – 'blowing shit up'[1] – is a very familiar
spectacle and utterly routine practice, whether in capital city
parades or in Hollywood blockbusters. However, those whose
communities, homes and bodies are shattered or extinguished
as a result are in a very different position. As human beings they
suffer through uncountable miseries, but through the media they
become just part of the picture, mere characters in a narrative.
For them it can't be much compensation being a sacrifice to
'history' as an ongoing academic and political project. As a
threat and as a practice this use of weaponry all 'makes sense'
within the hierarchy of competitive state-actors known as the
'international system'. But considered in isolation from that
national/international framing, 'blowing shit up' doesn't look
at all constructive or admirable. Indeed, unless that destructive
power is framed in national security terms, it signals criminality,
gangsterism and terrorism.

By contrast, militarized and glamourized hypermasculinity
is upfront in state-sponsored strategies for physical and
economic security, as states define these things.[2] Together
they create a stable zone of mutual legitimation: the state
legitimates militarized masculinity and endorses its alpha male
pretensions; the militarized masculinity legitimates the state
as a powerful actor in its competitive relation to other states.
That familiar configuration projects governmental prowess
to an international audience and mirrors the self-imaging
fantasies of politicians, who are overwhelmingly men. All
of that militarized firepower and masculinizing regalia is put

on display in celebrations, ceremonies, media images, feature films – often produced in cooperation with national militaries – that are consumed as entertainment, popular culture, even fashion.[3] Militarized masculinity is a major mode through which legitimated history making and racializing homosociality merge as a didactic political/patriarchal force. That familiar set of representations dominates the digital news media, nation-making mythologies, required curricular textbooks and history channel streaming services.

Thus this gendered conjunction of boys-and-toys is normalized to the point where gender seems to disappear, and men and maleness become a generically human ideal: self-protection, defence of the realm, the strong protecting the weak. As we have seen, it is difficult to imagine a state that doesn't repetitively perform the definition and representation of statehood in this way, instancing generic humanity and the human predicament. However, those representations also self-evidently instance male bodies and a moralized masculinity. Masculinity flickers between the two in the mind so rapidly that they merge into one idea, normalized through repetition, and invoking consent, that is, tacit unthinking acceptance, or at least disinclination to active contra-engagement. It is difficult to pull this apart analytically, never mind as a practicality, because it so pervasively tells us what it is to be human, modern – and male.

In these performances, states aspire competitively to subordinate other states within the nested hierarchies of warrior-protector masculinity through which they understand their role as international actors. Or, in other words, the security dilemma – through which a supposed human nature is understood as always-already threatening a war-of-all-against-all, a war of every man against every man – is actually about militarized masculinity understood as the state and figured in its leaders. Even presidents and prime ministers, who are elected as civilian heads of government, are, by definition, commanders-in-chief of their armed forces, even though they are generally not uniformed up as such. And in some cases, of course, the commanders-in-chief are de facto/de jure heads of government, taking more or less time to restore control of the state, and of its military, to civilians.

Something that isn't so regularly displayed and performed within this warrior-protector framing is the money. Gender constructs the warrior-protector state – men as protectors of womenandchildren. And the state legitimates the weaponry and the militarism, which cost huge amounts of money.[4] Staging national days and heroic displays is certainly part of the story, using spectacle to displace economics and to keep the money invisible. Budgetary discussions about money are consigned to 'talking heads' in media analysis at best, and highly secret 'deals' that appear only when leaked at worst. Hypermasculinity thus occupies public attention, and stigmatizes economic investigation. Cost–benefit analysis then looks unpatriotic and risky.[5]

The technologies of waging war, of inflicting and facilitating violence, are part of a hypersophisticated, multibillion-dollar industry that, until the 'opening for signature' of the international Arms Trade Treaty in 2013, was less regulated than the international trade in bananas.[6] The trade in conventional weapons, which includes small arms and 'everything else', is dominated by the five permanent members of the UN Security Council – China, France, Russia, the UK and USA – along with Germany and Spain. Although many arms companies were nationalized during the 20th century, the majority are once again private enterprises, many global and multinational, incorporated to make money from the business of insecurity and war. The relationship between global insecurity and corporate profits is evidenced by the fact that, since the 2015 stadium attacks in Paris and the UK's decision to bomb Syria, share prices of multinational arms companies rocketed.[7] Annual sales of arms and military services by the world's 100 largest arms-producing and military services companies total well into the hundreds of billions of dollars.

Although arms companies are corporations driven by market imperatives, states are still embedded within, and crucial to, the arms trade and industry. As central to national security, they are generally too important to fail. This is because the major great powers in this hierarchy regulate and influence these commercial activities, they authorize export licences, and they are also the main customers. States facilitate arms sales to other states, thus creating client networks and political traction. That traction is both international and domestic: 'no company can pull off a major international arms deal without the diplomatic support of its "own" government'.[8] While it is the illegal and illicit trade that is often portrayed as 'the problem', the majority of global arms sales, including those to human rights-abusing governments, are legal and actively supported at the highest levels.

'Blessed are the deal-makers'

To create the national days and heroic displays, as well as the destructive firepower and mass deaths and injuries, producers must meet consumers, and sellers must meet buyers, such that goods are sold and bought. Competitive wealth accumulation, whether national, corporate or personal, drives the process over and above the legitimating narratives of national security and patriotic pride. But we don't generally see the very human, hence very gendered, interchanges, where military spending meets arms manufacture, because these transactions of mutual desire take place behind closed doors.

Gaining access to self-styled arms fairs, or 'defence exhibitions', as they are usually termed in the trade, where corporate power, state power and economic power come together to 'strut their stuff', is not that easy. Suffice to say at this point, that those meaning-making interactions, using any and all performative means and technologies, are not open to the public – not because what is inside the venues poses any particular risk to life and limb; it is because the public might be, and sometimes is, a risk to the activities involved as they take place. That risk threatens to undermine the provision of weaponry, through which the state and its politicians construct their legitimacy, on both practical and symbolic levels.

Making all this arms trading invisible to the public eye tracks the taboo that morality is a world apart from money, and that what the state does is the moral exemplar: national heroes don't do it for the money, and profiteering would sully the shiny weaponry. What the state does with its weaponry cannot be in vain, as the state is the moral arbiter of innocence and guilt, dutiful service and cowardly betrayal. The death it causes cannot be judged otherwise than by the state itself, in and through its pageantry, memorials and displays, which are wholly validatory. Judgements from the outside, whether personal, religious or ethical, are subjected to ruthless marginalization, barely tolerated at best, and they become targets for assiduous co-option. Imagined communities of national identity are powerful mythologies against which citizens are unlikely to vote, because the question is almost never put to them.[9] In a world of competitive states that kind of question is nearly meaningless and thus dangerous, verging on insanity. Such subversive and seditious ideas, if visible at all, are subjects for satire and black comedy, made safe as – supposedly – mere entertainment.

Having identified arms trading as a promising site within which to investigate and analyse the threefold conflation that we have so far established – masculinity with legitimacy with political power – it's clearly necessary to present analysis and evidence. We can see how public displays of warrior-protector masculinity perform the legitimacy of the state and validate its leadership, but what role does gender play in the hidden world of national/commercial weaponry? Or, to put it another way, what does using the gender lens, with particular attention to masculinity, tell us about what arms-trading activities actually mean? Answering that question will tell us why arms fairs are not family-day-out attractions, open to any and all.

To understand that circumstance we will need to watch how the overtly gendered masculinity of moralized patriarchy interacts with the covertly gendered humanness through which money making is sanitized. That interaction would not take place without the present-absence, and also literal presentation of, femininity and females, very much as an 'other'. However, it requires some further analysis to understand exactly how gender operates, and in particular, how masculinity operates, so as to produce the national days and heroic displays. These displays are generally backed up by news media spectacles showing off hi-tech destruction. The repetitive performances construct the legitimacy of hypermasculinity within the gender-order hierarchy, because they invoke and guarantee widespread consent to it. At the same time these performances also project the legitimacy of great power politics within the international system, because they demand and guarantee consent with menace. The arms trade is key to this.

This chapter considers the legal framework and international discourse of arms control through which the legitimate arms trade is defined and monitored. It then considers the UK as a particular state agent within the industrial production and sales exchange of legitimate weaponry, ancillary technologies and servicing support. Having set that structure in a gendered analysis, in the next chapter we take the reader inside the 'closed' arms fairs and corporate enterprises not normally on public view. Or rather, the public view, as much as there is one, expresses the normalization that makes the closed doors seem appropriate and enforceable.

The view here, by contrast, derives from an understanding of masculinity as competitive structures of nested masculinizing hierarchies. Behind closed doors, then, we will see the work of legitimation going on right where the money is. What is being legitimated is the corporate–governmental nexus. From that nexus arise the national days and heroic displays as a repetitive spectacle, and thus the miserable deaths and widespread destruction chronicled repetitively as world news.

The legitimate/illegitimate dichotomy

The first step in this journey is to tackle the legitimate/ illegitimate dichotomy. We do this in texts and images so as to draw out the way that a negative 'other' already legitimates a positive phenomenon. Although the text and images constituting the international arms trade do not always explicitly differentiate between the legitimate and the illegitimate arms trade, those texts and images nonetheless still constitute the dichotomy by alluding to an 'absent other'.

The international Arms Trade Treaty, ratified in 2014, is the most recent important international agreement designed to regulate the manufacture, selling and buying of weaponry in global commerce. It endeavours to draw an explicit line textually between what is legitimate and what is illegitimate. Although that line may be fuzzy, open to interpretation and certainly up for debate, the dichotomy itself represents a power resource for strategic manoeuvring in a competitive marketplace. Regulating the international arms trade means identifying aspects of it that are illegitimate, in order to constitute what is actually legitimate, and thus that which is legitimated by the treaty. An emphasis on what is deemed problematic, and thus associated with the illegitimate arms trade, helpfully distracts from other things that, by implication, become unproblematic. Hence legitimation proceeds by implication and default. Additionally, of course, the legitimate/illegitimate distinction can be weaponized by one competitive arms-seller against another in masculinized market competition, so it is hardly 'merely semantic'.

Within the NGOs concerned with the legitimacy of the arms trade, there are two main positions: transformists and reformists. Transformists question the legitimacy of the *entire* trade and industry, thus working to overthrow the whole system. They are therefore not part of the arms control discursive community, although they certainly have a lot to say about it. The best example of this is the UK-based Campaign Against Arms Trade, which sets out its position:

> Governments like to give the impression that it is the illegal trade that is damaging, while the legal trade is tightly controlled and acceptable. In fact, the vast majority of arms sales to human rights-abusing regimes and into conflict areas are not only legal, but actively supported by governments. Many of these 'legal' sales violate the selling countries' own arms export laws.
>
> It is true that there is also a large illegal arms trade, with arms smuggled across borders, stolen, or sold from military or police stocks without government authorisation. While also causing severe harm, it is much smaller than the legal trade.[10]

Reformists, on the other hand, see the existing trade in some weapons, deemed conventional, as legitimate, albeit with flaws that can be corrected by national legislation, improved national and international policies, and more transparency at the highest international level of treaty making.[11] They are advocates of increased arms control, which is a further step necessarily predicated on the legitimate/illegitimate distinction. Examples of reformists are Amnesty International, Saferworld and Oxfam, which are behind the Control Arms campaign. Reformists affirm the legitimate/illegitimate distinction, which is as much about the moral character of state-actors as it is about the weaponry itself, where further moral hierarchies and taboos are operative. The moralized, masculinized, militarized warrior-protector is clearly invoked in and through the rhetoric of arms control: 'So is Oxfam against all arms sales? No, Oxfam is not against all arms sales.' Its position is that it recognizes the production, stocking and transfer of arms for legitimate purposes under international law, such as legitimate self-defence, protection of its own charity worker civilians, or as armed support for duly mandated peacekeeping operations set up to protect civilians caught in conflicts.[12]

Focusing down with the gender lens

A number of themes arise in arms control discourse that link together intertextually. Intertextuality refers to the ways that meanings made in different discourses, for example, in texts or images, are linked to, and depend on, meanings made in other discourses.[13] These themes link together to constitute what and who are legitimate, even though the negative, illegitimate side of the dichotomy is not usually made visible through explicit references and signifiers. Rather, it is the presumed, negative norm through which the positive, legitimate side of the dichotomy becomes visible by inference.

The dichotomies and categories listed in Table 3.1 represent analytical abstractions that order principles of thought. That discursive ordering has real significance for how the international arms trade is to be understood, controlled, contested and legitimized. Table 3.1 illustrates typical descriptive and moralizing dichotomies through which the illegitimate constructs the legitimate, even if implicitly.

These binaries are both gendered and raced, and in that way the moralizing reflection from illegitimate to legitimate

Table 3.1: Dichotomies in arms control associated with legitimate/illegitimate

Legitimate	Illegitimate
State	Non-state
Rational	Irrational
Conventional weaponry	Small arms and light weapons
Us	Them
Licit	Illicit
Public	Private
Soldier	Civilian
Order	Chaos
Successful	Fragile
North	South
Humane	Inhumane
Just war	'New wars'
Discriminate	Indiscriminate
Militarism	Failed states/new wars
Neat	Messy
Clean	Dirty
Law	Crime
Developed	Developing
Global 'north'	Global 'south'
Military	Civilian
Modern civilized warrior man	Frenzied barbarian savage man
Modern	Medieval
Responsible	Irresponsible
Respect for human rights	Abuses of human rights

reflects back on femininity and on non-whiteness. Any privileging discourse that positions the superior in relation to the inferior is always already gendered as inferiorizing and thus feminizing, even if the sexed bodies of men and women are not mentioned. Gender does not produce the dichotomies; rather, the dichotomies 'are the foundation stones of a process of "othering" via metaphorical projections, with which the metaphors that produce gender importantly intersect'.[14] Many of these dichotomies are based on racialized categories of whiteness, against which darker 'others' *do* appear as 'race', while whiteness goes unnamed. And they are also based on Eurocentric-Weberian Anglophone conceptions of states and security that are repetitively cited and ubiquitous. Media news and academic theorizing generally reproduce those definitions, with only rare qualification.[15]

Racial 'othering' against unmarked whiteness is familiar to postcolonial scholars as informing the dichotomies associated with orientalism: rational/irrational, us/them, order/chaos, developed/developing. The premise of much postcolonial scholarship is that national identities of former colonies, declared or de facto, are 'constructed in opposition to European ones, and come to be understood as Europe's "others"'. It is gender that allows hierarchies, which are inherently raced and classed, to be naturalized into physical bodies and bodily representations. In that bio-material manner they are thus depoliticized as immutably physical, historical and cultural.[16] Invoking the '"natural" inferiority of the feminine', as Peterson argues, 'plays a powerful, though not exhaustive, role in legitimating these hierarchies'.[17] Gender and race are thus entwined in what Rowley identifies as 'a logic of intertextuality'. However, that logic also 'functions to *obscure* this intertextuality', because most often one side of the dichotomy evokes its silent 'other'.[18]

While some of the negative poles of these dichotomies could certainly be identified as hypermasculine (such as indiscriminate, irrational, criminal, frenzied, barbarian, irresponsible), hypermasculinity can still be feminized, because its configuration is relational. It depends on which kind of masculinity is being privileged at that discursive moment, and on who is doing the defining and evaluating. Where masculinity is equated with control, hypermasculinity can always be feminized as a lack of control. Integral to dominant masculinity, as Connell explains, is 'the ability to impose a definition of the situation, to set the terms in which events are understood and issues discussed, to formulate ideas and define morality', in short, to assert domination.[19]

Carver identifies a myth of 'unitary masculinity' or 'masculinized being' existing over and above the gender dichotomy itself, and constituting the '"man" in the hu*man*, the hu*mane* and the hu*man*itarian'. That generic 'man' is the self-subsistent masculinity from which 'others' are constituted in opposition and in subordination. Although this masculinized being remains unseen, the 'others' to it are made hypervisible and problematic. That logic animates the distinction between the 'humane power of civilization' and 'the inhumane power of the barbarian', which, in turn, legitimates warrior-protector masculinity. Accordingly, the emphasis on the weak and vulnerable in the discourses of international politics is somewhat self-subverting. Centring the weak and feminized leaves the strong and masculinized at the margins, lacking visibility and looking unproblematic. But to look unproblematic is to gain power, the exercise of which is not necessarily tied to protecting the weak and vulnerable, which was supposedly the central point. The strong and masculinized, and strong *because* masculinized, are thus hiding in plain sight.[20]

This is precisely what is occurring in the dominating discourses of the arms control community. Masculinity legitimizes itself by centring non-masculine, or less masculine, 'others'.[21] In constructing an image of the illegitimate, which is linked to feminized/racialized 'others', arms control discourse is also constructing an image of the legitimate, which is discursively linked with the masculinized use of money and technology by dominating white males. A focus on illegitimacy thus legitimizes the positive pole of these dichotomies *and* displaces attention away from exactly what that positive side actually is, and therefore from what it actually *does*. At the same time, displacing attention away from the positive pole increases its legitimacy, as it therefore does not come under scrutiny.

This binary logic of feminized 'otherness' also means that forms of violence associated with richer countries, on the one hand, and different forms of violence associated with poorer countries, on the other, are somewhat at a remove.[22] Agathangelou and Turcotte argue that 'the consolidation of Western identity formation depends on the division of the world into spaces that seem to be disconnected from each other'.[23] In richer countries – self-styled as humane and civilized – the concern with an unrestrained masculinity that they locate in poorer regions, imagined as the 'frenzied barbarian' and 'heart of darkness', constitutes an identity that is benevolent, paternal, progressive and legitimate, namely modern, civilized, 'warrior man'.

The legitimate/illegitimate dichotomy in arms control discourse thus sanitizes the commercial trade and industrial manufacture of weaponry. That is, the threat of violence is the operative presumption of masculinized competition within the marketplace, notwithstanding protestations that market exchanges are inherently peaceful, and that peacemaking is a goal that is mutually desired.[24] The role of gender and race in this political meaning making is crucial.

CITS–UGA briefing paper

In order to demonstrate how these concepts are deployed to generate legitimacy, we analyse a briefing paper on the international Arms Trade Treaty. This briefing paper, entitled 'The international Arms Trade Treaty: A win–win for the defense industry', was produced by the Center for International Trade and Security at the University of Georgia (hence CITS–UGA).[25] This text is one of the few that distinguishes between the legitimate and the illegitimate arms trade, using those terms explicitly. Thus it performs the distinction between the legitimate arms-trading industries as opposed to their illegitimate 'other'. Furthermore, this briefing paper is the only document that emerged in our research that is specifically aimed at the weapons industry rather than at politicians or members of the public.

The briefing paper appears on the website of the Arms Control Association (ACA), an American organization that describes itself as 'a national nonpartisan membership organization dedicated to promoting public understanding of and support for effective arms control policies'.[26] The ACA is a member of Control Arms, a global civil society alliance which, for over a decade, has advocated the adoption of 'a bulletproof Arms Trade Treaty'. As a document published by an academic institution, this briefing paper carries considerable prestige and authority for the intended audience. That audience is clearly marked as 'Industry' at the top right corner of the first page, where the reader learns this:

> The Center for International Trade and Security
> at the University of Georgia, USA endeavors to

promote peace and prosperity through the use of research, training, and outreach focused on the mitigation of threats posed by the trade of weapons of mass destruction materials and technologies and other military-related transfers as well as the illicit trade in conventional arms. The Center (CITS) carries out its mission by engaging and informing policymakers, industry representatives, educators, students, and the general public, both in the United States and abroad, about the dangers of trade in and theft of weapons and weapons components.[27]

For a reader within the arms-trading industries, the fact that the document has been produced by a university centre masculinizes it in relation to what, for that audience, is an 'other': the 'do-gooding', hence feminized, NGOs also working within the broader Control Arms coalition. Through the use of defence industry terminology – trading partner, trade advantage, trading route security, technological gains, technological advantage, legitimate business conduct and suchlike – the authors are working hard, using textual and visual means, to persuade a sceptical audience of weapons producers and arms traders that the international Arms Trade Treaty is beneficial to their interests.[28]

The CITS-UGA briefing paper states that the 'production and procurement of the means of defense, based on the national right of self-defense constituted in Article 51 of the UN Charter, is a necessary and legitimate business'. This is a clear claim to unarguable legitimacy, given that almost all states in the world have consented to those articles as a condition of membership. 'But', it continues, the situation is 'one which poses very specific challenges'. Those challenges relate to trade routes where a lack of regulation and control 'creates a risk that weapons might … end up in the wrong hands causing devastating effects on civilians, perpetuating conflicts, and undermining development'. Moreover 'these loopholes are meticulously exploited by illegitimate arms traders, generating a hazardous environment for the legitimate and responsible members of the defense industry'.[29]

Having positioned the audience rhetorically on the side of legitimacy, by marking illegitimacy as physically dangerous and disruptive to trade, the briefing paper proposes that a treaty 'could effectively level the playing field in international arms transfers, ensuring that legitimate transfers are held to consistent standards, and that there is a clear distinction between the legitimate and illegitimate arms trade'.[30]

Self-defence is the classical basis of moral doctrines that legitimize the use of force by people or states against illegitimate, that is, non-defensive, unprovoked aggression by an 'other'.[31] The defence industry is thus articulated to the public as a legitimate enterprise at the outset. Indeed, its denomination as an *industry* inversely invokes an 'other' realm of enterprises that do not enjoy that legitimizing description, namely criminal organizations and illegal activities.

However, the briefing paper further reinforces its moral legitimacy by positioning itself and its target audience as potential victims. It advises that 'illegitimate arms traders' will generate 'a hazardous environment for the legitimate and responsible members of the defense industry'. That invocation of victimhood pushes the briefing paper and its target audience into an even higher position in the moral hierarchy.[32]

That moralizing argument is reinforced through visual rhetoric. At the head of the briefing paper is a montage of four images of men and women, pictured in head and shoulders view, arranged in a row.[33] While the images blur into each other, it is clear through foreground signifiers in costume, and background signifiers in props and foliage, that the individuals are from different places. The caption, 'We all want an Arms Trade Treaty', cements this visual trope for the reader, with the implication that diverse individuals, from seemingly different geographical zones and cultural worlds, are all interconnected because they all want the same thing.

That montage is entirely lacking in signifiers that might excite even the suspicion of behaviour or character that would challenge the simplicities of the readily intelligible moral vs immoral framing. The row of images – photogenic faces performing an appeal – hail the viewer/reader into agreement that the international Arms Trade Treaty is needed, not just wanted. Over and above textual tropes, then, visuality evokes emotions as powerful persuaders. Anyone in the target audience not in favour of the international Arms Trade Treaty would fly in the face (literally) of a globalized moral consensus and humanity's most deeply felt moral intuitions.

While this document does not mention gender or race in its text, nonetheless these signifiers are crucial to its intended impact. The faces in the montage look at the audience and communicate their individual and collective need, while radiating their mutual agreement. But when the audience looks at the faces in the images, they see gender and race. Analytically we apply the gender 'lens' to this montage to see what narratives it produces about the international Arms Trade Treaty.

Of course, multiple and varied readings of any conjunction of text and image are possible. Our reading, however, reveals what Lazar describes as 'the complex, subtle, and sometimes not so subtle, ways in which frequently taken-for-granted gendered assumptions and hegemonic power relations are discursively produced'.[34] And, as has been established through feminist testimony and critical race studies, race and gender are experienced intersectionally and performed as an inseparable imbrication.

The first image is a young, smiling, black woman. She has a black headwrap, seemingly tied at the back, and wears a short-sleeved, fairly low-cut top that would not be uncommon in the westernized world, a signifier of similarity to the intended audience. However, on her head she is holding a large bowl or bucket, although we can only see part of it, as the image is cropped. This item is clearly a signifier for a less industrialized, less westernized society, probably in formerly colonized Africa or the Caribbean. That set of signifiers links intertextually with other images in media reports and charity appeals relating to so-called 'developing' societies. As the woman is smiling, and unlike the other images, there are no other signifiers that predicate conflict, the image argues that effective arms control brings real safety to those who have little. This is just as the briefing paper states; an uncontrolled trade in arms leads to violent conflicts that kill non-combatant, innocent people.

The second image is of a white male with grey hair wearing a shirt, tie and suit jacket. Those signifiers identify him with bourgeois-rational, business masculinity, and mark him as someone with power, authority and resources.[35] That reading is reinforced by its juxtaposition with the woman pictured to the viewer's left, since he does not look threatening or aggressive. His benevolent smile interpellates him as a 'good guy' from an industrialized society. That man could work in the defence industry, but he could also be a UN or government official, or even the person writing the report. The ambiguity here is a hermeneutic 'hook'. If he is a member of the defence industry, then he is what the briefing paper refers to as a 'legitimate and responsible' member of the industry. He is also someone with whom white men in any position of power could identify, so he mirrors the target audience. In Anglophone-Eurocentric, white-raced terms, he also performs the generic man in hu*man*.

The third image, the largest of the four, is of two people, making it seem central to the whole series – a white male soldier carrying a young girl. It could be a young boy, but the child's hair appears to be long and tied back. That signifier of femininity, in conjunction with the delicate cream crochet material around the neckline, predicate her as female. She has brown skin, dark hair and appears to be about seven to ten years old. The man carrying her wears camouflage and a helmet, marking him unambiguously as a soldier. In that pose and conjunction he exemplifies warrior-protector masculinity.

Photographs such as these play a mimetic role, as McAuliffe argues, so 'the connotations … bring the individual story into a wider discourse of understanding in a complex and contingent manner such that the meaning of any image shifts relative to its consumption'.[36] Not everyone would know that this man is an American soldier, but the image links intertextually with images of recent wars in Iraq and Afghanistan. Given the global target audience, those associations are risky, but the risks are displaced, because the girl looks happy, and the soldier is smiling, carrying her paternally. The story that this image is telling is one of rescue and protection of brown females/brown children by white men, a trope that the target audience would likely endorse as a moral exemplar.[37] Even if the target audience were unsure of the morality of particular American interventions, the iconic

Hollywood masculinity in warrior-protector narrative mode signifies a gender-ideal.

The fourth image presents a girl in a headscarf or veil, signifying Islam and 'otherness' from the target audience's presumed white-raced and Christian cultural perspective. From that perspective, the veil has come to embody, epitomize and symbolize the supposed and presumed backwardness and oppression of Muslim women.[38] The girl stands next to a barbed-wire fence, predicating a refugee camp. The image thus represents what Mohanty characterizes as the 'third world woman', 'a singular monolithic subject',[39] poor, oppressed, uneducated, victimized, passive and culturally enslaved.[40] While the men pictured are clearly from a privileged class position, attained within competitive masculinizing hierarchies of power, the women default to lower social status, lower social class, lower 'third world' positioning in the hierarchy of great power politics.

Thus masculinity, as the dominance of men over women, and some men over others – in this case via state competitiveness and rank ordering within the international system – is the master signifier of the montage. In representing armed force and charitable assistance as mutually compatible and necessarily linked, the images figure the way that the target audience wants to see itself and how it wants to be seen by others. The viewer is positioned to gaze straightforwardly into unproblematic images that project an ideal and are their own reflection.

To secure this reading the four images presuppose common knowledge about victims of modern-day warfare who are visible on media news networks, and about their rescuer-agents from their innocent, agent-less victimhood. The two men are positioned in the middle of the frame, so the women are marginalized to the side. Men are thus the subjects with power and authority, whereas womenandchildren are defenceless victims of war and poverty. The men are interlinked, because warrior-protector masculinity is linked with bourgeois-rational masculinity, and the two masculinities are thus merged as the technological/industrial solution to the problem. In that way both masculinities acquire political agency and exemplify moral justification. The just deployment of arms and men resolves conflict and brings peace, and peacetime technological development in the national economy brings prosperity and happiness. Viewers really do not need to be told that they, too, would want an international arms trade treaty.

What is missing from this montage are any black or brown women whose innocence cannot be presumed secure, as would be the case with older women, or women in any position of authority. Also missing are the human agents causing conflict and inflicting violence: the 'nefarious actors' using the 'diverted' arms. They are absent, because they clearly do *not* want an arms control treaty. Hence they are a present-absence through which the image argues the legitimacy of what it is representing through visual narrative.

Accordingly, in the montage there are no adult brown men or male children, who would represent the global south. For the viewer those 'missing' subjects link together subconsciously and significantly because 'good men can only appear in their goodness if we assume that lurking outside the warm familial walls are aggressors, the "bad" men, who wish to attack them'.[41] Viewers experiencing that absence can understand it as the presence of a threat, and so can easily fill it in with dangerous dark-brown men as the brown 'other' to the vulnerable brown women in need of white protection.

Moreover, the inclusion of men/boys would introduce problematic references to the competitive masculinities through which some men gain power over others, notably through and within violence and criminality. The 'other' to that subliminal chain of signifiers in equivalence and difference is white men in white collars.[42] In that visual and subliminal clash of civilizations, and indeed modes of production, the white men featured are not only warrior-protectors, they are also bourgeois-rational businessmen with access to modernizing, westernizing technologies and knowledge. It is their legitimated burden not only to rescue brown women and children from brown men, but also to civilize them all as well, specifically through weaponry. This montage, and in particular, the central placement of the white-man-in-the-suit, invites those in industry to participate in a fantasy life as heroic-manly rescuers of brown women and children. Gender and race are thus instrumentalized as a means to sell the international Arms Trade Treaty to the weapons industry. But the treaty also represents a legitimation of the great-power international system, a legitimation of masculine dominance in the gender-order hierarchy, and a legitimation of the ordering hierarchies through which some men dominate others. While all the images and tropes are readily intelligible to the target audience, the crucial mirror of self-recognition is the kindly, rational-bureaucratic civilian businessman as warrior-protector masculine hero.

Due to associations with morality and internationalist good will and suchlike emotional rhetorics,[43] the international Arms Trade Treaty could be coded as feminine. This is because treaties rely on mutual trust and are notoriously difficult to enforce, either through international agencies or national actions by individual states or several states in a consortium. Applying the gender lens intersectionally to this document reveals how those supporting the international Arms Trade Treaty are masculinized even though advocating its ratification. That legitimizing result is achieved by positioning the male-self in relation to feminized others, and in relation to the subordinated, excluded and delegitimized masculinities that cannot be pictured, but are nonetheless there. In that way the montage performs male-gendered, white-raced masculinity as morally good, but also argues that generic humanity is legitimately performed as masculinized whiteness.

The UK – bourgeois-rational warrior-protector

In this section we focus on a particular state that has championed the international Arms Trade Treaty, and is thus supposedly an exemplar of the legitimate arms trade – the UK. However, the transfers of weaponry and money made under those auspices set up contradictions within the UK government itself, and for that government within the international system. To smooth over those contradictions, gender, and in particular, masculinity, play a significant part in the processes through which the UK's exemplar status is defended and maintained. For comparable 'players' in great-power politics, and in the national-commercial manufacture and sales of weaponry, the dynamics are necessarily the same.

The fundamental right of states to purchase weapons is legitimized in international law. States that sell weaponry are thereby providing a necessary and legitimate service. But, in reality, states such as the UK, whose industry is now privatized, are not sellers as such. Rather, they subsidize arms industries, overtly as a matter of policy, and somewhat less obviously through university departments and similar 'defence' establishments. On occasion states also authorize sales that would otherwise not be legitimate, such as exports to close allies whose aggressions and incursions have been internationally condemned. Both activities – purchase and sale – require legitimation, and in the case of the UK, both are legitimated together as the defence industrial base (DIB), a concept understood in great-power geopolitical strategic terms, and concurrently within the great-power terms of a major world G7 economy.

As we have seen, states are understood as personified masculine actors. It follows that the sale and purchase of weaponry – overwhelmingly associated with men – that takes place within the international system can be read as the performance of masculinities. Warrior-protector masculinity and bourgeois-rational masculinity are together an analytical common denominator and a readily intelligible intertextual linkage. Given the powerful and obvious contradictions involved – making war to bring peace, causing death to preserve life – it follows that warding off a legitimation crisis requires some powerful discursive weaponry. Gender, understood as the gender-order hierarchy, is a more readily understood and easily communicated grid of intelligibility than the supposedly authoritative terms of international law and the argumentative logics of legal reasoning. This is so particularly as these international laws and conventions are always already cross-cut with declared or implied conceptions of national interest and strategic advantage.

The UK prides itself on its role as a legitimate international state-actor, and thus in necessarily promoting the international Arms Trade Treaty. Yet the legitimacy of its arms sales to other states, such as Saudi Arabia, is regularly scrutinized with regard to alleged violations of human rights. Those violations occur internally in the domestic order and externally in relation to other states.[44] The latter are typically airstrikes that constitute an illegitimate use of any weapons sold to them, and are contrary to the terms of sale through which the trade in arms is understood to proceed legitimately.

The terms of that legitimacy are enshrined in Article 51 of the UN Charter of 1945 and in the international Arms Trade Treaty itself.[45] According to international law, sovereign states have the right to defend themselves and to obtain the means to do so. States are therefore, at least in principle, deemed to be fundamentally legitimate participants in, or customers of, arms manufacture and trade. As such they are entitled to buy weapons in order to maintain their own security, unless such purchases or sales are otherwise deemed illegitimate. High technology industry therefore provides a necessary and legitimate service, authorized and facilitated by states, most of which are buyers rather than sellers of such weaponry. The legitimacy of the international arms trade rests on the legitimacy of the state system itself, where sovereign states are recognized as controlling the means of legitimate violence. The international law that legalizes the arms trade is therefore fundamentally based on an understanding of security that is state-centric, rather than founded on some other principle of protection.[46]

Arms provide a symbol of masculine status by showing that the state has the capability to use force, both domestically and internationally, and, just as importantly, by showing that the state has the credentials that make it bourgeois-rational in major commercial markets. While 'bourgeois' relates to commercial prowess, 'rational' relates to science and technology, and indeed, to the way that commercial technologies finance and drive scientific discoveries. Histories of science, awardees and prizewinners, visual modelling as 'men in white coats', have all contributed to the exclusion and marginalization of 'others' not consistent with the very white model of rationality.[47] Highly technological militaries 'symbolise modernity, efficacy, and independence', or, in other words, successful as opposed to fragile statehood. According to Eyre and Suchman, the spread of weaponry can be explained by 'institutional normative structures linking militaries and their advanced weapons with sovereign status as a nation, with modernisation, and with social legitimacy'.[48] This explains why states often procure 'highly sophisticated, expensive weapon systems and technologies, despite well-known absorption handicaps' while rejecting 'equally serviceable but cheaper and perhaps less sophisticated options'.[49]

Certain recipient states are often feminized within the academic literature on arms. Many explanations for the propensity for so-called 'third world nations' to buy expensive, unnecessary equipment 'tend to emphasize the inadequately rational nature of third world military decision making rather than the potential inadequacies of the rational explanation'.[50] That discursive subordination intersects with orientalist and racialist assumptions through which the masculinity, agency and capabilities of the so-called 'first world states' are reinforced.

Military purchases by poor countries are often constructed as the 'squandering of precious resources by profligate elites', but when understood in the context of global militarism and militarization, they are ultimately 'activities sanctioned by the global military culture'. Capital-intensive militarization 'in the Global South is a product of ... the dominance of western models of militarisation that have been exported'.[51] Because the purchase of weapons is legitimated within the international system, it follows that states legitimate themselves by purchasing weaponry, much of which is unlikely to be used, for legitimate purposes anyway. That nested hierarchy of competitive state-actors mirrors the way that masculinization works in the economic register, as well as in more visible displays of marching and weaponry.

The power of marketing must not be underestimated here, as Enloe remarks: 'not only Nike, Sony, BMW, and Dunlop are globally marketing their products and encouraging potential customers to develop needs and desires they might not have thought they had. So too are manufacturers of heavy and light weapons.'[52] The host nation of those industries also plays a crucial role in encouraging other states to purchase. We turn now to the consideration of the UK as a 'seller' state.

Mutual legitimation: state and industry

Many national, although privately owned, arms industries seek to 'transcend their national origins and to manoeuvre for survival and supremacy in a global arena'. These companies must sell weapons to other countries in order to make enough profit to maintain a competitive edge and to keep themselves in the market. States regulate the exports of corporate players, and the 'home' state is often the main customer. Through that support and subsidy, Stavrianakis concludes, 'the capitalist state is crucial in legitimising the formally private arms industry'.[53]

The UK government facilitates arms sales to other countries by granting export licences and providing assistance at both ends with supply chains. It provides export credit guarantees, which means that if the buyer-state does not pay, UK taxpayers cover the cost. The UK government would then attempt to recover this debt from the buyer-state, including recovery from democratic states that were formerly dictatorships.

The UK government also overpays on some purchases in order to buy from domestic industries: 'In any other industry, World Trade Organization rules and other free-trade legislation would prevent such spending distortions as unfair competition. ... Politicians and civil servants freely admit their preference for "buying British" to maintain the DIB [defence industry base].'[54]

The UK not only facilitates arms sales to other states, but UK representatives also actively encourage them, becoming militarized, necessarily, in the process.[55] The prime minister and members of the royal family 'frequently serve as unofficial arms salesmen abroad'.[56] While arms sales account for a very small amount of the total value of UK exports, and sustain just a tiny fraction of the national labour force, the UK maintains very large complements of civil servants and advisory consultants devoted to promoting the sale of weaponry.

In a verbal briefing, a civil service official from the UK government, on secondment from the UK military, stated that the UK supports companies in 'the mission to succeed abroad ... helping the big guys such as BAE [Systems] and Rolls Royce but also the smaller guys'. In the presentation we were told that 19 UK embassies have UK Trade & Investment Defence & Security Organisation staff working there who 'do what we [UKTI DSO] ask them to'. UKTI DSO also has 'part-share' of UKTI staff in other embassies, but only 19 have military expertise – 'they speak the language [of the military] the others don't'.

The civil service official emphasized the legitimate and legitimizing role of the UK state in building 'G to G [government to government] relationships in order to open doors ... to allow industry to have the right kind of conversations'. Here 'right' refers to right as defined and thus legitimated by the UK government, in contrast to unmentioned backroom deals. He also stated that 'we have to be careful with our companies. ... We need them to be careful with the media and export controls, things like that.' He continued: 'It's your [industry's] responsibility to get an export licence if you are exporting defence and security type things. ... Ethics is always an issue ... everything we do is open and transparent ... it is not about doing deals quietly.'[57]

The state's role in determining and enforcing the legitimate arms trade is echoed by industry. In an interview regarding its sales of weapons to Saudi Arabia, the chair of BAE Systems, Sir Roger Carr, stated: 'We have relationships on a government-to-government basis. So, we only make and sell equipment to those allies that the government of the United Kingdom say that we should deal with in the interests of the preservation of peace for the United Kingdom.' At the BAE Systems annual general meeting in May 2016, in response to questions by protestors over BAE sales to Saudi Arabia, the chair stated: 'We will stop doing it when they [the UK government] tell us to stop doing it.'[58]

While industry indeed relies on the UK state for survival and profit, because it authorizes and subsidizes exports, states are also concerned to justify their intrusion into the realm of commercial autonomy: 'If we do not make clear which industrial capabilities we need to have onshore (and this includes those maintained by foreign-owned defence companies), industry will make independent decisions.'[59]

The maintenance of the DIB in the UK certainly involves close connections between the state, the military and the weapons industry. This is described as a revolving door of government–corporate collusion,[60] which reveals how 'the ambitions of profit-seeking companies are enmeshed with questions of high political strategy'.[61] Furthermore, there is a highly disproportionate share of national research and development funding given to the arms industry, in relation to 'the amount of employment and economic activity that defence companies actually provide'.[62] As Steans reports, 'the use of concepts like "autonomy" and "national interest" ... rely upon masculinised notions of rationality as a technique of control'.[63] Governments support their arms industries because 'a strong defence industry is seen as a symbol of power in world affairs'.[64]

Being a seller-state gives the UK a superior position in the hierarchy of states, as it has some power to control who gets what. Due to the Russia–Ukraine situation, Russian arms manufacturers were not invited to the UK Defence and Security Equipment International arms fair of 2015, despite usually being 'a big feature at these events'.[65] That performative act constituted the host seller-state, the UK, as powerful, able to determine and impute the rogue state identity to Russia, and thus demote it in the competitive hierarchy of masculine state-actors.

Masculinity and legitimation

The UK arms industry conjoins corporate enterprise and state facilitation. It is overwhelmingly dominated by men, although masculinization – which patently excludes and marginalizes women – does not immediately explain the processes through which this powerful nexus of international business and great-power politics operates. Those processes are not only constitutive of the presumptions through which the militarized arms trade makes sense; they also legitimate both the soldiers and the traders as national warrior-protectors. That, in turn, legitimates masculinization as the process through which hierarchical structures of power and authority operate in general. And again, this is mirrored in the overwhelming male dominance of those in charge and at all the higher levels.

The ubiquity of this dominance enables masculinity to fade into a supposedly generic humanness and functionality, into which women are being strategically admitted, although only in the US on any scale.[66] Some women may question what they are being admitted into, as indeed do some men, on any number of grounds. The discussion below explores the way that masculinization of men, and among men, makes this questioning difficult, because legitimation forestalls critique, wherever it comes from. Legitimation makes such questions unsayable in the insider context, and, as we will see in the next chapter, outsider critique is made to appear pathetic or crazed.

The masculinity historically associated with manufacturing and technology becomes even more potent, prestigious and legitimate through its link to the sanctioned use of violence.[67] Carrying arms has been articulated as real men's work, that is, protecting the womenandchildren of the feminized nation. The links between industry, the nation and the military are made argumentatively and rhetorically by employees working for major suppliers as a means of legitimizing what they do. This understanding of the nation's business, and of the business of being a nation, is projected by the managing director of a weapons firm: 'There is a strong sense of pride in what we do here, allowing our armed forces to carry out their duties around the world.'[68]

The fact that the weaponry is sold to other countries does not seem to be a problem, because it can be narrated as in the national interest. However, that narrative relies on the notion of the industry functioning as 'workshops for national armed forces' rather than 'corporations driven by market imperatives'.[69] That erasure removes any question of negative effects that arms production might have on the national economy and on human beings elsewhere. Having a strong arms industry, and thus the capacity to sell weaponry, promotes the UK to great power status within the nested hierarchies through which the international system of masculinized state-actors operates.

As a great power seller, the UK is also an advocate for international arms control. As we have seen, the apparatus of arms control is a platform through which states compete for the moral high ground, as well as for control within a regulatory framework. That framework will inevitably structure the trade in ways that will favour some players over others. Indeed, the UK's export controls and involvement in the international Arms Trade Treaty legitimize its own arms sales within the market conditions and the terms of trade that it has a hand in setting.[70]

On 2 April 2013, when the UN General Assembly adopted the treaty, David Cameron, then UK prime minster, invoked warrior-protector masculinity as the moral high ground of great power politics: 'This is a landmark agreement that will save lives and ease the immense human suffering caused by armed conflict around the world. ... We should be proud of the role Britain has played to secure this ambitious agreement, working with international partners to secure this momentous step that will make our world safer for all.'[71]

The UN Charter commits member states to promoting 'universal respect for and observance of, human rights and freedoms' in order to achieve 'economic and social progress and development' and 'to promote ... international peace and security with the least diversion for armaments of the world's human and economic resources'.[72] This morality, formerly subordinated to geopolitical national interests and thus feminized, has been repositioned as masculine by grounding it in the legality of human rights and humanitarian principles. From those principles the international system of masculinized state-actors claims its legitimacy and articulates its conception of the moral high ground. That supposedly de-gendered moral high ground has thus become the public face of the nested hierarchies of competing state-actors, understood as personified men.

As a major advocate of the international Arms Trade Treaty, the UK government saw itself (or at least wanted to be seen to be) burdened with the responsibility to protect subordinated states from making unnecessarily expensive purchases. It also aimed to protect citizens within other states from stereotypically hypermasculine governments, where nested hierarchies of competing males had become too sharply exclusionary and too violently oppressive. Yet, less than three years after the UK signed the treaty, it stood accused by eminent authorities in international law – associated with Amnesty International and Saferworld – of not only breaking EU and UK arms export policy, but also violating the treaty itself, which it had once championed.[73]

It is no secret that British-made and British-traded arms have been used to facilitate and commit what have been deemed violations of international humanitarian law. Documents passed to WikiLeaks in June 2015 reveal that a secret deal, initiated by the UK, had been concluded between it and Saudi Arabia, whereby each would vote the other onto the UN Human Rights Council.[74] Amid reports of systematic violations of human rights in Saudi Arabia, that deal clearly makes a mockery of an important UN agency. The UK–Saudi Arabian relationship has come under even closer scrutiny since then in the context of terrorist activities in the Middle East. After a brief moratorium on arms sales to Saudi Arabia in 2019, the UK resumed trading in July 2020, resulting in £1.4 billion worth of exports. Shortly after taking office in January 2021, President Biden banned similar arms sales, a contradistinction seized on by Campaign Against Arms Trade and similar critical agencies and interests.[75]

UK policy thus poses a contradiction in terms. On the one hand, it promotes human rights and the international treaties that oblige signatory states to implement their protections, and certainly not to violate them. On the other hand, it blatantly contravenes its commitments to humanitarianism and international law, as Basham summarizes: 'Though Britain has time and again been characterised as a "welfare state", it has waged war more frequently than most other countries, and consistently undermined the welfare of "others" to promote that of its own citizens.'[76]

The logic of masculinized competitive state-actors legitimizes both terms of the paradox by performing 'tough and tender' masculinity.[77] That persona combines 'deliberately "hard" military initiatives' and 'realist foreign policy tools' with feminine '"soft" humanitarian concerns' and 'idealist humanitarian relief'.[78] However, the warrior-protector model, within which state-actors compete for dominance, ultimately wins out when a state breaks the rules and does 'whatever it takes',[79] unleashing a 'tough', unrestrained military action.[80] That pattern mirrors the nested hierarchies through which masculinized actors compete for whatever the current terms of competition dictate as ensuring the dominance of some states over others. Those terms of dominance represent the current hegemony through which the gender-order hierarchy is legitimated as commonsensical. That dual legitimacy makes critique, from either angle – anti-militarism or gender oppression – very hard work.

It is with this highly familiar and well-financed repetition of that ordered authority, in and through the popular and educative media, that any questioning and political critique must contend. The confusions and contradictions are themselves made to appear natural and invisible, while also sanitized and depoliticized. Different traits of humanity are masculinized and thus privileged according to the shifting consensus through which the legitimate/illegitimate distinction is articulated at a particular moment. Thus other traits are discredited.[81] This protean conceptual rhetoric manifests itself differently, depending on context, as Smith explains: 'At one stage the man is meant to be rational and in control and at another to allow his "natural aggression" to come out. In some instances he is meant to act as the protector of the "other", the female-and-child; in other situations it is accepted that the spoils of war include the rape of the conquered.'[82]

Therefore, despite the UK's 'tender' commitments, Cameron was able to defend the UK's relationship with Saudi Arabia by using the trump card of masculinized national security and the protection of 'our people':

> We have a relationship with Saudi Arabia and if you want to know why I'll tell you why. It's because we receive from them important intelligence and security information that keeps us safe. The reason we have the relationship is our own national security. There was one occasion since I've been prime minister where a bomb that would have potentially blown up over Britain was stopped because of intelligence we got from Saudi Arabia. Of course it would be easier for me to say: 'I'm not having anything to do with these people, it's all terribly difficult et cetera et cetera.' For me, Britain's national security and our people's security comes first.[83]

Here Cameron presents the events of the secret deal over the UN Human Rights Council as a UK security issue and political success. While the term 'relationship' is applied in this instance to the UK and Saudi Arabia's arrangement over the human rights pact, it could also arguably encompass the arms deals between the two nations. That relationship is justified by appeals to national security – the ultimate role of states as protector. Cameron therefore articulates a masculinizing identity that is prepared to do 'whatever it takes' in order to protect the femininized nation and its womenandchildren, even if that means dealing with nations that abuse human rights, and even if it means contravening UK commitments elsewhere.

This is also the strategy in relation to criticism of the UK's indirect involvement in airstrikes, which Cameron legitimizes by directly connecting them to the UK's national security: 'we are backing the legitimate government of the Yemen not least because terrorist attacks planned in the Yemen would have a direct effect on people in our country'.[84] His appeal to protection of the feminine nation thus legitimizes his questionable foreign and economic policies via the masculinizing logics of the male state-actor. It is, of course, reasonable to question exactly how that relationship works, and which ways the flows of power operate, given that Saudi Arabia brings its wealth to a buyers' market, where the UK state–corporate arms industry has very real competitors.

While supporting the international Arms Trade Treaty, the Cameron government was still facilitating transfers of weaponry that impacted negatively on security and development and/or facilitated human rights abuses. This was contrary to the work and interests of UK government departments, particularly the Department for International Development and the Foreign and Commonwealth Office. The UK is known to have exported weapons to many of the same countries considered 'of concern'.[85] Stavrianakis argues that the UK's own arms export licensing system creates the image of control and benevolence, 'whilst allowing the government to get on with business as usual'. Thus it is 'a ritualised activity that functions to create the appearance of restraint rather than significantly restrict the arms trade'.[86]

The appearance of control and registering of concern for others legitimizes the UK's role in the arms trade. Simply having these rules and regulations in place, and ratifying them as a signatory, implies that they are being adhered to without self-contradiction, thus legitimizing UK arms sales. That carefully constructed image projects the honourable and noble character of warrior-protector masculinity in classically stereotypical terms. Exporting weapons to Saudi Arabia thus appears as evidently an exception to the moral rule, rather than a starkly self-contradictory moral wrong.[87] As Nordberg notes: 'there is an obvious double standard in how western leaders stress the importance of both human rights and women's rights but mostly fall silent on these issues as soon as immediate economic interests and political alliances are at stake'.[88]

Compliance with the international Arms Trade Treaty, and with the apparatus through which human rights violations can be alleged and may be confirmed, is very much an on–off affair. Through that process, then, national self-interest – cashed out in the interchangeable currencies of great power prestige and influence, and corporate profits and market shares – is a very visible thread, official denials and explanations notwithstanding. UK weaponry sales to Saudi Arabia were halted, by court order, for a time in 2020, subject to a ministerial review. That review concluded that actual violations, related to Saudi airstrikes in Yemen, were only 'isolated incidents'. By holding the review, and adhering to that perhaps foregone conclusion, the government authorized BAE Systems to resume sales of airborne bombs and missiles used by British-made jets.[89]

Conclusions

Arms control discourse explicitly recognizes the legitimate need of states to purchase weapons for their national security. According to that logic, industry plays the part of providing a much-needed service. State-centric, nationalist and militarist discourses are therefore crucial to legitimizing the state's and industry's involvement in the arms trade.

This chapter has demonstrated how gender is a key explanatory tool in understanding how it is possible for arms purchases and sales to be considered legitimate, even if the weapons are unnecessary, and even if the buyer is using them to violate human rights. That legitimation happens as a result of the pervasive privilege of masculinity within the gender-order hierarchy. This hierarchy is articulated through the warrior-protector masculinity of the state-actor, and through the bourgeois-rational masculinity of the weapons industry elite. Those parallel hierarchies of male privilege together legitimate the UK's major and defining role in the arms trade, even if, and particularly when, self-contradiction arises.

Constructions of masculinity function as an intertext between the different modes through which the legitimacy of the UK arms industry is secured as a state–corporate conjunction. The arms industry confirms the UK as a male state-actor positioned high up in the nested hierarchies of masculinizing competition. That outcome does not arise just because the UK has a controlling role in establishing who gets what, and because it celebrates weaponry in national displays and at international venues. It also arises because advanced science and technology, integrated with corporate industries, are masculinized and masculinizing. Those practices and representations are merged with, and imbricated within, the military at the highest level. Thus they militarize national cultures quite directly. In that way the nested hierarchies of male dominance – warrior-protectors and techno-commercial rationalists – achieve hegemonic status because consent gives them legitimacy.

Because this chapter has focused on the UK, it is important to recognize and consider how its historical national identity – achieved through vast imperial and colonial violence – has been constructed by, and participates in, that legitimation. Understood, and projecting itself, as a global power, the UK legitimizes itself within the international context. In that context white-raced elite males are overwhelmingly dominant. Basham notes that the UK's 'erasure of [the] colonial and postcolonial bodies with and on which it has waged many wars, has also reinforced the notion that Britain has but a small-scale volunteer military separated out from society and that, in consistently punching above its weight, Britain deserves to be heard in the world'.[90]

While identities are constructed in relation to difference, particularly those in an international realm of 'others' to be subordinated, the UK also constructs itself in relation to its domestic citizens and residents. Through its promotion of the international Arms Trade Treaty, the UK has constructed a paternal, measured, responsible identity by comparing itself with the US. The US did not actively support the treaty, signing but not ratifying it, and then unsigning it in 2019. Making that contrast the UK then prides itself on being a model advocate for domestic gun control, showcased by a largely unarmed police force. In that way it frames itself 'as a more mature, less "cowboy-like" international power', that is, the 'tender' and 'rational' side of masculinized dominance.[91]

This chapter has provided a contextual foundation for the empirical studies that follow in the next chapter. Those studies will show how the legitimation of the arms trade occurs in practice at arms fairs, and also through corporate promotional videos. The relevance of the theoretical models of dominant masculinities – warrior-protector and bourgeois-rational – to the arms trade has thus far been analytical. Those theoretical models for masculinizing processes are reproduced in practical, real-life terms at two important sites to be investigated in the next chapter. While women and the feminine were largely missing in the present chapter, other than referenced by femininization, they are made visible in the empirical studies that follow. The gender-order hierarchy rests on much more than just the nested hierarchies of male-centric competitions.

Further reading

Cerelia Athanassiou (2014) '"Gutsy" decisions and passive processes: The warrior decision-maker after the global war on terror', *International Feminist Journal of Politics*, 16(1): 6–25.

Allison Howell (2018) 'Forget "militarization": Race, disability and the "martial politics" of the police and of the university', *International Feminist Journal of Politics*, 20(2): 117–36.

R. Claire Snyder (1999) *Citizen Soldiers and Manly Warriors: Military Service and Gender in the Civic Republican Tradition*, Lanham, MD: Rowman & Littlefield.

Anna Stavrianakis (2010) *Taking Aim at the Arms Trade: NGOs, Global Civil Society and the World Military Order*, London: Zed Books.

J. Ann Tickner (2014) *A Feminist Voyage through International Relations*, New York: Oxford University Press.

4

Gender at Work!
'Get Pissed and Buy Guns'[1]

The previous chapter demonstrated how legitimizing narratives
are gendered, and in great-power politics how they specifically
invoke warrior-protector and/or bourgeois-rational forms
of masculinity. These are nested within the competitive
masculinizing hierarchies of the gender-order hierarchy of
masculinity over femininity. The present chapter builds on this
by exploring how masculinity works in practice, specifically
in major international arms fairs and in the international
corporations that manufacture them. Competitive masculinizing
commercialisms are awash with the gender-order dynamics
through which masculinization secures corporate activities to
state-controlled markets. Those are the markets through which
huge sums of money change hands in hard-to-trace contracts
and offshore accounts, in which international relationships are
nurtured and severed, in which the civilian–military binary
well and truly dissolves. All this is legitimate, repetitively re-
legitimized, and nearly invisible, because the action takes place
behind closed doors.[2]

Arms fairs are the key physical conventions of the international
arms trade, contributing to the mutual legitimation of great
power politics *and* the competitive hierarchies of masculinization.
They bring together the buyers and sellers who represent states,
and other legitimated actors. Indeed, arms fairs legitimate those
non-state and nation-state-actors that are allowed admission via
inclusion/exclusion criteria that are internal to the hosts and

organizers. The products, industries and trading companies involved in these international fairs of deal-making are celebrated and glorified, but only to each other and select representatives of the media. They are thus a performance of legitimacy and political spectacle, but barely visible to the public, and then only in highly sanitized and authorized media reports. Contextually the reporting of these events is already framed with legitimated authorizations and dignitary personalities, sometimes royal personages on state-sponsored visits, and regular reportage from trusted defence experts.

Clarion Events, which organizes many arms fairs, declares that: 'All defence and security exhibitions … can serve only the legitimate defence and security industry which is the most tightly regulated industry in the world.' Legitimation here is somewhat tautological, in that the UK government, with its defence, foreign and business ministries – a top-rank participant in all major arms fairs – is said to guarantee the conformity of the whole exercise with international law, regulatory agencies and domestic legislation.[3] The unreferenced 'other' to this performance of legitimation is a presumed illegitimate and unruly realm of gangland criminality, offshore banks, secretive accountancy, rogue states and terrorist networks.

Authorization to attend confers legitimacy on the attendees and exhibitors, with the implication that those who engage in the illicit/illegitimate trade are not allowed in. Furthermore, this zone of self-regulation legitimizes the products that are displayed and advertised there. The strict application procedure for individual, corporate and national participants is also designed to keep out anyone who, or anything that, might contest the legitimacy of the fair, the trade and the products. That exclusion is compounded by security clearance on arrival, and a visible securitizing presence at the fair. Thus points of entry are secured, and the event is closed to the public, open to insiders only.

However, there have been occasional 'undercover' observers, notably Gibbon, an artist and political activist, who writes from immediate experience: 'The police bow deferentially as I arrive in a suit, their eyes searching only for threats – "anyone in trainers holding a banner, anyone without a pass".' After these visits to arms fairs as a 'war artist' were rumbled (she was observed sketching individuals), Gibbon 'set up a fake business in security consulting, and returned in a suit and pearls', noting that her 'pretence is a metaphor for a performance of respectability in the industry'. Thus respectability has its unsavoury 'other' present rather than absent, but *sotto voce* and not part of the spectacle: 'I overheard an arms trader say, "You can't do deals in this business unless you are drunk".'[4]

Gibbon's sketchpad, and the promised visibility it portended, merited summary exclusion. Photography is also not permitted without permission from the individual stand managers. Effectively this erases anyone who, and anything that, could potentially question the legitimacy of the trade within its self-legitimating, securitized space. However, the legitimacy of the weaponry itself, and the trade in it, is visibly called into question by protestors who stand at the gates, entrances and exits with signs and banners, often shouting slogans and comments. Protestors are a fact of life for those attending arms fairs. They are monitored and restricted by police and private security.

While protestors may momentarily make participants uncomfortable, they are easily forgotten by attendees and exhibitors once inside and immersed in the spectacles that await them. However, protestors are there again at the end of the day as people leave. Attendees talk about them in embarrassed tones, and there are attempts to avoid them and the awkward moments that they create. Sometimes individual attendees are advised by security workers to leave through a secret 'backdoor' exit in order to avoid the protestors outside.

While protestors provide a brief encounter with the public politics of legitimation and its critique, on the inside arms fairs excise any sense of politics from the visible paraphernalia of warfare, which is understood wholly within the international nation-state system. This sanitized, hermetic and inward-looking environment enacts a metaphorical mirroring of the abstracted and rather similarly enclosing discourse of strategic interaction and bloodless anarchy that is foundational for 'realism' in International Relations.[5] Corporate videos for weapons companies are very much in the same genre, as we will see.

This chapter will demonstrate what the gender-order hierarchy does in these sites of legitimation, how it is performed, and how it legitimizes states, corporations, traders and products. It also legitimizes itself as a competitive hierarchy of masculinities embodied in sellers and buyers, with femininities and women marginalized in passing and obviously exceptional. Analysis will reveal how performances of the gender-order hierarchy in sanitized exhibition spaces erase the violence and death of the great power politics that the whole exercise necessarily presumes. Conversely, those spectacles – whether in-person in real time, or in video mode in narrative time – erase or marginalize the racialized realities of death and destruction. Concomitantly they dramatize whiteness as the presumed and effected great-power economic and military domination of the globe.

All the fun of the fair

Our focus here is on three arms fairs, typical of the international trade in legitimate weaponry sourced from legitimate suppliers and sold to legitimate purchasers. One such event is the Counter Terror Expo 2012 (later known as the Security & Counter Terror Expo), which takes place annually. It describes itself as 'the event for any professional tasked with protecting assets, business, people and nations from terrorism'. Participants will view the 'latest developments, share best practice and ensure that their threat mitigation strategies are effective', with access to 'over 300 leading suppliers'.[6] The biennial Defence Procurement Research, Technology & Exportability (DPRTE) expo 2014 was described as 'a unique educational and engagement platform for MOD [UK Ministry of Defence] and industry to connect'. In making those connections the aim is 'to explore the key challenges, programmes and future opportunities that exist within the defence acquisition supply chain'.[7]

The other event in focus here – from which much of the material in this chapter is drawn – is the biennial Defence and Security Equipment International (DSEI) exhibition. This is one of the largest arms fairs in the world, attracting 'the largest international community within the sector'. It describes itself as 'a global showcase of innovative defence and security equipment and technologies for land, maritime and air applications, as well as the latest developments for the security, unmanned, medical and disaster relief sectors'.[8] In 2015, there were over 34,000 attendees, including 1,683 exhibitors from 54 countries comprising global defence and security suppliers, set up in 42 international pavilions.

While DSEI is owned and organized by Clarion Events, it 'receives major financial, logistical and political support from the UK government, most notably through the government's arms sales unit'.[9] The event typically includes a series of specialized workshops and showcases, 'offering additional opportunities for further learning, discussion and debate', in addition to a drinks reception for 'rising stars' in the arms industry, along with strategic conferences requiring additional payment. According to DSEI, its events include 'top level international military staff, major procurement officials, and the entire industry supply chain, from large prime contractors to supplying companies ... bringing the entire supply chain together on an unrivalled scale'.[10]

Warrior-protector man meets bourgeois-rational man

Dominant and subordinate masculinities are constructed in transnational arenas such as multinational corporations or sites of war.[11] These include both warrior-protector and bourgeois-rational model masculinities, the latter encompassing both 'transnational business masculinity'[12] and 'techno-scientific' masculinity.[13] Arms fairs feature a range of exhibitors that display actual, replica or mini-models of their products and/ or advertising materials in order to promote their brand. Many exhibitors are advertising overtly militarized warrior-protector products for sale, such as guns, tanks, drones and bombs. Others are recognizable civilian brands that are already, or easily become, militarized, such as Oakley sunglasses or Nikon cameras.[14] As Gibbon notes, political repression is also treated as 'a sales opportunity',[15] so there are aisles displaying CS gas, riot guns, batons and surveillance equipment commonly deployed against civilians in public demonstrations.[16]

Arms fairs feature many physical instances of warrior-protector masculinity, including actual tanks, guns and other conventional weapons, as well as actual human bodies in military dress, and similar images in advertising material. The fairs themselves are ultimately organized like any other trade show in the business world. As one observer notes: 'Walking around DSEI, I was struck by its similarity to IFA, a tech trade show I visited earlier in the month. The booths, the lanyards, the men in suits discussing specs and prices; they were all the same, but instead of smartphones, everyone was looking at guns.'[17]

Like all exhibitions and trade shows, there is a hierarchy in the size and arrangement of stands and exhibition spaces. Smaller companies have small, standard-issue exhibition spaces that they decorate with their own banner or display rigs. At DSEI the major arms companies, such as BAE Systems, Saab, Lockheed Martin, Finmeccanica and Rafael, all have huge, imposing, impressive and sleek pavilions that include different areas, usually with a separate seating area for business deals. As platinum sponsors for expo, BAE Systems has an upstairs VIP area, and the UK MOD has a separate lounge. Those spaces are business-like and sanitized, evoking the experience of modern offices, business lounge retreats and corporate waiting areas.

At the same time, other areas display major pieces of 'kit', such as tanks or other vehicles, as well as the latest drones. The hierarchy of stands mirrors the class hierarchies of masculinities, through which some men subordinate others. There is thus a different kind of dominant masculinity on display in the larger stands compared with the smaller ones. While there is obviously some overlap, the larger, more powerful companies generally do not use as many overtly hypermasculine advertising techniques as the smaller companies. The difference is that their brand names usually speak for themselves, and this is reflected in the size of their stands. As everyone knows, size really does matter.

Furthermore, while the small companies often use gimmicks in order to draw people in, the spectacular displays mounted by large companies are often actual tanks or missiles. Because of their size, authenticity and destructive capabilities, those props pack more punch. Getting up close and personal with such items requires proof of insider access, and for many civilian participants it is a privileged chance to cross over into the rigidly guarded, taboo and out-of-view realm of the military.

Dressing to impress

Gender is performed most authentically and recognizably through embodiment; for example, in many situations 'a man's body gives credibility to his utterance, whereas a woman's body takes it away from hers', as Smith affirms.[18] Further sociological studies demonstrate that what people choose to wear on their bodies can be likened to a theatre costume, or to a fashion show, which conveys 'gender and power, respect and authority, modernity and authenticity'.[19] What people wear 'is highly effective in endlessly constituting but never fixing identities'. Because clothes are usually 'the visible social marker of gender difference',[20] they are therefore crucial in establishing a person's legitimacy as an authority, always already dichotomously gendered. In context, then, clothes are not just 'metaphors for power and authority' but 'literally *are* authority'.[21]

Performing gender is performing legitimacy, and thus legitimating the hierarchy of masculinity over femininity. The inverse is well exemplified through the concept of cross-dressing. Men wearing women's clothes and vice versa perform a violation of the gender-order hierarchy, removing any claim to legitimacy that an activity would otherwise have, apart from circumstances understood as comedic or parodic. Moreover, violence towards cross-dressers, and others identified as violators of the hierarchical gender order, is understood by perpetrators as legitimate because such aggressive, criminal acts dramatically re-legitimize the hierarchy.

In the business world, as in the military world, cross-dressing – without proper accreditation and performed with proper dignity – would be decidedly out of place. The gender order is deadly serious, and we know it when we see it. Moreover, interpersonal violence, or any provocation that might inspire this, is, of course, also out of place in sanitized and securitized exhibition spaces. Violence in these weaponized spaces is referenced verbally as a human essential, but is kept very distant from the site, and portrayed materially there as inertly safe and consumer-friendly.

At arms fairs the general run of gendered, classed and raced identities is repetitively cited and performed through different styles and types of clothing, serving different functions in relation to the products and the fair itself. Participants perform their legitimacy to attend the event, in part through what they are wearing, as well as through lanyards and badging, which are compulsory. At DSEI it is clearly stated, on the website and in other promotional literature, that attendees must wear business dress/attire, that is, the uniform of transnational business masculinity.[22]

Dress serves a function of legitimation immediately on entering the arms fair, especially in relation to the protestors outside. They are persistently visible there because they wear more casual clothes. Some of those outfits could be described as an alternative to normalized commercial attire, often featuring someone dressed as the grim reaper. The scene is certainly not what anyone would understand as readily compatible with business or military uniforms, which would stand out among the protestors. However, on the inside, with the attendees and exhibitors, the situation is reversed. Protestors are therefore performing a mocking, individualistic parody of corporate-military uniformity and group-think conformity. This continuous charade is a public strategy of delegitimation, in particular of older elites and their hierarchies of orderly rank authority. When undercover protestors have managed to get into arms fairs, they have necessarily dressed in business attire in order to both get in and fit in.[23]

Gibbon writes that gender 'plays a contradictory role in arms fairs', where many exhibitors 'use myths of femininity to convey fantasies of power'. Yet renegotiations of gender are also in evidence, sometimes in conjunction: 'a female manager might be discussing a deal on one stand, while a woman is offered as an erotic spectacle on another'.[24] At DSEI the attendees and exhibitors fell into these gendered subject positions: (1) bourgeois-rational men who constituted the overwhelming majority, approximately 70 per cent; (2) warrior-protector military men (uniformed women are rarely present), perhaps 20 per cent, although some military men and women may have chosen not to wear military uniform; and (3) women.

Women probably constitute less than 10 per cent of attendees, occupying their own distinct categories (explored below), thus marking the 'other gender' in relation to the dominant and dominating men and masculinities. Their presence secures the scene for heterosexuality, safe from any suspicion that the homosocial gathering – as it appears and as it functions – could possibly signify the unnamed 'other', that is, male homosexuality.[25] That 'other' destabilizes 'normal' masculinities, because it destabilizes the gender-order hierarchy, not just the numerical, cultural and political dominance of heterosexuality. That dominance secures the gender-order hierarchy itself.

To function as a social marker, uniforms rely on shared understandings as to what they represent, just as gender does, and the two are co-constitutive of the gender-order hierarchy.[26] De Casanova argues that 'white-collar men accept conformity and constraint in their work clothing because doing so helps them maintain their privileged status', naming it a 'strategic embrace of conformity' which ensures 'continued access to … privilege'.[27] This commonplace fact of the commercial and military worlds signifies the might of the gender order, given the enforced binary of suited-and-booted masculine uniforms over and against female 'business' attire. Female businesswear is necessarily parodic, rather than identical. Identical outfits, for otherwise identifiable men and women (typically hairstyles, facial features and [non] make-up), would signify disorder, even unintelligibility, and threaten panic.

At DSEI, the military men project uniformity but also a hierarchical ordering of nationality, rank and service, for example, army, navy, air force, marines. There are further cross-cutting hierarchies, for example, combat service, commandos and suchlike. In the military, the uniform is considered, in Craik's words, 'an apparatus to instil discipline by training the body and mind in specified ways'.[28] As in most public places it is not a normal occurrence to see military personnel in uniform, apart from their presence at special events, such as certain parades, weddings and funerals. Following anti-terrorist threat warnings against wearing uniforms in public, or after highly publicized one-off murders of service personnel, perhaps these casual sightings are less frequent. At least this is so in civilianized countries with volunteer armies; in militarized nations, with conscription, it might be more normal to see males, usually youthful, on the street or in the metro.

However, at an arms fair a panoply of stripes, insignias, badges, ribbons, braids, feathers, hats and colours, and further coded accessories, all deriving from the world's militaries, are on display. The scene thus presents a strange mélange of uniformed diversity. Men wearing military uniforms are specifically respected and treated differently from those in businessman uniform: people move out of their way, and some stare at them, as they are a continuously changing spectacle, and clearly useful to exhibitors as a 'draw' to their stands. The Official Event Preview actively encourages the wearing of military uniform: 'Military Personnel are encouraged to wear uniform. Changing facilities will be available upon request. Ask at the concierge desk ... for further details.'[29]

In this context, a 'forces' uniform marks a person as someone with evident military knowledge and experience, a warrior-protector, but also a 'knower' and expert. The glorification of warrior-protector military masculinity, implicit in the encouragement given to uniform wearing, underscores the legitimacy of the arms trade, in contradistinction to its illegitimate 'other' as a present-absence. That present-absence is a presumed shadowy world of diverse and un-uniformed criminality, even more hidden from public view than the expo fairs. This is where idealized masculinity drives the legitimation processes that this unarticulated 'guilty conscience' requires.

Men in uniform are a visible reminder of how the military of the nation-state links with idealized masculinity, and certainly not with criminal gangs, which are also overwhelmingly male.[30] This is fulsomely articulated in promotional materials by hypermasculine youthful male bodies in warrior-like action mode. It is possible to hire army members to attract people to stands, drawing on unstated desires for eroticized and fetishized alpha-maleness. Uniforms represent this ultimately legitimizing form of masculinity, even if at the event the bodies wearing the clothes do not always live up to this publicized ideal. The gap between the ideal and the visible, of course, keeps one looking and checking against the blockbuster poster-warrior index.

As gender is relational, the military men in uniform are masculinized in a superior hierarchical relation to the somewhat subordinated bourgeois-rational men and to the much more subordinated women, just as the gender-order hierarchy ensures a familiar normality. The military men make the bourgeois-rational men appear somewhat lacking in relation to an iconic ideal of militarized masculinity and to the well-understood and ubiquitously advertised processes of hypermasculinization, which merge male physicality with deadly weaponry. That hierarchy makes it obvious that most men do not live up to the blockbuster-warrior male ideal in their daily lives, even if those daily lives are military ones.[31]

Moreover the military hierarchy erases class hierarchies that are visible elsewhere in civilian life. Class signifiers within bourgeois-rational 'businessman' masculinity are effected through suit tailoring, bespoke shirts, 'clubby' silk ties and other more or less expensive accessories, such as luxury watches and hi-tech gadgets. Gibbon observes: 'This is best quality pinstripe. It drapes gently as he moves. He sweeps back his jacket. He has contacts, he can pull strings.'[32] These items are markers for social class through a variety of aesthetic signifiers that are most easily accessible through higher education and social background.

The *Financial Times* weekend edition provides advisory columns on high-class business fashion shopping, a curated business-and-leisure 'Technopolis' feature in the glossy magazine, and considerable amounts of 'How to Spend It' lifestyle advertising. This is aimed at the aspirational, not-yet-super-rich *homme d'affaires*, highlighting luxury gifts and jewellery classics to bestow on women, thus objectifying them as high-value 'worth it' sexual acquisitions and status signifiers.

Although in a very marked and distinct minority, women are a significant presence. As Sjoberg argues: 'the presence of women draws attention to gender dynamics. How are women seen? What are women seen to signify? What does that mean for how men are understood? For how situations are understood?'[33] In this situation the small minoritized, very unthreatening presence of women makes bourgeois-rational men look, and probably feel, more masculine, as they are somewhat feminized in subordinate relation to the military men. Thus some men will be secured in relation to the gender-order hierarchy overall and assuaged in relation to their superiors in the nested hierarchies of masculinity. At the same time they can feel the gender superiority of maleness that is secured through the heterosexuality within which masculinity, as the dominating gender, 'makes sense'.

Moreover, the minority presence of women reflects the now familiar reality – in certain parts of the world – of some women serving alongside men in the armed forces, and indeed, doing the same in the arms industry in the corporate and political hierarchies of salary, wages and value. Both the minoritized presence in relation to the male majority and the subordinated position in relation to male-dominated hierarchies of reward are mirrored in, and projected by, the arms fair spectacle. Some women seem to be assistants, there to serve drinks, while others seem to be the equivalent of the men, there to sell and give information about the products. And some are simply looking at the products as buyers or competitor-sellers.

Perhaps surprisingly, the women at DSEI, who are one way or another inside the industry – rather than the cleaners, food servers and similar on-site female service workers – are not all blending in with the civilian men by wearing dark coloured business 'suits' or by power-dressing as executive females. While the men in suits generally blur into one normalizing mode, what constitutes business attire is much more flexible for women. Much of it is overtly feminine, colourful and patterned, even occasionally frilly, rather than projecting masculinized versions of female tailoring. That 'look' is individualized on their female bodies as objects of heterosexual male interest, using variety and diversity to draw in the male gaze, over and above other markers of female 'difference'. This gendered difference is always already hierarchical and political in opposition to the ways that conformity protects bourgeois-rational men. Rather than a monolithic force to be reckoned with, the already marginalized minority of women are further fragmented as disparate individuals and de-subjectified objects.

The spectrum of women's identities, parsed as attendees and exhibitors, falls roughly into these five bands:

- Those who blend in with the bourgeois-rational men yet are still recognizable as women, but in corporate attire, which is de-sexualized by being masculinized in a suit-like way, that is, trousers or skirt with black tights. They are the least visible and least visibly feminine. Their clothes mark them as experts/knowers, much like the bourgeois-rational men in suits.

- Those wearing corporate attire, that is, dressing in a dark suit but with some kind of visibly feminine, decorative touch, such as colourful high-heeled shoes, making those women quite distinct as sexual objects. But a corporate clothes style also marks them as experts/knowers.

- Those wearing corporate, smart dress, but sexy, with flesh on show. This is corporate because the tailoring is dark and fitted, yet sexually distinct and enticing at the same time.[34] Here the bare female body is exhibited in stark contrast to the sea of men in body-covering suits. Tight smart dresses in dark colours reveal bare arms, legs, cleavages and backs, making these women very visible. Sexiness is tempered, evidently, since technically this counts as business attire. Only a minority of women dress like this.

- Those presenting themselves as overtly feminine but primly respectable, covering the body, yet colourful in patterned dresses or white tailored suits. Those women are very visible amidst the dark suits and offer interest and decoration for the male gaze. Often women in these clothes would appear to be in supporting roles, such as receptionists or drinks servers, or what are often termed 'hostesses'. Sometimes they are wearing a common 'event' uniform similar to airline flight attendants.

- Those who are present as hypersexualized objects to entice, either through being physically there or through cartoon or poster-type imagery, but, unlike the hypermasculine bodies, not linked directly to the product. That type of female presence appears to be decreasing over time, for reasons discussed below.

Evidently there are unspoken dress code rules about what constitutes corporate attire for women. It appears that women could be in non-business attire, such as coloured or patterned material, but must then be covered and respectable. Alternatively, flesh could be showing, as long as the clothes worn could be considered corporate/business, that is, dark, monochrome, fitted, formal. Looked at the other way, men gain power through marking their dominance visibly as a phalanx of uniformity. But in that uniformity they present nested hierarchies. Within that mode they enact the male gaze of domination that elicits and constructs heterosexual objectification.

In addition to the attendees and exhibitors, there are other women at these events, but they are not legitimated as participants. Rather, they are serving the event and its official participants in different ways. This presents an immediate social class hierarchy, through which female subordination is commonly enacted and experienced in the inseparable way that intersectionality signals and highlights.[35] Massage therapists, mainly women, but sometimes men, wear branded T-shirts and trousers, but are not overtly sexualized. They are rather carefully de-sexualized as knowledgeable professionals. Young women and men are working in the food outlets. Of course there are cleaners, who are mainly female, contributing to the sanitization of the event in literal ways, but also signifying its legitimacy as a clean and wholesomely respectable activity.

Such women are visible, but also invisible. They are visible because of their bodies and cleaners' uniforms. Unlike the military/corporate uniforms, the cleaners' attire is marked sartorially as hard and dirty work by hand, but not very much – supposedly – by brain. That work is invisible in relation to the sanitizing mode through which the event operates, and is thus, in a metaphorical contradistinction, 'behind the scenes'. Those women are understood as having a service mentality, not in authority, not someone to talk to. They are inside, but not insiders.

Warrior masculinity and the erasure of violence and death

The potential for violence and death, caused or facilitated by the products that are advertised for sale at arms fairs, represents an important threat to its legitimacy. The erasure of violence and death is therefore an important part of the legitimation of the international arms trade, particularly in the actual spaces that are constituted as being part of it. Such possibilities are silently directed at its rarely mentioned illegitimate 'other'.

That erasure takes a number of remarkable and unexpected forms. At DSEI, 'goody' bags are handed out on entry, as is typical at trade shows. Rather than an official bag branding the event, however, this is a bag advertising, for example, one of the companies exhibiting – Kent Periscopes. The company's catchphrase is, 'Designing, developing & manufacturing sights and observation systems for armoured fighting vehicles'. The goody bag contains a 'build your tank' cut-out template. Once you have built your tank, you can enter a competition to win an iPad by sending in a picture of your model.

Both the cut-out tank and the competition are reminiscent of prizes and 'draws' in cereal boxes – dating back to the 1950s or earlier, and still aimed at boys in the 1980s or 1990s – except that on the other side of the cut-out template there is an information leaflet about products and services for 'fighting vehicles', as well as the terms and conditions for the model competition. Thus national officials and businessmen attending the arms fair are being invited to indulge their boys-and-toys fantasies and sensibilities, including a 'freebie' stick of branded rock candy. This evocation of boyhood and seaside holidays renders arms fairs non-threatening and non-lethal, thus enhancing the legitimacy of commercial weapons production. Gibbon also catalogues this 'fun feature' of arms fairs:

> Many companies also offer gifts as an alternative to business cards – pens, key rings, sweets stamped with arms company names. A gasmask manufacturer gives away condoms with the slogan, 'the ultimate protection'. Caterpillar has a line of toy bulldozers alongside the huge versions that are used to clear homes in the occupied Palestinian territories. There are stress balls in the shape of grenades, military vehicles, and a bomb with a string fuse.[36]

While DSEI self-identifies as an exhibition in serious museum-type parlance, it is also, in fact, a fair, a place of entertainment and fun. This direct mixing of business with pleasure, and war with amusement, performs a sanitizing and therefore legitimizing function. This happens immediately on entry, where many large, imposing and intimidating military vehicles are displayed. Weapons in that setting are presented as harmless toys to be admired and played with, abstracted from any sense of politics or war, as is the case in wider militarized culture across many contexts, including film and video games.[37]

Interestingly the technology is usually not named, for example, drone, tank, missile. It is assumed that everyone knows what everything is by name, rather as anyone would know a common household item. That sense of playfulness is also apparent in a number of interactive opportunities available to visitors. For example, a small rubber company puts a sign on its stand saying 'Please touch' next to some rubber products. This is an open invitation, in stark contrast to 'Do not touch' signs commonly found in gift or craft shops. There are numerous displays of replica guns and rifles that visitors can pick up, play with and aim at each other.

While these displays give military personnel a chance to sample the products, they also provide an opportunity for non-military attendees to experience what it would be like to touch, and to some extent, use, the technology, and possibly participate in war-hero realities. Although these chances to play with the products enable attendees to get physically close to them, they also function to further separate the products from violence and death, since they are replicas that do not actually shoot bullets or explode, and the context is clearly a non-violent one. This tactic of sanitization transforms these technologies of death and destruction into toys or video games, harmless and fun. It is possible, and no doubt intended, that the person participating should experience a thrill and a sense of power, an aspect of 'a militarism of consumption and pleasure', as Power explains.[38]

Militarized video games are a clear point of reference, enabling visitors to enjoy fantasies of killing without consequences, because even the dead die discreetly in such sanitized circumstances.[39] Cockpit technology is a good example. First, in the cockpit the technology learns to sense the visitor's eye movement, after which the 'look and shoot' game begins. As explained by the company 'rep' this is a development far in advance of conventional technologies, which require manual movement of a joystick in order to select the target prior to shooting. Simply looking at a target doesn't 'kill' it, however, since manual button pushing is still required, so the experience grounds itself in familiar human physicality and centuries-old technologies, very familiar to boys.

At the arms fair, however, this dual fantasy, boyhood and soldierhood, induces a subjectivity of full participation and emotional immersion in the event itself, mirroring in individual subjectivities the legitimizing strategies deployed there. This immersive seduction echoes Cohn's classic experiential account of her secondment with nuclear defence intellectuals at the Rand Corporation. That kind of immersion makes the destruction-oriented environment at the think tank, or at the trade show, seem safer, more reassuring, quite normal. The 'disembodied simulation' of 'virtuous' war sanitizes the violence of war and weaponry.[40]

Bourgeois–rational masculinity and the erasure of violence and death

The very recognizable bourgeois-rational, transnational business masculinity that turns 'war into a business' at the trade fair allows participants to mask the consequences of so much state-sanctioned violence and destruction. If the arms trade is just another business – as DSEI proclaims with every branded give-away USB stick – then it's all too easy 'to forget what the business is all about'. Furthermore, as Vincent relates, the bourgeois-rational, transnational business context means that 'there's also a normalising effect going on here, where guns and bullets are packaged in the familiar language of consumerism'.[41]

In this context, then, the language of militarism, weapons and war quickly becomes normalized, sanitized and, in some cases, glorified, which, in turn, reinforces the legitimacy of weapons, militarism and war, by forestalling the obvious critique and making it unsayable. Gibbon echoes this point: 'A string quartet competes with explosions video-looped at that moment when earth and light collide. The impact of such explosions on lives and communities is not shown or spoken [or heard, presumably]; the language of grief and pain does not exist in a world of clean metal.'[42]

Arms fairs are civilized and ordered by contrast to warfare itself, which many people know, if somewhat abstractly and distantly from media reports, rather than from experience, is messy and violent. The disconnect between the visuality of broadcast news and everyday normality in manufacturer-countries is thus quite stark. Moreover, manufacturer-countries are protected from the bloody and dirty destruction that these weapons cause because of the wealth and self-arming through which their role in the weapons industry is secured. So by contrast and inverse example, countries and regions subjected to this dirtying destruction appear guilty and pathetic.

Many of the pavilions are glossy white, projecting a sanitized and minimalist ambience, making whatever is on display stand out even more against the white background. Glossy, white, hyper-clean surfaces refer intertextually to scientific laboratories as temples of hygienic white rationality, mirroring the bourgeois-rational government-backed research and development behind the technologies actually on display. This assemblage of intertextual referencing performs a science-framing halo of sanctified knowledge all around the personnel and contents.

Violence and death are nowhere to be seen at arms fairs, apart from displays within the medical exhibits. Displaying objects behind a physical barrier of glass, as if they are artefacts in a museum, further removes them from functional actuality. Gronning, a visitor, comments on the scene, summarizing the situation: 'What the exhibitors really lack is a joining up between the tools and their actual purpose: the evisceration of flesh and the righteous punishing of enemies.' The advertising 'focuses far too much on the technical specs of the merchandise and hides away from any hint whatsoever of bloodshed or actual violence (except in some of the more gnarly medical exhibits)'. Factually Gronning notes that, 'over the course of the day, I can only find one reference to death. ... The high-energy laser gun has "scaleable lethality", almost making it seem boring. Almost.'[43]

As much as an arms fair can be understood as one giant display of warrior-protector and bourgeois-rational masculinity, traditionally feminine signifiers are also apparent. In and among displays of weapons there are bowls of fruit and flowers in vases. These are not hypervisible, as are the weapons, yet such decorative touches do significant gender work. Bowls of fruit and vases of flowers have classical associations with femininity, and indeed with 'still life' as a genre of peaceful domestic contemplation, that are similarly persistent today.

Moreover, as artefacts they are traditionally found in homes or in settings made to seem homey, thus associated with domesticity and women, understood through heterosexuality and the male gaze. This femininity effectively frames the 'hard-ass' techno-masculinity, making it friendly, welcoming, healthy and paternal, in stark contrast to the realities of militarization and war, as well as to the ideals. Thus we have the warrior-protector's home life, at home but not of it, referencing what is to be protected, not what that protection is presumed to require.

A large proportion of the stands typically offer bowls of sweets for casual grazing, evoking childhood innocence and adult nostalgia, as well as a something-for-nothing frisson. As Vincent notes: 'It makes me wonder whether a piece of Haribo ever cinched the deal on a shipment of assault rifles.'[44] Many stands will offer coffee or wine, served by women, and sometimes later on in the day, a stand-up beer-bar atmosphere. And, as Gibbon observes, sometimes 'later in the day' comes quite early: 'By late morning many stands have opened a few bottles of beer and champagne, and filled bowls with grapes, nectarines, nuts and chocolate.'[45] That sort of installation promotes an after-work atmosphere, rather reinforcing the idea that stand visiting earlier in the day had been focused on serious work, thus erasing some of the guilt over earlier frivolity. As a comedian and anti-arms trade activist, Thomas remarks of DSEI: 'The message "Get pissed and buy guns"... seems at odds with the organizers' message that this is "high tech".'[46]

Summing up/moving on

The violence and death caused by warrior-protector masculinity in action is made highly visible through news media images and imagery, photography and cinematography, history documentaries and the like. Some experience of its representation is therefore deeply embedded in everyone's consciousness. However, that experience is embedded there in a way that still contrasts, for example, with rather more taboo realms of violence and death, such as aerial bombardment and terrorist executions, even via media images. When shown on news broadcasts such images and video recordings are preceded by stern warnings that they 'might upset some viewers'. Many such grisly representations aren't shown, and appear, if at all, only as evidence in the highest zones of international inquiry.

International arms fairs occupy a liminal realm, such that even without protestors a change to full public access and news video reports would be unwelcome. The exhibition of weaponry, however sanitized with corporate seriousness, heterosexist hierarchies, nods to nostalgia and frissons of frivolity, is still one of visceral, unexpressed taboo. Within that space everything for sale relates to warrior-protector masculinities, military and civilian, in a visible imbrication. The familiar commercialism of things-for-sale is yet another way that the taboo liminality of the space negates one of modern society's most fetishized boundary lines, namely wartime/peacetime, what can be shown and what can't, when shopping is appropriate and when it's not. The large-scale actualities of genuine tanks and functioning, albeit unloaded, weaponry are metonymies for the realities experienced 'out there' in conflict zones and 'over there' in foreign lands.

Rather similarly metonymies of femininity and domesticity – fruit, flowers, sweets – and everyday normality – coffee, wine, beer – are surreally counterposed to blood-and-guts ordnance, rather as if military recruitment videos had seamlessly merged with advertising commercials and then materialized in real time. The shiny white and spotlessly clean exhibition zone radiates health and happiness, commercial success and secure domesticity, rather than any dizzying nausea of unfamiliarity and terror.

The physicality of the scene, bright lighting, familiar binary gendering in clothing and bodies, hairstyles and deportment, make orderly and peaceable normality into a specially potent set of signifiers, given the nearly unthinkable character of the constitutive 'other'. That 'other' is, of course, the violence and destruction that cannot be displayed, or even named or referenced with any clarity. Yet all that is in the air, a haunting spectre of horror.

DSEI and similar sales fairs are one of the highest peaks of bourgeois-rational masculinities, making rationality out of violence and death by abstracting all that warrior-protector physicality into geofinancial/geopolitical calculations and corporate reports. This is accomplished in a parody of an office-like, business exhibition atmosphere of competitive men and subordinated women. This is replete with in-work and after-work homosocial opportunities for men, and heterosexualized awkwardness and objectification for women. The arms fair is effectively a stage setting, a real-life 'improv', through which studied articulations of masculinities and femininities make the whole thing work. Gibbon meditates on this: 'I may be wearing a suit, but I know that I am a fake. ... Like the arms traders around me, I am careful to act the part. ... And yet while engaged in this covert charade, I have come to realize that parody is not necessary in this setting.'[47]

Corporate players in the weapons game

We now move on to explore in detail how the weapons industry and arms trade legitimize themselves to the general public. BAE Systems is the largest arms producer in the UK and the seventh largest in the world, as of 2020.[48] It is quite close in turnover to the next-higher ranking three, so in league table terms it is approximately joint fourth.[49] It posts promotional videos on YouTube, so, in choosing two of these, each with a different target audience, we are now in very different territory.[50]

The arms fairs are about weaponry and money, through which sellers meet buyers. Elites in both spheres, as we have seen, are playing their parts in affirming the legitimacy of the arms trade. They do this by repetitively citing the familiar hierarchies of the gender order themselves, and indeed, their legitimizing spectacles also work the other way round. Powerful elites, overwhelmingly white and male, are using weaponry and money, once legitimized, to endorse and maintain the legitimacy of the gender-order hierarchy of masculinity over femininity. That order operates hierarchically in nests of competitive subordination, privileging some states and corporations over others, privileging warrior-protector military 'brass' over bourgeois-rational executives, privileging white-raced elites over 'others' deemed non-white. It privileges men over women by minoritizing them in numbers and positioning them within the male gaze.

Making a video of all this activity would not be a good promotional strategy for a company, because some within the general public would be adept at spotting the great-power politics of these unholy conjunctions: taxpayer funding for violence and destruction, unpublicized deal-making with corruptible deal-makers, corporate profits trumping the national interest – no matter how sanitized the appearances.

How, then, do corporate players in the weapons 'game' legitimize themselves for much more sceptical, and much less handpicked, worldwide 'outsider' audiences? To answer that question we turn to two promotional videos. Both address the ongoing legitimacy deficit[51] that BAE Systems faces simply by doing what it does. What it must do, therefore, is construct repetitive, legitimizing narratives to make up the ground.

Race–gender–class

As we have seen, warrior-protector and bourgeois-rational masculinities, as understood and practised within the world of weapons manufacture and arms trading, represent pressing moral liabilities, briefly summarized as deathly violence and commercial-political corruption. It follows that those two masculinities are the signifiers – words and images – through which legitimation must necessarily be pursued. Otherwise BAE Systems would be unrecognizable as a legitimate business, rather than the hyper-dirty illegitimate opposite.

Moreover, both masculinities are themselves at risk, as is the masculinizing ordering of hierarchies, which operates within, and is the result of, nested hierarchies of domination and subordination among men. Boys-and-toys warrior-protector masculinity marks the pinnacle of idealized maleness as an aspiration, precisely because nested competitions ensure that very few men attain the alpha-male positions. BAE Systems claims to be a 'top company' in bourgeois-rational masculinity terms, and also in its particular connection there to blockbuster Hollywood militarism. That militarism is also 'top tier', because those are the terms of the inter-state competitions through which the international system is understood.

The corporate world of bourgeois-rational masculinity mirrors this competitive militarism of state-actors quite precisely, albeit in a subordinated way, but only slightly. And even that slight subordination disappears in the smooth imbrication of personnel that is a feature of those two aligned, but supposedly distinct, male-dominated worlds: arms corporations and militarized states.

BAE Systems has posted two videos, referred to here as 'US' and 'global', both addressing its legitimacy deficits, albeit for somewhat different audiences. The interplay of race–gender signifiers is thus somewhat different in each, although the gender-order hierarchy of masculinity over femininity, and the nested hierarchies of some men over others, will appear, even if implicitly, as a common grid of intelligibility. That intelligibility flows from intertextual references that are voiced and visualized, thus constructing a legitimizing narrative from familiar materials. Other kinds of businesses, and virtually all nation-states, do the same, and for much the same reasons.

We identify four ways in which BAE Systems is legitimized in these videos:

- *Legitimation 1*: presupposing the inevitability, normalization and glorification of armed violence.
- *Legitimation 2*: sanitizing BAE Systems through the erasure of violence and death.
- *Legitimation 3*: narrating BAE Systems as a national symbol.
- *Legitimation 4*: articulating BAE Systems as a progressive, equal opportunities employer.

In our analysis we highlight the ways in which race–gender–class is implicitly and explicitly deployed in order to produce these legitimations.

Legitimation 1: Armed force as inevitable, normalized and glorified

The inevitable, necessary, normalized and to some extent glorified character of armed force, understood as security for the nation-state, is the fundamental premise for BAE Systems' existence. That premise must be repetitively signified and unquestioningly accepted by the target audience in order for any further legitimating narratives to make any sense.

In the US video the use of the definite article in 'the next front' ensures that, before viewers even click 'play', they are aware that not only is another war inevitable, but that wars will always continue to happen. The sub-heading of the YouTube version substantiates this assumption: 'The world continues to change. New threats emerge. New fronts arise.'

Once the viewer has pressed play, that narrative of the enduring inevitability of war is compounded by the timeless concept of 'the bad guys', introduced in the second spoken line: 'the name of the game is staying one step ahead of the bad guys'. By referring to the 'bad guys', BAE Systems establishes an 'us and a them', good guys and bad guys, self and other.[52]

Who the bad guys are 'goes without saying', which presupposes and affirms pre-existing knowledge. Yet that hermeneutic 'hook' involves the viewer in puzzling out who the 'bad guys' currently are, and what their 'badness' consists of. The viewer is thus subsumed into the subject position of someone who can identify with 'us', that is, the aims, values and purposes of the company, in other words, one of the good guys.[53]

We do not see any bad guys in the video, but we do not need to. Our imaginations can picture them for us, and indeed, the ambiguity of this empty signifier leaves us to do the enjoyable interpretive work, assisted no doubt by numerous Hollywood archetypes. Moreover, by not visually identifying any particular bad guys, that discursive strategy makes them even more threatening. They could be anyone at any time, thus referencing other narratives of national paranoia about 'others' who are not 'us'. 'Others' aren't 'us' because, following stereotypical narratives, they don't share 'our values', which are unspecified, other than being 'good'.

The 'global' video refers to 'bad people', which presupposes by contrast that the people at BAE Systems are good. This hails the viewer into the good person-subject position aligned with the company. Again, we do not see any bad people, although there is a verbal reference to pirates, familiar outlaw/outsider figures from childhood action-adventure fiction and films. Those abstract, yet potent ambiguities avoid any conflict with the diverse political perspectives and conflicting national interests in the targeted global audience. Their views would be less easily predictable than is the case with an American one.

The hero worshipping of soldiers and glorification of armed force is central to, and essential for, the militarism without which there would be no warfare and no arms industry. Hence BAE Systems videos will sustain this view and spectacle.[54] Through both videos, BAE Systems gives viewers the opportunity, in O'Neill's words, 'to assume and become subsumed by a story of masculine heroism'.[55] In the US video, hero worship and respect for the troops are key points of reference, including statements such as: 'we're serving those who serve us'; 'I feel what we do is important to lives. To the men and women who put their lives on the line'; 'We solve problems – big problems, for pilots and the troops they carry. And I'm so proud to be a part of that'; 'me and my crew … we served on these vessels, and so we take a lot of pride in the work that we do now'; 'They're [our soldiers are] keeping us safe and I'm doing my part to help them the best I can.'

The global video features less hero worship and deference to the military, although it occurs more generically: 'Knowing soldiers are counting on you, that's what keeps me going.' When BAE Systems positions itself as subordinate in this way, it is masculinizing the armed forces and feminizing itself. It is more than just what is said that achieves that gendered positioning. By including female BAE employees, both visually and audibly, BAE Systems is able to subordinate itself in relation to the military. Although the military are correctly referred to throughout the US video as 'men and women', we see only servicemen using the products. When BAE Systems positions itself in the service of, and therefore subordinate to, the male-dominated global military, this gendering trope adds to the glorification of military men, and to the understanding of masculinity as importantly militaristic.

The global video focuses on the ways that armed forces rely on BAE Systems' work. That video is less emotional than the US one, because it is less about the people doing the fighting and more about how the technology itself is going to 'do great things'. Nevertheless, armed force is glorified in statements such as: 'you see these ships go off to chase pirates or on a disaster relief mission. It's a source of great pride amongst us'; 'we are making sure those who are defending us are ready'; followed by 'that's what inspires me, all of us really. We're doing something that truly matters'. Here the speakers are explicitly saying that preparation for war is something that 'truly' matters. This echoes the sentiments of an earlier worker: 'What my team and I do is really important and it really matters.' By glorifying armed conflict, BAE Systems is legitimizing its business and guaranteeing demand for its weaponry.

Legitimation 2: The erasure of violence and death

In these videos some things and ideas are erased by being omitted, or by being replaced with something else or some other meaningful reference. Although war is presumed inevitable, and armed force is glorified, what is missing from both videos are any of the effects: violence, destruction, injury and death. Instead, the videos highlight BAE Systems' technologies in quite a worshipful way. Visual citations of protection produce a rhetoric that sanitizes BAE Systems' products. Hence that rhetoric legitimates weapons production, while also legitimating warrior-protector masculinity. BAE Systems must trade the products it produces, but those commercial roles in the company are also not pictured or mentioned. That omission erases any thought of 'dirty money', thus sanitizing the arms trade. This legitimates the bourgeois-rational masculinity through which it operates. Actual hands exchanging actual money is an age-old taboo affecting visuality as well as narrative.

The use of positive language is explicit from the start in the US video, which opens with the line: 'I feel what we do is important to lives.' Here BAE Systems is explicitly challenging any negative reference to the arms trade and weapons industry as, say, merchants of death. The positive language erases death by emphasizing life. Although the next sentence adds that the lives referred to are those of military personnel – 'the men and women who put their lives on the line' – the positive, inclusive connotation of the opening banality frames the qualification. That framing closes down the thought that lives – other than the viewer's – will be destroyed: civilian lives, lives in other militaries and indeed the lives of those serving 'us' in the military. The company, as warrior, protects the viewer.

The global video also features repetitive positive language: 'these amazing machines'; 'something special'; 'really important and it really matters'; 'exciting'; 'the amazing submarines made here are a big part of our hearts'; 'these aircraft, they're very advanced'. That focus on what is positive and active closes down negative notions of destruction and death. The video also uses the words 'feel', 'love', 'carry', 'serve', 'provide', 'help', 'giving', 'trust', 'touch' and 'inspire'. Those terms are characteristically feminine and stereotypically maternal. To that rhetoric the video adds the visual deployment of female bodies and the aural testimony of female voices, so as to sanitize BAE Systems' business and make warrior-protector masculinity paternal and husbandly.

BAE Systems sanitizes its products by displacing the language of weaponry with that of technology. The word 'weapon' is never mentioned. Instead, weapons and allied hardware, software and wetware (that is, trained human beings) are referred to in the US video as: technology, vessels, critical hardware, combat vehicles, technical solutions, microprocessors, Mars rover, things, technologies and services. While the products are quite determinate as objects, even that materiality is displaced in favour of this mixture of abstract and concrete references.

In the global video, the word 'weapon' is similarly never mentioned, and similarly the language evokes familiar tropes and artefacts: vehicle, machine, something special, ships, cabin systems, round (that is, ammunition), Black Hawks, submarines, aircraft, ships, technology. However, some of the terms are explicitly related to the American military, for example Black Hawks – a reference that the target audience is likely to understand from the hero-rescue Hollywood blockbuster film *Black Hawk Down* (directed by Ridley Scott, 2001). But some are overtly civilianized, for example aircraft: 'we're using our skills to improve cabin systems, fuel economy, everything that helps the airlines be more competitive'.

In both videos the erasure of the humans who are on the receiving end of the technologies is accomplished by emphasizing the humans who use and make it: 'We provide critical hardware for our soldiers'; 'We solve problems – big problems, for pilots and the troops they carry'; '[in] building these combat vehicles … I'm giving these boys an edge' (US video). Thus the technology is humanized by these constant links: 'we put ourselves in the soldier's shoes to create a vehicle that stops at nothing'; 'you work on these amazing machines for months'; 'you see them in action'; 'we'd been working on it in secret for many years'; 'I know that it was me, it was us that helped them, to complete their mission' (global video).

The technological language that we hear links with the technological images that we see. The picture moves swiftly from shots of fighter planes and ships in motion to behind-the-scenes shots of the technologies of production, as weaponry is being manufactured and assembled. Much of the technologies we see are harmless and sanitized, because they are familiar items in civilian society, such as planes. We see missiles, but only when being tested, not when being used, and similarly we see soldiers carrying guns and driving tanks, but not actually using the weaponry.

The discourse of defence-and-protection runs throughout both videos. BAE Systems is protecting the troops; the troops are protecting 'us'. Both the military and the workers are repetitively masculinized. Even a man in a suit working to neutralize cybercrime – something that could be considered quite nerdy, and even, as a subordinated masculinity, somewhat feminized – performs this function by never letting his guard down: 'It's so important to never let my guard down, to always be searching. Bad people, they work in the shadows, but they always leave a digital footprint, and that's where we find them, buried in the data.'

Indeed, the arms trade is often referred to as the 'defence industry', closing down visualization and conceptualization as to just how that defence is achieved, and who decides authoritatively that force and violence are the appropriate means with which to pursue it. In the videos, defence requires warrior-protectors, and warrior-protectors require weaponry. Otherwise, the narratives tell us, protection won't happen, and warrior-protector masculinity will dissolve. Once that is gone, then the nation-state no longer 'makes sense'.

That mode of representation makes BAE Systems sound like a positive, inspiring place to work. The use of positive language and the focus on technology – which signifies progress, development, positivity, enlightenment – closes down negativity and scepticism. That erasure is a first step in securing legitimacy, so that BAE Systems cannot subsequently appear as a merchant of death. The universalizing inclusion of 'us' versus 'others' is only universal to the nation of the audience. The 'others' to be protected elsewhere do not appear, even though great power militarism supports interventions into subordinated states on various grounds and in various guises. Non-combatant casualties in those situations sometimes obtain public notice as so-called 'collateral damage', whereas, in the falsely inclusive world of BAE Systems, they do not even exist.

Legitimation 3: BAE Systems as a multinational symbol

The US video, from the American subsidiary BAE Systems, Inc, represents BAE Systems as stereotypically 'All-American'. Even though that idea is never explicitly stated, the video constructs this illusion by ambiguating the boundaries between military and industry, nation-state and multinational company, in order to give the impression that the company and its subsidiaries are a workshop of, and for, the American military. That patriotic narrative erases any unpatriotic suspicions that commercialization and profit-making could tarnish the investment in the Anglo–American 'special relationship'. Or, more specifically, that generating super-profits from government, that is, taxpayer funding, from either the home-side or the foreign-side, could possibly be an alternating perspective. That is a key point of criticism directed at weapons manufacture and the arms trade, so it requires erasure.

That illusion of Americanness encourages the American viewer to believe that what is being produced is going to the right people, and only to the right people. That rhetorical construction generates an inclusive realm of unquestionable moral certainty rooted in patriotic exceptionalism. Of course weapons could later be sold on and even used against Americans themselves. For example, the US armed the Afghan Mujahideen in the 1980s but then the weapons went to 'individuals and organisations that went on to form Al Qaeda'.[56]

Every time the military is referred to, the voiceover has an American accent: 'the men and women who put their lives on the line'; 'pilots and the troops they carry'; 'our soldiers'; 'we're serving those who serve us; 'boys'; 'the men and women down the line'. The video features white soldiers, stereotypical to American imagery, riding in combat vehicles that the viewer will know are American. This national framing is then confirmed by a shot of an American flag on one of the uniforms. Underscoring the conviction of moral certainty is the virtue of moral sacrifice, repetitively instanced. Viewers will know that American lives have been lost that cannot – in the national framing – have been other than virtuous.

Some speakers in the US video have 'foreign accents' that accurately reflect the range of countries in which BAE Systems operates. Yet it is made absolutely clear that BAE Systems is making things for America and Americans. The 'foreigners' do not say 'our' or 'we'. They do not talk about the company's mission; rather, they talk *about* the technology and the people they work with. That discursive strategy makes all the more visible the American accents in talking about 'our soldiers'. Dramaturgically these foreigner 'bit'-players are showing how BAE Systems exploits hi-tech talent from other parts of the world to American advantage. Thus 'our soldiers' (the US military) and 'my team' (the BAE Systems workers) are securing the nation for the target audience. America figures as global warrior-protector, needing BAE Systems' helping hand. Dramaturgically this narration works intertextually as a bromance or buddy film, another commonplace Hollywood genre.

In the US video the state resolves itself into warrior-protector masculinity, thus depoliticizing both, because together they are inevitable, necessary, moral and virtuous. The world order and the gender-order hierarchy merge, and neither provoke any problematic thoughts. The global video, however, has a harder job. That video treads a careful line in referencing several nations by name: Australia, Saudi Arabia, the UK and the US. And it refers visually to issues that are specific to certain nations, for example, protecting the kingdom of Saudi Arabia, flying American Black Hawks in Iraq, boosting the UK economy.

By contrast, national security threats are abstract enough to affect anybody anywhere: bad people, pirates, cybercrime. BAE Systems needs new markets in the competitive states of Asia and South America,[57] so to some segments of the global audience the reference to piloting planes in Iraq could well be highly contentious. Consequently that reference is very personalized, marking the pilot's dutiful experience of service and virtuous moral action. Thus the activity and its consequences are depoliticized: 'When I piloted Black Hawks in Iraq, it was technology that came out of this very building and out of this company that helped really save my life and the lives of my soldiers, someone was looking out for me, and now I get to pay that back.'

The reference to the Iraq war is also sanitized because the pilot is an attractive, white, middle-class woman, and thus somewhat at odds with the 'blow shit up' masculinizing imagery. Militarization itself is further sanitized by presenting it as an important economic activity: 'this shipyard – it's critical to the [UK] economy'. Moreover, disaster relief marks the military as quintessentially the nation's protector, even when 'bad people' are not involved. Thus moral virtue and depoliticization merge, so warriors and weaponry are then fully sanitized and legitimated.

Legitimation 4: BAE Systems as a diverse, progressive, ethical, equal opportunities employer

As Enloe reminds us, recruitment into the military is highly selective. Some men will be encouraged or coerced to enlist, and others discouraged.[58] The military is thus a crucial manager of the nested hierarchies through which elite selectivity reproduces itself. To do that the military projects an ideal in order to legitimate realities that may be otherwise, even quite contrary. The US video uses race–gender–class in different ways to make the 'right' kind of men visible, and to legitimate the selectivity involved.

By featuring women, 'non-whites'[59] and non-Americans, both visibly and audibly, BAE Systems represents itself as a progressive, inclusive, equal opportunities employer. Those representations articulate another layer of legitimacy to set against its legitimacy deficits. That layer of legitimacy is parasitic on the liberal democratic values that the US, its allies and some other states have made hegemonic among themselves – that is, they express a common sense that cannot be denied, because it is legitimated by consent. That legitimacy is then invoked in targeting some nations as failed, rogue or threateningly 'other'.

The US video features a wide range of skin colours, social classes and gender markers of masculinity and femininity, making visible its inclusivity of bodies. These are to be understood through familiar categories of intelligibility. By making women and non-whites visible, the video narrates, for its American target audience, that it is not just white men who are good and whose views and actions are thus morally legitimated. Rather, some women and some non-whites are good, too, or at least good enough.

However, the US video also represents and normalizes hierarchies of race, gender and class so as not to disturb stereotypically American political convictions. As Eisenstein notes: 'Imperial democracy uses racial diversity and gender fluidity to disguise itself – and females and people of color become its decoys.'[60] In this video, females and people of colour are decoys, distracting viewers from registering the gender-order hierarchical dominance of white, middle-class, warrior-protector males.

The gender-order hierarchy is secured as legitimate by the masculinizing nested hierarchies – of race and class – within which some men are subordinated in two ways: as feminized inferior, and as hypermasculinized 'other'. Yet the workers of BAE Systems, female or otherwise, are articulated as manly heroes, but in varying degrees. Presenting women and men, whose class, race or nationality is hypervisible, creates or reinforces the normalized hierarchy of stereotypical subject positions.

It is through those subject positions that BAE Systems, similar industries and the arms trade generally legitimate themselves. Those subject positions are also stereotypical for the warrior-protector masculinity projected by the 'top players' within the international system. The international system, overwhelmingly dominated by men, then legitimates itself, and its own nested hierarchies, by mirroring the commercial-military hierarchies that the BAE Systems' videos are articulating.

In the soundtrack of the US video we hear middle-class non-Americans talking about arty craftwork and aesthetic revolution, rather than about science and technology in a 'hard ass' way: 'This technology, it's dynamic, er, it adapts to the environment, er, it's revolutionary'; 'I'm amazed on a daily basis in that the people that I work with inspire me, they make technical solutions almost into an art form'; 'everybody that works here is a true artist and a craftsman, and we all take pride in every piece of technology that we touch'. These voices are somewhat softer than American-accented ones, and they do not refer to the military. They do not invoke heroism in defence of the nation, and they are feminized in talking instead about art and aesthetics.

We also hear some Americans who are hypermasculinized as 'other' in terms of their marginalized subject position. That subject position is signified by their working-class status and thus the increased potential of racial ambiguity, that is, non-whiteness: 'Well, me and my crew we work hard, we love these vessels, in fact a lot of us, we served on these vessels, and so we take a lot of pride in the work that we do now. We're no longer serving, but we're serving those who serve us.' That speech is accompanied by images of a large ship and a white welder (presumably the speaker), indicating an already subordinated working-class

121

position in the competitive nested hierarchies through which masculinity is articulated. Despite this hypermasculinization as muscly workers, these men are ultimately feminized by the very attributes that hypermasculinize them. By their class, they are subordinated in and through capitalist society, which values brain-workers over hand-workers. But they are further feminized by their emotional attachment to the military: 'we love these vessels'; 'they're gonna come home'. By contrast, the higher value scientists talk with a cool detachment of intellectual *hauteur* and thus an air of disembodiment.

In both videos what we hear does not strictly correspond with what we see, leaving room for ambiguity. But sometimes there is a suggestion that the person we hear is also the person we see, offering by contrast a more determinate point of reference. Because idealized manhood in the US is 'fundamentally constructed around perceptions of whiteness and heterosexuality', as Kimmel has explained,[61] African American men have historically been stereotyped as hypermasculine, hypersexual, violent and aggressive. These are traits that are often explained by a lack of restraint, a traditional colonialist signifier of 'civilized', that is, white men.[62]

Thus the imagery of race and class, for the American target audience, will merge, hence BAE Systems' US video reflects that ordering device. However, non-whiteness is not always immediately apparent. When our first non-white man appears, the viewer might not notice his 'blackness' because he is positioned at the side of the shot. The Asian woman at the other side of the shot is slightly further forward, and the two white men in the middle dominate the picture-space. The black man, wearing a shirt, is in a room with sophisticated technology, including screens and maps. That setting places him in a dominant position in terms of class and makes his race less immediately visible, or at least backgrounds it a bit, so that it isn't hypervisible against American norms of stereotypical whiteness.[63] He is thus an example of a 'good black man', 'a token member of the corporate world or a conservative post-race spokesman', as Cooper puts it.[64]

However, that black man's position on the left of the more active-looking white men in the middle of the shot marks him as subordinated within the nested hierarchies of competitive masculinization. He is off to the side, observing and listening to the white men, not actively participating in their efforts. Men of colour are thus legitimated, but in terms of liberal values of non-discrimination and civil inclusivity, without undue disturbance to the ideals and realities of elite, white male domination.[65]

The next non-white man, presumably African American, is either a pilot who has just finished work or a passenger who has just landed – the phrase 'pilots and passengers' occurs on the voiceover. He appears to be at an airport. Even though the suggestion is that he could be a pilot, we do not actually see him flying a plane or wearing a pilot's uniform. The previous shot featured two pilots flying, but he was not one of them, and they were both white. The responsible exercise of power is a constituent of white-raced masculinity, thus marking black men as subordinates. That subordination, the viewer may surmise, however subliminally, results from a presumably 'fair' – although in fact racialized – competition.

The African American man is shown greeting a middle-class, nicely dressed woman and young girl who are also black, albeit light-skinned. That family *mis-en-scène* confirms his heterosexuality, a crucial marker of idealized manhood. In the setting and by their clothing, he and his family are clearly middle class. That configuration of race–gender–class 'whitewashes' him, defined as making something undesirable 'seem legitimate or acceptable'.[66] More specifically here it refers to 'a process or result or act: when a person who is considered a minority adopts a lifestyle (including speech, mannerisms, clothing etc) that is attributed … to those of European descent, white people'. Hence there are no contrasting white people in the shot, thus reducing the visibility of raced non-whiteness. As Ahmed explains, even bodies that might not appear white still have to inhabit whiteness if they are to get into white-raced power structures. These are the structures through which the global economies of wealth creation, and the international order of great-power politics, currently operate.[67]

Another man is non-white but appears to be of East Asian origin. First we see him looking over the design of what appears to be a tank or other military vehicle. He is wearing a business shirt and working at a computer, so he is clearly removed from manual labour. Then we see him physically working on the tank, wearing safety goggles, although still in the white-collar shirt. He is hierarchically positioned in the shot over and above a white-raced worker, who is wearing a T-shirt and baseball cap, signifying less educated employment. But the East Asian product designer is visually lower down and physically smaller in the picture-space. The voiceover talks solely about technology, feminizing him as subordinate to an unseen world of white-raced science.

A further non-white man repeats the hierarchizing tropes of race–gender–class. For a split second we glimpse half of his face, just enough to see that he is black. We cannot actually see what he is doing because he is secondary to the subject of the shot – a white man working on a rocket, a phallic mirror-image. Whiteness is constituted through presumed superiority in knowledge and know-how, visibly confirmed in relation to the male workers we have seen and what they do. While the first three non-white men are white-washed by their class position, full equality is denied to them visually so as not to disturb the stereotypical hierarchy. All of the non-white men are positioned lower or at the side of white American males in the shot, and similarly in the 'black middle-class family' scene with respect to the present-absence of the white exemplar. By contrast, the class position of white American males disappears tropologically into a presumed equality, mirroring the way that whiteness dissolves into an absence of race. As Ahmed says: 'We do not face whiteness'; it 'trails behind bodies, as what is assumed to be given.'[68]

Class and race are thus used to mark subordination, whereas dominance reigns through their absence as signifiers.[69] That exercise of visual and aural rhetoric, in turn, makes whiteness as certain as the merger of science with industry. Through that merger BAE Systems presents itself as sanitized, that is, cleansed of any connection with violence and destruction, and thus moralized as a good warrior-protector. Overall the US video naturalizes global dominance as white male uniformity, and moral virtue as an attribute of their prowess in producing weaponry. They are in control of an industry that, through a presumption of competitive success in the commercial marketplace, dominates the international order of great-power politics.

The women featured in the US video actually function to reaffirm rather than challenge the dominant masculinity of the men, given the *relational* way they are positioned. By contrast, what is strikingly different about the global video is the centrality of women – this is also the case in a subsequent US video,[70] which overlaps with this global video. This shift in the representation of women reflects the way that masculinizing processes reaffirm the gender-order hierarchy even when politics pushes against it.

In the global video, using women to dominate the first half is a bold statement that completely contradicts the traditional image of the arms industry, rebranding it for the contemporary era. BAE Systems appears to be a progressive, diverse and women-friendly employer committed to equal opportunities, which, apart from trying to appeal to women to improve the diversity of its workforce, also functions to negate its legitimacy deficits. By including different types of women, classed and raced in stereotypical ways, and indeed men, similarly graded along the same criteria, BAE Systems is striving to broaden its appeal, and leave as few hostages to fortune as possible.

Looking ahead

However, what are the contrary processes pushing against the masculinizing, male-dominated hierarchies of race–gender–class? And, rather similarly, what are the contrary processes pushing against the international order of great-power politics and the international system? We have seen how the corporate–national trade in weaponry works to legitimize both orders as mirrors of each other. Who or what is threatening either or both? In our concluding chapter we explore the alternative politics of race–gender–class in delegitimizing the arms trade through which great-power politics sustains itself.

Further reading

Paul Amar (2013) *The Security Archipelago: Human Security States, Sexuality Politics, and the End of Neo-Liberalism*, Durham, NC: Duke University Press.

Zillah Eisenstein (2007) *Sexual Decoys: Gender, Race and War in Imperial Democracy*, Melbourne: Spinifex Press.

Marsha Henry (2017) 'Problematizing military masculinity, intersectionality and male vulnerability in feminist critical military studies', *Critical Military Studies*, 3(2): 182–99.

Charles W. Mills (2017) 'White Ignorance', in Charles W. Mills, *Black Rights/White Wrongs: The Critique of Racial Liberalism*, Oxford: Oxford University Press, pp 49–71.

Brittany C. Slatton and Kamesha Spates (eds) (2014) *Hyper Sexual, Hyper Masculine? Gender, Race and Sexuality in the Identities of Contemporary Black Men*, Farnham: Ashgate.

5

Looking Back/Pushing Ahead

The arms trade is both a product, and productive, of global militarism.[1] Militarism, as Ling cogently argues, is based on 'colonial-capitalist practices of race, gender, sexuality, class, and nationality'.[2] It underpins global hierarchies of business power and military weaponry. Importantly, and at the highest level of destructive firepower, nation-states legitimate themselves in a hierarchy independent of democratic forms of legitimation. Or, to put the matter simply, there are very few opportunities to vote against either the weaponry or the militarism or the state, as activists have been pointing out for many generations. Henry David Thoreau's much cited refusal to pay taxes to support the American seizure of Mexican territory in 1848, as well as W.E.B. Du Bois' very powerful condemnations of subsequent American imperialist incursions and occupations, make spirited reading on this subject.[3]

The preceding four chapters have demonstrated that un-de-gendering this picture puts the male dominance in state rulership and weapons manufacture into sharp focus. Once this 'flickering' between generic humanity (as if de-gendered) and gendered maleness/heterosexual masculinity (as morally good) is understood, an imbricated set of nested hierarchies emerges. This is what in practice legitimizes the gender-order hierarchy of masculinity over femininity, and some men over others. Besides interlocking, overlapping and interleaving personnel, the corporate and military nested hierarchies mirror each other in well-disciplined, business-like structures of production, finance and marketing.[4]

Of course President Dwight D. Eisenhower's coinage 'the military-industrial complex' references this concisely, but – as one would expect, and as is still overwhelmingly the case – the gender dimension, namely masculinity in behaviour and maleness in body, isn't made explicit. It suits men generally to have this conflation both assumed and erased, and to make it seem odd, even weirdly redundant, to point it out. Pointing this out, and stating the supposedly unremarkable obvious, then marginalizes those who do so, and delegitimates their activism. That strategy is what activists must face into, and very notably many persist, despite blowback and flak attack, as we explore in this chapter.

Bottom-up/grass roots

These un-de-gendering and anti-militarism advocates, of course, divide on as many issues as they agree. At one end of the spectrum we have comprehensive pacifism, including rather unsung conscientious objectors to military service.[5] And there are certain campaigns within the feminist-framed 'new men's movements'.[6] At the other end of the spectrum many anti-militarism activists, in highly qualified ways, support both conventional nation-states and their self-legitimated interests in weapons trading, but as a matter of tactics. Those activisms focus on much closer monitoring by international agencies, with sanctions operating through the international legal system, leaving abolition to the future.

This is where self-defence, national defence and human-person defence meet in a clash of moral principles. Throughout this conflictual melée is an array of masculinities, necessarily, because so many of the activists are men, and because they have experienced masculinity themselves, one way or another. Because women are largely, and so often completely, excluded from masculinity as a practice, their knowledge of it, and views about it, can be very pertinent. Or, to put it the other way, men are already implicated in masculinity by identity and processes of identification.

Gender identity is not a pseudo-physical property of a single body/mind conjunction. Rather, it is thoroughly and paradigmatically reflexive. On the one hand, it consists of identifying other-directed projections of selfhood and bodily legibility. And on the other, we all experience binary gender identifications projected back onto our own bodies.[7] Men find it difficult to struggle out of this self-other, other-self identity circle, even if the idea occurs. And when they write about their experiences, they often struggle to get a respectful hearing, not least from other men.

For over a hundred years at least, feminist and gender scholars and activists have worked to delegitimize the world military order, demonstrating the links between masculinities, violence, soldiers, war, militarism, sport, and men in general. These understandings and practices are performatively defined against the feminine 'other'. Repetitively they stabilize and sustain a globally destructive conjunction of men-in-arms, celebrated as an imbrication of warrior-protector with bourgeois-rational masculinity.[8] That is how gender projects itself as an ordered hierarchy.

Looking back to the 'war to end all wars', that is, the 'Great War', later termed the 'First World War', historians have recorded that many activists believed that the 'the profit from arms sales must be eliminated to preserve the peace'.[9] The availability of weaponry, and the unrestrained traffic in arms, was seen in part to have caused and to have exacerbated the war. Weapons manufacturers and arms merchants who dominated the manufacture and trade had often sold to both sides in the conflict and had used neutrality as a convenient base.[10] As profiteers they were labelled 'merchants of death'. That sentiment was captured by the League of Nations Covenant (1919), which stated: 'The Members of the League agree that the manufacture by private enterprise of munitions and implements of war is open to grave objections. The Council shall advise how the evil effects attendant upon such manufacture can be prevented'.[11]

Edgerton asserts that 'the greatest campaign waged by the interwar peace movement was against the private arms industry and the international arms trade'.[12] The campaign for the Peace Ballot in Britain in 1934–35 succeeded in establishing a Royal Commission on the Private Manufacture of and Trading in Arms that sat during 1935–36. As Anderson states, this 'was probably the closest Britain has ever come to banning the private sale of arms. Despite its importance, its recommendations were buried at the time and are little remembered today.'[13]

Scholar-activists have also shown the relevance of the gender-order hierarchy and queer exclusion to livelihoods, markets and the international political economy, including multinational corporations, and in particular, so-called 'private security agencies'. These are the means through which notable great power incursions have proceeded via outsourcing and covert 'black ops'. Activists have thus made visible academically, and in the serious media, the relevance of the gender-order hierarchy to public policy on weaponry. They have done this by protesting nuclear weapons, but also by protesting embodied technologies and technological embodiment. And in recent years this work has extended to disembodied technologies in aerial weaponry such as drones.[14]

Like anyone else, scholar-activists have observed the effect of warrior-protector militarized masculinity on the symbolic activities and budgetary management of nation-states. Their contribution is to make this problematic rather than normal. Typically this is done by historicizing what seems merely obvious in order to show exactly how, and in whose interests, this evident normality has come about. Another powerful strategy is to follow the money through the political and military hierarchies, so as to make visible exactly how nested hierarchies of men maintain their power. Both those strategies are developed in the previous chapters in this book, showing how the hierarchy of some men over others, differentiated variously by race, class, (dis)ability and similar markers of presumed devaluation, arises so powerfully and so legitimately.

While race and class have generally been visible as categories of inclusion and exclusion as military masculinities have variously developed, (dis)ability has generally been invisibilized. This is because militarism itself is founded on a selection of abilities, not just deemed masculine, but also cultivated as quintessential to manliness itself. Hence in that hierarchy of 'ableisms' of inclusion and exclusion, disability doesn't even register as a category in the first instance. Rather, it registers as a category of expulsion. It is through those various hierarchical distinctions – often styled identities of relative subordination and exclusion – that activists aim to form coalitions and gather strength.

Whether it is useful then to identify 'different masculinities', in making descriptive political reference, may emerge in particular conjunctures.[15] But how useful this is, and to whom, isn't a given or a necessity. Invoking the gender-order hierarchy, even subversively, is sometimes a hostage to fortune, dividing men from women, rather than invoking human commonality. It may also inadvertently reinvoke masculine and masculinizing presumptions of gender superiority. That dilemma will be explored below.

The gender-order hierarchy excludes and devalues women, although those men already within it can be pressed and pressurized by women, and sometimes by some men, to include suitably masculinized women, whether heterosexual or lesbian. They are thus higher in the power ranks than subordinated women-and-others in supportive roles. Women's equal and identical involvement in the military therefore threatens to 'trouble' the gender-order hierarchy, as does the 'open' inclusion of gay men in relation to the heteromasculine exemplar. Gendered identities of superiority and subordination, understood within the heterosexual norm, are central to the creation and reproduction of militarism. And they are persistent for that reason.[16]

Consider the non-inclusion of female masculinities, where female physicality begins to merge with male-identified gender behaviour. Or rather, where masculinity comes unstuck from the male body – as distinct from female bodies that are masculinized in parodic dress and behaviour. Military and business contexts now include masculinized women, signalling complicity and co-option, as detailed above. However, female masculinity profoundly 'troubles' the stability of the gender-order hierarchy. That hierarchy founds itself literally and symbolically in an enacted identity between the idealized male body and the idealized norms of warrior-protector/bourgeois-rational masculinities.

Female masculinity appears as a performative reality rather than a performative parody.[17] Parodies can be 'taken on board', as female inclusion in the military and business have shown;

realities that contradict a founding conflation are much more threatening, at least at present. Female masculinities could easily disrupt even the queerest protesters on the outside at arms fairs as much as they would upset the gender conformities of the military businesspeople on the inside.[18]

Enloe has highlighted the crucial roles that women and femininity have played in sustaining militarism – as diplomats' and soldiers' wives, as prostitutes and nurses, and in any number of servicing occupations, paid and unpaid. Women have also played significant roles in mobilizing support for war, encouraging men to be 'real men', and in sexualizing the man in uniform.[19] But exactly how and why some men are recruited into, and selected within, the most powerful and destructive hierarchies on the planet is a further focus for analysis. Once in those positions they exemplify the highest national ideals and control access to huge commercial rewards.

Making visible the gendered activities of men-as-men doesn't merely expose the workings of power; it crucially removes the naturalized 'merely human' character of those interlocking institutions and structural networks. In that way it reveals the gender-specific way that nested hierarchies of exclusion and subordination produce the elites that we see in the news, and indeed, the ones that are less immediately visible. That way of looking at international-interpersonal politics is thus resisting the all-too-automatic division between politics and economics. It also resists a view of international politics as an equality of nation-states, as presumed by the doctrine of sovereignty. Because it is focused on warlike rearmament, it resists the commonplace conflation of commerce with peacetime. Moreover, it resists the ordered normality of conventional news values, because pertinent information comes instead from leaks, scandals and revelations.

Over and above the pushback against global militarism that should result from this method of historicization and problematization there is the question of hegemony, that is, domination *by consent*.[20] How is it that competitive national defence, to the point of mutually assured destruction, operates with such élan? Engenders such pride? Defines what a state is? Creates hierarchies and gradations of citizenship? Has such resilience? Defends itself with such vehemence? Why is deadly violence the archetype for manliness? Elite males subordinate other males, feminizing them as the contrast to iconic militarized masculinity, pushing men down the ladder and towards the women. This subordinating motion in the gender-order hierarchy is very effectively outlined by Schippers:

> When a man exhibits ... feminine characteristics – as in having desire to be the object of masculine desire, being physically weak, or being compliant – he becomes the target of stigma and social sanction, much like women who embody features of ... masculinity. And, like pariah femininities, possession of one characteristic by a man is culturally defined as contaminating.[21]

Why, specifically, do men consent to this, knowing that the hierarchy also subordinates them as men, indeed, as what they are personally and socially? Why does the icon – the general-politician, the obediently 'brave' soldier, the fabulously successful businessman – have such power over men at large? And why are so many women consenting to such an exclusionary and destructive pyramid of power?

This mesmerizing imbrication of the military hierarchy with nested hierarchies of men (sometimes including suitably masculinized women) is repetitively constructed in popular culture – films, computer games, toys, fashion, boyhood stories, all the way back to the *Aeneid* and the *Iliad*. In identifying the problem, big as it is, scholar-activists are suggesting quite a broad front, chipping away at any and all modes through which consent is secured, tacit or otherwise. The strategy is to delegitimate at least some aspects of elite empowerment.

As Cockburn and Enloe explain, 'militarism cannot coherently be opposed without also working to resist patriarchy, heterosexism, and racialised configurations of queer inclusion/exclusion'.[22] Essential to the 'value systems, practices, rationalities and subject positions' through which militarism is constituted, as Rossdale argues, are 'particular configurations of gender and sexuality'.[23] Or, to put it another way, resistance to those specific structures is not an activity removed from militarism, because those gender-sexuality hierarchies are themselves constitutive of it, both symbolically and performatively. The military-industrial order *and* the sex-gender order very much hang together, mirror each other, support each other, and manufacture normality. Typically this happens through strategic control of national ceremonies of celebration and remembrance.

Summing up the gender-order hierarchy – nested hierarchies of masculinity over femininity, and some men over others – by using the single word 'patriarchy', is useful. But then so is refining the concept of patriarchy as a way of making activism more specific, and more specifically targeted at weak spots. Cockburn writes that, 'patriarchal gender relations predispose our societies to war. They are a driving force perpetuating war. They are among the causes of war.' But then, of course, 'gender is not the only dimension of power implicated in war'.[24]

Economic interests and commercial incentives, as we have seen, are an important part of the national story. Through that means nation-states attain not just their identity, but also more pertinently their relative positioning in the hierarchies of great power politics. Not that the UN is without influence, but no one really thinks that the equality among nation-states, as mandated and displayed in equal voting rights at the General Assembly, tells us all – or indeed much of anything – about the way nation-state-actors understand global politics. Cockburn outlines the relevant power systems: 'War-makers and their apologists are capitalists, but not only capitalists. They are phallocratic, but not only patriarchs. They are white supremacists, but also located advantageously in other power systems (cultural, religious).'[25]

Consent/complicity

The systems that Cockburn outlines are not just accidentally male-dominated; the system-within-the-systems is one of nested hierarchies. In those hierarchies most men consent to, and thus legitimate, their own subordination. This is relative, yet relationally locates men within masculinity. This situation arises because – so far in history and to an almost universal extent –

it isn't very easy otherwise, or indeed often very possible, to be visible and intelligible as male. That is because referencing those masculine and masculinizing hierarchies repetitively *is* one's gender.

Gender-resisters have made themselves visible, albeit as gender-traitors and gender-criminals, as it were. But insofar as they are in some way male they will have to contend with the terms of militarizing-commercializing masculinities. These include male-exclusive international super-sporting hierarchies, as well as other hierarchies of achievement. Those are the reference points through which someone is seen and understood as male-masculine. And from those hegemonic terms – hegemonic because they inspire so much willing consent among men and women – gender-resisters are easily marginalized as 'odd' individuals and 'deviant' minorities.

Most women are outside those terms, hence feminist activism has led the way against militarism, understood as male-gender hierarchies of imbricated political-commercial power. Tracing these counter-hegemonic and self-consciously subversive activities historically is difficult, owing to their omission from, or denigration within, male-written conventional histories. Getting these alternative perspectives and that kind of authorship into academic curricula is still a struggle. Almost by definition conventional histories still operate within the nation-state, empire-building, great battles-and-victories framing of what counts as historical knowledge, even if lately this framing is somewhat qualified and avowedly inclusive of diverse testimonies.

While grieving mothers, wives and sisters are the conventional normality for women in classic male historiography, resistance to the gender-order hierarchy – when noticed – was generally marginalized as futile and insane, even ignorable as feminist *avant la lettre*. Feminist politics in the 20th century has tried hard to change this, forging a new understanding of history, making militarism and weaponry more problematic, and so working to delegitimate the militarized nation-state. Delegitimating those political-commercial projects is itself a feminist act, precisely because those activities would not be what they are without the gender-order hierarchy through which they 'make sense'.

They 'make sense' because they are so repetitively constitutive of nation-state and male-personal normality.

Actions make identities: Cockburn found that 'women antiwar activists, with few exceptions, [were] unhesitating in naming themselves feminist'.[26] And Acheson contributes this report from experience:

> One tactic deployed to sustain patriarchy is for men in dominant positions to establish and maintain themselves as authorities by denouncing and denigrating the views of others. In the case of the TPNW [Treaty on the Prohibition of Nuclear Weapons], those representing nuclear-armed states berated other governments for supporting the ban, ridiculing their perspectives on peace and security, and accusing them of threatening the world order, risking total chaos. Prohibiting and eliminating nuclear weapons is neither practical nor feasible, these 'realist' governments assert. Those who support the prohibition of nuclear weapons are delusional. They are 'radical dreamers' who have 'shot off to some other planet or outer space'.[27]

Courageously the Women's International League for Peace and Freedom, founded in 1915, has as its ultimate goal a totally demilitarized global society. 'Reaching Critical Will' is its disarmament programme, undertaking 'analysis and advocacy for disarmament, the reduction of global military spending and militarism, and the investigation of gendered aspects of the impact of weapons and of disarmament processes'. It confronts 'violent masculinities and gender discrimination', and among other tactical aims, it is 'committed to creating change by altering discourse'.[28]

Perhaps in relation to fiery destruction, and the threat thereof, this looks feeble, even nugatory. But it isn't. Discourse, that is, words made meaningful through repetitive practices, and practices made intelligible through wordy repetition, are the ways that masculinized hierarchies come into being. And it is within and through those hierarchies that men continue to consent to their own subordination relative to other men and masculinized women. At any given time and place there are masculinities that secure the gender order by generating consent to men's and masculine dominance. The nested hierarchies within that dominance are then secured as ranks of relative subordination, and of super-elite domination, through the same consensual process.

Scholar-activists have identified 'missile envy'[29] and tracked the heteromasculinizing terms, tropes and activities through which the links are made: personal to political, national to commercial, male to male.[30] In relation to India's nuclear testing programme, for example, the Hindu nationalist Balasaheb Thackeray said: 'We had to prove that we are not eunuchs.' This is quite a normal kind of statement amid the posturing of nation-states, in this case when they are jostling within and just outside the 'Nuclear Club'. In that clubby configuration they insulate themselves in various ways from the goals and terms of the TPNW, adopted by 122 states in 2017. Looked at analytically, however, the quite surprising and reality-disrupting emergence of this treaty is also an attack on patriarchy, understood as the gender-order hierarchy of masculinity over femininity, and some men over others. On that point Acheson writes:

> Two aspects of the ban-treaty project posed particular challenges to patriarchy. First, the treaty was brought about through a deliberate discursive shift by concerned activists, academics, and diplomats – from a discourse centred on the alleged security benefits of deterrence to a discourse centred on the urgency of disarmament. Second, the ban was promoted through the empowerment of women, diplomats, and activists of the global south … banning nuclear weapons can be read as an act of challenging patriarchy.[31]

Nuclear weaponry is the highest and most destructive way of defining and representing militarism within the nested hierarchies of great power politics – the 'Nuclear Club'. Militarism at that level was, and is, overwhelmingly male-dominant, and is the ultimate badge of warrior-protector masculinity. Pushing back on that took years of struggle, necessarily from outside military establishments. It was wholly undertaken by women and – relatively speaking – feminized men occupying diplomatic positions and a varied and racialized set of marginalized political circumstances. The UN itself was founded as a political force for war prevention, including – but privileging – the 'great' nuclear powers and their 'nuclearized' clients, as the situation developed. Thus since the 1940s the world has witnessed a very notable pushback on militarism, hence on patriarchy in a very visible way. However, the term 'patriarchy' does not in itself, and at first glance, reference the gender-order hierarchy that dominant masculinities work so hard, and so effectively, to legitimate.

The mutual imbrication of masculinity and militarism, through which the gender-order hierarchy is legitimated, and consent is effectually asserted, has critical political implications. It is deployed to justify arms expenditure, and even spending increases, while austerity measures, consonant with shrink-the-state ideologies or other budget-cutting exercises, are promoted and implemented. Legitimation in effect overturns what would otherwise be obvious, namely that competitive weaponry is most often a higher priority than individual and collective wellbeing. National defence and security is conceived within the hierarchies of great-power politics and competitive 'arms races'. Anna Stavrianakis argues the radical but comprehensive view that 'human security is a form of militarism rather than the antithesis of it'.[32] Through repetitive media representations, competitive weaponry is presented as coincident with any individual voter-taxpayer's self-interest. Thus it trumps any number of other things that government spending might afford.

This dynamic interaction of masculinity and militarism increases and normalizes existing inequalities. These are already differentially experienced through hierarchies of disadvantage, typically organized along race/gender/class/(dis)ability and similar lines of hierarchy-making discrimination. Research funding that goes into weapons development is most often at the expense of other projects, such as the mitigation of climate change or the development of cleaner energy resources. While crossovers and spin-offs may occur, the trade-offs are far more predictable.

The apparent delegitimization of nuclear weaponry, albeit to a degree and only with considerable instability, has made conventional weaponry look less threatening by contrast. Activists, with some notable high-profile and female celebrity participation, have pushed to delegitimize landmines and cluster munitions, for example, even to the point of mandated bans in manufacture and trade. Those devices are small, inexpensive and 'conventional', that is, non-nuclear, although again, the gap between delegitimation and non-use is considerable.[33] And there are further discrepancies between use and liability, and between liability and sanctions or reparations. But the violence done to human bodies is very tangible and wholly regrettable. The most common means for the violent destruction of human life are, in fact, small arms and light weapons, which have been dubbed the 'real weapons of mass destruction'.[34]

Big boys/small toys

The international, great power community is apparently on the case. UN Security Council Resolution 2117 on Small Arms and Light Weapons, adopted on 26 September 2013, echoes the sentiments of the international Arms Trade Treaty. The resolution notes 'the disproportionate impact on violence perpetrated against women and girls, and exacerbating sexual and gender-based violence', in line with UN Security Council Resolution 1325 on Women, Peace and Security. To get that resolution passed, feminist activism – against violence, whether interstate or interpersonal – was crucial at the international level. The international Arms Trade Treaty requires exporting states to consider whether there is a risk that conventional arms for sale and purchase in the legitimated trade will be used 'to commit or facilitate serious acts of gender-based violence or serious acts of violence against women and children':

> The exporting State Party, in making this assessment, shall take into account the risk of the conventional arms covered under Article 2 (1) or of the items covered under Article 3 or Article 4 being used to commit or facilitate serious acts of gender-based

violence or serious acts of violence against women and children.[35]

Note that the locution 'gender-based violence' leaves the reader to infer the place of men and masculinity within the term 'gender', illustrating the discursive strategy that is the focus of this book: where are the men? This trope of erasure is the rule, rather than the exception. The international Arms Trade Treaty is the first to make gender explicit in linking the 'licit' international arms trade to violence against womenandchildren, and also with gender-based violence in that context. This is a hugely significant gain – not just for women and children, but also by implication for anyone at risk of interpersonal violence. A focus on masculinity and men, however, encourages enquiry into how the problem arose in the first place.[36]

This very first reference to gender within the main body of a global, legally binding treaty represents an opportunity to promote awareness of masculinity and the inclusion of men as a *problem* in analysis and action. They – that is, men and masculinity – are a problem, not just in relation to women, but also in relation to individuals and groups marginalized through sex/gender/sexuality non-conformity. This is because they are judged against the masculinized norms through which heterosexuality and male dominance are most often understood.[37]

This is not an easy move to make, or even to make intelligible, given the way that men are positioned already within the gender-order hierarchy. But then awareness and inclusion could concomitantly promote activism against the gender-order hierarchy as such. That kind of resistance could derive support and participation from within the male ranks of nested subordinations, as well as from the binarized subordination of females. And indeed, activism could also arise from those resisting the binaries of bodily sex, gender performance and sexuality categorizations.

Moreover, small arms and light weaponry are the most iconically masculine and masculinizing artefacts and tropes of all, but at the level of the individual rather than the state. That kind of weaponry constitutes an entire male-oriented genre in popular culture, effectively, the gendered opposite of 'rom-com'.[38] Activists have successfully focused on this kind of weaponry, which figures significantly in the global arms trade. That activist focus makes crucial boundary lines problematic, because the defining realm for great-power politics is top class, hi-tech, large-scale weaponry. From that perspective, then, anything small in size and lightweight isn't really visible, nor are the mere individuals and motley gangs involved a major priority.

The perpetrator–victim model, rather than the state-to-state model, frames the conventional understanding of small arms and light weapons as commercial technologies of interpersonal violence. Nonetheless activists, NGOs and think tanks have registered some success in merging the otherwise distinct great-power understandings of violence and weaponry into a more general account of violence. Specifically, they relate it to loss of life and limb. In that way state actions and inactions, hi-tech weaponry and security threats, are thrown into a somewhat different focus. This happens when a narrative shifts from states and individuals, as abstract entities, to human physical and mental trauma and death. That tactic rather disarms the power politics of supposed collective insecurity, where the collective is the nation-state. Sometimes the nation-state is figured metaphorically as a physical body politic, but nonetheless, that conception is highly abstract compared to individual injury and obvious grief.

Violence has very wide-reaching effects on social structures that impact on both women and men. Those effects are crosscut with the hierarchies of advantage/disadvantage marked by race and class: it is 'young, poor, socially marginalized men most of all – who are killed or injured through gun violence'.[39] And individual injury and death is not the only social consequence and cost:

> In some countries, gun-related violence leads to demographic imbalances. Brazil currently has nearly 200,000 fewer men than women in the age range 15–29. It is estimated that in 50 years' time, there will be six million men missing from the Brazilian population mostly as a result of death in traffic accidents and homicide – the vast majority of the latter being gun-related.[40]

Or rather, the personal here becomes political all the way up: the weaponry, commercialism and state involvement, one way or another, all snap into a single place of scrutiny and critique, namely loss of life and limb. What does not snap into place with that shift in focus is the structuring role that masculinity plays in making all this violence actually take place with such high degrees of legitimation. Even though it is obvious that the vast majority of perpetrators – in the widest possible sense – of this violence are male, why is masculinity not more often the structuring principle for analysis and resistance? Resistance, which should be focused on the problematic obvious, namely the heteronormative masculinity through which consent to the gender-order hierarchy is secured, is most often deflected instead to the gender binary. Once that move is made, the next, supposedly logical inference is often to acknowledge the realities of female perpetration, which – although an important and very political acknowledgement of female agency – actually doesn't bear much comparison.

Male focus on masculinity most often takes the form of pushback in defence of the conventional norms of the gender binary, and in explicitly heterosexual terms, for example, #NotAllMen are like that in using or threatening violence in relation to women. That phrase thus brackets some men off from so-called 'toxic masculinities' that are assigned to male perpetrators. There is, of course, considerable traction in the idea that the posturing and tweets of Donald Trump, Jair Bolsonaro and numerous other men on the world stage are instrumental in securing legitimation for the gender-order hierarchy as a violent form of domination.[41] That is, legitimately *violent* when other forms of intimidation don't work. But that line of debate doesn't set up an enquiry into how 'all men' are *like what*.

Although these dialogues in and across the gender binary do raise issues, and do mark out masculinity as in some sense a problem, nonetheless, this analytical gendering presumes the binary men/women. In that way it doesn't focus *precise* attention – as this book does – on the gender-order hierarchy as a structure of male dominance. That hierarchy is graded: some men and masculinized women over others. Implicitly, some masculinities emerge as non-toxic by default, but then reinvoking the de-gendering discourse of humanity, nation-state, society. Through these and similar abstractions maleness magically disappears. That move, as argued above, misses the critical focus that masculinity should offer, since empirically men – in their nested hierarchies of subordination – are overwhelmingly dominant in great-power politics and commercial wealth accumulation.

Without detracting from the importance and quality of the activist-driven campaigns concerning small arms and light weapons, it is important to note that the focus within that frame is usually on vulnerable bodies in locations where violence is found and suspected. These are often in the global south and thus in conflict zones lower down in the competitive hierarchies of commercial, political and military prowess. These hierarchies are dominated, as we have shown, by the great powers and their military-industrial establishments.

Within the critical literature on the arms trade, case studies focus largely on the 'illegitimate' arms trade, that is, what arms control discourse terms illicit or irresponsible. Adding gender to arms control discourse has created certain figures, images and expectations. Importantly this gendered discourse is not just the trope of women-as-victims, but also women-as-agents who sometimes use or transport weapons. But the focus on vulnerable bodies as female then makes it easy to generate a mirror-discourse of male vulnerability. That vulnerability then supposedly has similar moral validity and emotional appeal, even if those claims are easily critiqued as a misleading sort of gender equality.[42]

The move to the gender binary again shifts attention away from elite males, whose ranks include masculinized women. It also shifts attention away from the political invulnerability of the male-masculine power structures. That invulnerability arises from concurrent engines of legitimation: the naturalized gender-order hierarchy, and the ordered system of competitive nation-states.

Visible/invisible/hypervisible

This gendering move to the male–female binary has also created the hypermasculine marginalized man who uses and trades in small arms and light weapons. In that way gender is conceptualized in what is presumed to be a minority of men, whether a tiny or sizeable number, but doubled-down, gender-wise, as the disavowed 'outside' to an otherwise normal and moral mode of being. Amar defines 'hypervisible subjects' as 'fetishized figures that preoccupy public discourse and representations but are not actually recognizable or legible as social formations and cannot speak on their own terms as autonomous subjects rather than as problems to solve'.[43]

As previously argued, this discursive ploy allows the presumed majority of non-criminal men to occupy both the moral positioning of good husbands, fathers, brothers, sons, and so on, and also to continue to figure as the de-gendered, generically human, public person. Thus in this dual way masculinity backgrounds women as domestic, subordinate, private and 'other'. Because men have traditionally been awarded generically human status as implicitly de-gendered, with women solely having or embodying gender in most contexts, there is a distinct risk that when racialized or marginalized 'others' are figured as visible and problematic, this then also reaffirms a de-gendered white image of *both* generic human agency *and* masculine moral goodness.

Even the term 'gender' itself is made complicit with the whiteness, or more specifically, non-blackness, through which the nested male-dominated hierarchies of great-power politics operate. In arms control discourse the term 'small arms and light weapons' is linked intertextually with illicit activities. These are then most often studied academically in nation-states that are not highly ranked in the hierarchical tables of national success and achievement. Those poorer states are then measured against the self-defined achievements of the states that do the ranking. And these are the states that make and manage the nested hierarchies of nation-states through which weapons are manufactured and traded as legitimate.

Thus gender as a term reflecting an 'issue' is generally projected away from men and on to women, who thus become a further 'problem' requiring great power management. Women are then represented in clichéd portrayals in the international media, through which the dominant nations of the international order see themselves represented in self-reflection. In that gaze women become a super-synecdoche for national failures. Those conceptualizations are then a super-metonymy for the agency and issues occupying actual women in subordinated nation-states.

Although it is a very important contribution to discussions of gender and weaponry, in the scholar-activist collection *Sexed Pistols: The Gendered Impacts of Small Arms and Light Weapons*, the case studies are largely drawn from locations in the global south, identified as 'fragile states'. That term, combined with other signifiers, relegates them to a realm of subordinated illegitimacy: Albania, Democratic Republic of Congo, Haiti, Papua New Guinea, Sierra Leone, Somalia, Timor-Leste and Uganda. In the book there are three cases taken from developed states: Israel, Northern Ireland and South Africa.[44] However, those cases are put under the heading 'Militarizing the domestic sphere', thus organizing them into a separate category. That bracketing then puts their supposed crucial issues – relating to interpersonal gun violence – into a private-domestic context, already subordinated as a realm of human experience, given the top-down international perspective. Of course violence against women, presumed to be and figured as domestic, is a very real problem in those locations. While the work in that book is undoubtedly important, because it focuses on these cases, it implicitly reinforces hierarchies that preserve the normality and morality of great-power politics, rather than exposing them to genuinely comparative scrutiny.

There is very considerable violence effected on human bodies without guns, but gun violence – which is often disproportionately directed at racialized, subordinated, disadvantaged men, women and children – is a highly significant means for violent destruction of life and limb on a global scale. The analytical and activist focus on micro-sites of violence, where small arms and light weapons are deployed, sets them at a remove from conventional, more expensive, hi-tech weaponry *and* from the wider world of arms manufacture. That wider world is specifically the legitimate trade and industry operating within the highest ranks of great power politics and globalized commercialism.[45]

By making gender visible only in relation to illegitimate ownership or illegitimate use of small arms and light weapons, the legitimate trade and industry therefore remain de-gendered, so their gendered legitimation of the gender-order hierarchy passes unnoticed as apparently unintelligible. Making explicitly gendered issues a problem 'out there' constitutes a certain configuration of de-gendered/gendered identities for those 'in here'. Shepherd has demonstrated that in their national action plans, dominant states in the great power hierarchies, such as the UK, articulate 'the appropriate sphere of WPS [women, peace and security] activity ... [as] international, rather than domestic, hence "there" rather than "here"'. Accordingly, the 'not-here' states in these powerful discursive constructions are articulated 'as experts on the WPS agenda and champions of its principles', thus ensuring that anti-militarism is directed elsewhere.[46]

Gender as a term, articulated within this power/knowledge framework, thus legitimates both those dominant nation-states and the ways in which they construe gender as a concept. Moreover, that nation-state articulation legitimates both male authority as knowledge-makers, and indeed, their authority over the concept of gender-as-women in particular.[47]

Through that strategy of omission, the de-gendering of men as generic humanity, as well as the moralized gendering of men as masculine exemplars, is once again left untouched. So when men, and the institutions they dominate, nod to gender, they hand it on in certain directions to certain groups. Thus they make it mean whatever maintains their position in the gender-order hierarchy. What they are doing leaves what they do otherwise unexamined in its legitimacy, and thus resecured in presuming the consent that hegemony requires.

The circulation of small arms and light weapons within the global arms trade involves more than their use or abuse, their sale, purchase and deployment in specific locations where violence destroys human bodies and lives. So long as gender is defined and articulated with reference only to victims and perpetrators, arms traders and criminals in those marginalized and despised locations, it will remain underscrutinized. In that way it will remain safely gendered masculine as white manliness, which will stand in for generic humanity. The multimillion dollar deals between states and multinational companies, which were made visible in the preceding chapters, remove the men and masculinized women involved from violence generally. It also removes them from the sites where it occurs, whether through the use of tanks, bombs and aircraft, or small arms and light weapons.

Much more crucially, however, those practices of deflection, marginalization, demonization and erasure ensure that normalized and racialized masculinity is rendered respectable and emblematic. Thus it remains difficult to critique. A descriptive focus on individuals performing different masculinities, whether conventionally dominant or 'alternative' by contrast, misses the structural dynamics outlined here: the parallel hierarchies of nation-states and great power politics, imbricated with the gender-order hierarchy of masculinity over femininity, and some men over others.

How they get away with it

Until this book there were virtually no published feminist or gender studies texts that focused specifically on, and seriously engaged with, the legitimate trade in conventional weapons. The subject is sometimes briefly mentioned when the discussion is about gender and women. Or alternatively, women and gender are sometimes briefly mentioned when the legitimate trade is the subject of a study. We argue that these studies can proceed most effectively only by deploying a sufficiently nuanced understanding of masculinity. This requires a discursive strategy that names men as men, so as to resist their self-serving merger with generic humanity.

There is a very good, although actually quite rare, example of this punchy strategy: a masculinity-focused chapter in a gender-focused collection on climate change. Naming men as men is something of a breakthrough, rather than making reference to abstractions, such as structures and traditions, or to de-gendered signifiers, such as society or people. Hultman writes, as everyone really knows, that *some* men are the problem:

> As gender scholars dealing with environmental issues
> are all very aware, men are the big problem. Especially

white, middle-class, middle-aged, fairly rich men who travel too much, eat too much meat and live in energy intensive buildings. The truth is that if we quantitatively analyse per capita emissions and per capita ecological footprints, it is these particular men who are the problem.[48]

Rather similarly, Enloe focuses on men and masculinity, not just referencing them descriptively, but also telling us in detail how these nested and globally crucial hierarchies legitimate elite heterosexism and homosocial privilege. Top-level global finance, Enloe shows, is everything to do with men-as-men in gender terms. Those gender terms are performed as heterosexual masculinity of the everyday sort, as innumerable women have testified, and very publicly with #MeToo. Enloe's study also shows, conversely, how much effort goes into convincing the world that what isn't public isn't relevant, and that in men's lives money and sex aren't importantly connected. At the very highest levels of global politics, Enloe finds this scenario:

> Thus, while Wall Street's 'smartest guys' and London's 'Thatcher's children' were heralded as new, or at least relatively new, national breeds, Iceland's risk-taking male bankers were celebrated by the country's elites as a new incarnation of an ancient national breed. As in the United States, so too in Iceland: the masculinized culture that drove the banking firms to dangerous excess was promoted at the top by particular exclusivist masculinized groups. ... The all-male membership of the Locomotive Group collectively convinced themselves that pushing aside state regulators, maximizing short-term profits, and thinking little about long-term ramifications was the formula for success ... they announced their success by buying fast cars and dressing in expensive suits; they spent time together in bars and strip clubs.[49]

Women are, of course, capable of doing all the things, good or bad, that men do, if and when allowed by men to do them, or alternatively, by subverting or overturning male-dominated power structures. But as a matter of fact, in the hierarchies of great power politics it is overwhelmingly men, organizing themselves into nested hierarchies of male domination in masculinizing institutions, who are doing the damage.[50] As Dolan argues, 'there is a crucial connection to be made between state-level dynamics and micro-level behaviour, and the ideas which make up masculinity are a key connector between the two'.[51]

The Wallström affair or incident, as it has become known, is a good example – recounted in a separate section below – of how gender fades into a generic human normality. That normality is business deals and policy-making as usual, which continues largely undisturbed, despite the best efforts of activists. This lengthy narrative chronicles the frustration and incomprehension and, indeed, the failure of the intended pushback against the gender-order hierarchy. By contrast, crucially and politically, an analysis focused on men and masculinity identifies the exact and sadly predictable point where for activists 'it all went wrong'.

On the more hopeful side, possibly an activism that 'calls men out as men' in their normality – rather than as marginalized perpetrators – might sharpen up the struggle. No one in the Wallström narrative is a 'bad man' – that is the problem. And no one called out an institution as 'bad' because it normalizes violence – from hi-tech weaponry to small arms or even low-tech implements such as knives. In this case the normal administration of the practices through which human rights violations are regularly committed mirror each other.

The term 'patriarchy' is correctly applied to these arrangements, and politically it genders the situation. Yet deploying the concept doesn't get the traction that really effective change requires. This is because patriarchy references father-protectors, rather than how men, in nested hierarchies of power, re-empower the gender-order hierarchy in what they do every day, without needing to think about it.

Perhaps it's worth referencing here an activist campaign of historic significance that positioned itself up against the gender-order hierarchy of male elites at the highest national levels of political and commercial prowess – and won. Arguably the suffragettes got real traction when they targeted crucial male decision-makers as men, making their physical bodies and valued property frighteningly political. These tactics were determinedly personal, even targeting the sacrosanct zone of domesticity.[52]

Follow along with the Wallström narrative below, and ask yourself a number of pertinent questions: where are the men behind the de-gendering nominatives? What are they doing, or not doing, as they maintain the gender-order hierarchy such that treaty violations go unpunished and policy contradictions get smoothed over? How are all these national commitments, and international agreements, made to go away?

The Wallström narrative

An international political incident, or series of incidents, occurred in March 2015 between Sweden and Saudi Arabia, revealing the 'tension between Sweden's feminist face and its desire to maintain lucrative weapons contracts'.[53] This incident shows how gender can figure analytically and politically in contestation over what the arms control discourse refers to as 'irresponsible' but licit (that is, authorized) sales and/or transfers of weaponry. And it highlights the kind of gap that activists expect to close, since various treaties, policies and agreements on arms control already referenced gender, and indeed, gender-based violence, quite explicitly. This was hardly accidental or elite-driven. Over the years generations of activists had been working at any and all levels to get that result.

When she took office, Swedish Foreign Minister Margot Wallström (Social Democrat) announced that the country would be pursuing a feminist foreign policy. After Sweden declared that it would be the first EU member state to recognize Palestine, Wallström was invited as a guest of honour to the Arab League foreign ministers' meeting in Cairo. She was intending to speak about women's achievements, rights and representation. However, Saudi Arabia blocked her from doing so, because she had previously spoken in the Swedish parliament against the punishment of Saudi Arabian blogger Raif Badawi, who had been sentenced to 1,000 lashes and a decade in prison. Moreover, the Swedish government had deplored the subjugation and sequestration of women by the Saudi Arabian government.

Wallström is then reported to have complained to reporters in Cairo about the blocking of her speech. At that point the Swedish government was deciding whether or not to renew a memorandum of understanding, signed in 2005, on 'defence' cooperation with Saudi Arabia – in essence, a military trade agreement. An open letter, calling for the continuation of the memorandum, was signed by 'more than 30 of Sweden's business elite, including Jacob Wallenberg of Investor, Annika Falkengren of SEB bank, and Stefan Persson of the clothing multinational H&M'. Evidently Sweden's reputation as a partner in trade and cooperation was at stake.[54]

Although the Swedish government was divided over what to do, a decision was made to terminate the agreement, which the media referred to as 'tearing up of the arms deal'.[55] Saudi Arabia responded by recalling its ambassador and refusing to issue visas to Swedish businesspeople.[56] That response made explicit reference to Sweden's feminist foreign policy. Concurrently the Saudi action did not 'sit well' with some of Sweden's most powerful industrialists, who stood to lose out on significant income from a break in relations with Saudi Arabia.[57] Those businessmen and women included 'the likes of Volvo, Ikea, H&M, so popular with especially female consumers globally'.[58]

While the Women's International League for Peace and Freedom declared this a 'feminist victory',[59] it is important to note that the termination of the agreement with Saudi Arabia did not necessarily mean an end to all weapons exports. Actually, however, this was a non-affair, as Cohen concludes:

> Outside Sweden, the western media has barely covered the story, and Sweden's EU allies have shown no inclination whatsoever to support her. A small Scandinavian nation faces sanctions, accusations of Islamophobia and maybe worse to come, and everyone stays silent. As so often, the scandal is that there isn't a scandal.[60]

'Everyone' references the elite males and masculinizing institutions through which voices could have been raised. No doubt many non-elite males were also silent. And many women, and more than likely some feminists and other activists, had also tried to protest. But at the public level, that 'calling out' didn't happen. This apparent silence doesn't even seem to register as a puzzle, given that repetitive normalization of similar non-events gets no traction either, and indeed, the international and national press favours business-as-usual. This includes the legitimate sales and purchase of hi-tech and low-tech weaponry. Without those legitimate, and repetitively legitimated, deadly weapons, the violent destruction of lives and livelihoods would certainly be much less.

Sweden is a signatory to the international Arms Trade Treaty, which officially recognizes the link between gender-based violence and the legitimate arms trade. Moreover, it also covers other conventional weapons, and not just small arms and light weapons traded at the higher international levels. Yet, as we have seen, gender here references female victims:

> The exporting State Party, in making this assessment, shall take into account the risk of the conventional arms covered under Article 2 (1) or of the items covered under Article 3 or Article 4 being used to commit or facilitate serious acts of gender-based violence or serious acts of violence against women and children.[61]

That outcome leaves perpetrators in a de-gendered zone of generic human criminality.

Depending on what 'gender-based violence' is taken to mean, exporting arms to Saudi Arabia could potentially be considered to violate the gender clause of the Arms Trade Treaty. Definitions of gender-based violence there include: 'any act of gender-based violence that results in, or is likely to result in, physical, sexual or psychological harm or suffering to women, including threats of such acts, coercion or arbitrary deprivation of liberty, whether occurring in public or in private life'.[62]

Aside from the Saudi Arabian state's role in facilitating and condoning many other acts of gender-based violence on women – if gender-based violence includes arbitrary deprivations of liberty – then at the very least it could be argued that the state is directly perpetrating gender-based violence in any number of ways.

What is striking is that in the reporting on the Wallström affair, the link was made between Sweden's feminist foreign policy and the country's own rules and regulations regarding arms transfers. But little or no reference was made to the international Arms Trade Treaty itself, despite its provisions mentioning women/gender. Even so, the conflict between exporting weapons to a state that violates human rights, including women's rights, was noted as a problem. This could have been a prime opportunity for a nation to use the treaty to pursue a feminist, anti-militarist foreign policy, and to make good the treaty stipulations with respect to 'irresponsible' but still licit sales and transfers of weaponry. Here was an opportunity for states, and not just Sweden, to show their commitment to the principles that they had signed up to in treaties and resolutions at the highest international and regional levels.

Yet the other EU states 'stood by, silent by all accounts'.[63] But then, why is this silence not very puzzling? As an international Arms Trade Treaty monitor notes in a flurry of acronyms: 'There remains, however, an uneven understanding among States Parties of what constitutes or facilitates an act of GBV [gender-based violence], the ways in which the ATT [Arms Trade Treaty] addresses GBV and how GBV can be incorporated into Articles 6 and 7 risk assessment obligations.'[64]

'States Parties' here is a way of *not* referencing elite males, and also elite women in masculinizing, indeed, militarizing, institutions. If taken seriously, the treaty has the potential to be a very powerful tool for activists who campaign against militarism and what it does. The treaty has shifted terminology away from womenandchildren, as they figure in the UN Programme of Action on Small Arms and Light Weapons, to gender-based violence, which has further potential as a framing device. Possibly gender could function to delegitimize the international arms trade altogether, as Paul Kirby suggests:

Is there ever a conflict where arms flows could not be said to facilitate serious acts of gender-based violence – harms strongly correlated with, but not necessarily inflicted by, the deployment of weaponry? Is the use of white phosphorous 'gender-based' because it is indiscriminate, and therefore likely to inflict harm on innocent 'womenandchildren'? ... Are massacres of battle-aged males by AK-47s gender-based?[65]

Conjoining 'gender' with 'violence' could be interpreted to include LGBTQ+ and non-binary people, as well as straight, cis-men resisting militarization. That is precisely because it is the iconic and normalizing way of 'doing' the masculinity that is most important in legitimating the gender-order hierarchy. Focusing on men and masculinity would thus work both ways: elite male and masculinizing institutions would be called out, held accountable, targeted effectively; other men, feminist or otherwise, might then be emboldened to rethink and exercise a masculinity contrary to the norm that the nation-state works so hard to project as its defining self-image.[66]

Repetitively this 'alternative' masculinity could become a norm, or at least obtain some recognitional validity. Reforming masculinity, depending on how it is done, wouldn't necessarily reinscribe and reinforce the gender binary, if this is understood performatively in relation to multiple sexualities and possibilities. Insofar as some masculine alternatives 'trouble' heterosexuality, they also trouble the male–female binary paradigm, which is conventionally naturalized in the species as reproductive necessity. As with any political exercise, that sort of transformation would have to be painfully worked out, but having the concepts, and then the language to do it with, is the first step.

And how they fight back

Even though the arms trade and weapons industries may present themselves as, and also be presented as, gender-neutral, these agencies have been historically, and are still visibly and practically, highly masculinized. This seems unremarkably obvious on many levels: in the scientific research and development of technology, in engineering science departments, in the skilled people working in factories, and in the diplomats, government officials and businessmen who do the deals.

use of diversity, which is an apparently de-gendered abstraction. That abstraction erases the practices of exclusion and misogyny that caused the situation in the first place.

The 'business case' for investing in women and girls is not only used by corporations, but also by international institutions, notably the World Bank. It stated in 2012 that 'gender equality is important for both intrinsic and instrumental reasons', describing investment in women and girls as 'smart economics'. Discussions of gender mainstreaming in international security policies unsurprisingly echo this commercial economism.[73] Agnes Marcaillou, chief of the Regional Disarmament Branch of the UN Office for Disarmament Affairs, is reported to have said: 'It is not about feminism, it is about business. Member states give us money to implement projects, and if I implement a project that only affects 50 per cent of the population, that is bad business.'[74]

BAE Systems has made the company's position on diversity and inclusion perfectly clear:

> There is often some confusion over what diversity and inclusion means and why this matters – for us it is all about staying competitive and innovative. Many research reports have shown that diversity and inclusion lead to better employee retention and productivity. So having a diverse workforce and maintaining an inclusive working environment are key to the sustainability of the Company.[75]

BAE Systems is thus not seeking to become more diverse because it is ethically right, which, in gender terms, leans towards the softly and weakly feminine, but because it is better for business. In gender terms 'business' is easily referenced to hard-nosed competitive masculinity. That concept is understood in this book as the great power imbrication of bourgeois-rational with warrior-protector masculinities, as outlined in preceding chapters.

While benefiting from the inclusion of women as instanced by BAE Systems and outlined, at the same time, the arms industry also benefits from purple-washing, which is the practice of using women's rights and gender equality as 'femvertizing'. This is deployed as a means of legitimizing corporate–state policies, decisions, expenditures and actions. Purple-washing often leaves aside any critical consideration of women in relation to equal treatment, as well as women in relation to human dignity in male-dominated and highly masculinized workplaces. Roberts argues that transnational business feminism obscures 'the gender and class power relations that constitute the capitalist global political economy'. And further – through its 'instrumental use of gender equality' – transnational business feminism has become a 'useful means of legitimizing and depoliticizing the exercise of private power'.[76] As Acheson says regarding the women in top positions at US arms firms: 'These women are not challenging the patriarchal structures and systems that have created the militarized world order; they are actively maintaining it and profiting from it.'[77] In other words, 'You can militarise anything including equality'.[78]

BAE Systems, in common with the other industries of corporate–state weaponry, is thus addressing its long-standing, yet ever-deepening legitimacy deficit by adopting one of feminism's 'uncanny doubles', in Fraser's striking conceptualization.[79] That is, women are understood as needing men's help, benefiting from their largesse, and entering willingly into male-dominated power structures. Starting from that position, then, women's politics, that is, feminism, can be turned to the task of 'making up' a legitimation deficit.

As a signifier women can do this because – in contrast to the world that male dominance and commercialized-militarized masculinities have created – they are, in certain contexts/ discourses, understood as innocent, childlike, guiltless. In moral terms, understood through this powerful – if empirically flawed and hypocritically manipulated – set of metaphorical references, they can be deployed figuratively and bodily as an emblem of moral rectitude. Thus if women are visibly on board, then so is legitimacy, and further questions – about what is really going on – are again forestalled.

Rebranding the arms industry as women-friendly, in contrast to a former hypermasculine self-image, articulates it as progressively masculine. It is not only women who are made to purple-wash the guilt and make up for a legitimacy deficit. Pink-washing also figures in state–corporate strategies to make the arms industries live up to the label 'legitimate' and to forestall moral opprobrium. As noted, BAE Systems, and similar corporate interests, have made themselves visible in Gay Pride parades. This pink-washing tactic – deployed in order to gloss over militarized violence and any number of other injurious and discriminatory practices – shifts attention to issues and successes in LGBTQ+ inclusion into the workplace. Public declarations of support in sponsorship make it easy to advertise this.[80]

In effect this is a variant of homonationalism, the foreign policy practice through which some countries represent themselves as tolerant of sexualities, which they have formerly criminalized as deviant. They thus present themselves as progressive, so as to position other nations and peoples as intolerant, and therefore backward and malevolent. Racialization and demonization are then deployed to demarcate an image of white, secular, liberal virtue, legitimately threatening economic sanctions and armed intervention, and doing this from the moral high ground.[81]

As Rossdale says of BAE Systems, their involvement in Pride portrays western companies 'as always more tolerant, enlightened or progressive than non-western states'. This then licenses their privileged role as legitimated moral arbiters in relation to their own activities, products and partners, about which and about whom many moral qualms might otherwise be raised. This now commonplace state and corporate practice also reinforces racist and colonial attitudes about empowerment and privilege. And it renders the violence deployed by supposedly gay-friendly nation-states and corporate businesses a priori more civilized, controlled, proportionate and legitimate than the violence deployed by those whom they 'other' as rivals or enemies.[82]

This is where the relationality of sex, gender and sexuality, and their intersections with race, class and histories of colonialism and imperialism, become crucial in the anti-militarist activisms that target the arms industries internationally. In that context they are important as weapons of critique, yet they are also liabilities of complicity. With that in mind we turn to the ways that masculinities are figured and deployed by and within activist groups where – unlike now legendary feminist ones, such as the Greenham Common encampments – men are actively present.

Stand together/divide and rule

According to some witnesses, anti-militarism activists face a double liability in relation to gender and sexualities: in terms of effecting positive outcomes on targeted states and institutions, and in terms of avoiding negative relations among themselves. As Rossdale states, many activists are well versed 'in feminist and queer politics' and are thus 'often supportive of feminist politics, and might even self-identify as feminists'. Yet in activist groups this feminist/gender perspective is frequently conceived as politically distinct from their anti-militarism. In some instances gendered analysis simply doesn't feature in 'public-facing campaign communications and actions', hence the 'entanglement of militarism, gender and sexuality' doesn't emerge.[83]

Looking inwards, however, some among the activists are very ready to challenge sexist or homophobic conduct within anti-militarist spaces. Yet this happens without making visible the imbrication of militarism with sexism and homophobia as practised and constantly reinforced outside activist circles, namely in the world of great power commercial relations. Rossdale advises that there are 'compelling reasons to suggest that resistance to militarism' isn't possible without 'a corresponding encounter with heterosexism and patriarchy'. However, he concludes that, whether looking outward or inward, for many anti-militarists, 'questions of gender and sexuality might be important', but they are broadly understood as separate from 'matters of war and peace'.[84]

That cognitive separation, perhaps unsurprisingly, mirrors the newsroom and other journalistic strategies deployed to reassure readers and viewers that there isn't a connection to be made, since the two issue-areas are supposedly so different. Indeed the two areas are framed and understood as the one being wholly public and hardly private, while the other involves a struggle to get the private into the public at all. Categorical boundaries, and the presumptions of the gender-order hierarchy, are mirrored here. That imbrication is highly effective in discouraging curiosity because the fixity of those boundary lines makes a putative link across them seem weird and unintelligible.[85]

themselves as men, and to understand that their participation in these masculinizing and heteromasculinity-maintaining structures isn't merely a personal affair, even though that is the way it is experienced.

Making global change isn't so much a matter of working through individual male cathexes and disavowals as it is a matter of showing men – and everyone else – just how it is that normalized elite-male masculinizing hierarchies of destruction derive their power from the complicity and indifference of subordinated males, and further subordinated others. This is what makes resistance so difficult and risky.

'We can't even march straight'

A turn from male complicity and indifference to queer anti-militarism, which is set against and over-and-above the gender binary, might possibly help here. This could be a focus for anti-militarist activism such that masculinism/militarism snaps into focus as mutually constitutive. Rossdale gives three detailed case studies that are 'strong examples of how feminist and queer anti-militarists seek to contend with the banal or everyday dimensions of militarism while also targeting particular institutions'.[88] Some of the targeted institutions will be familiar from the preceding chapters, for example BAE Systems, which was enhancing its corporate image in a Pride parade in London, and also the Defence and Security Technology exhibition, where queer-identified protestors at the site suffered disproportionately at the hands of exhibition security and the Metropolitan Police.

However, one of the groups that Rossdale discusses is of particular interest here, because of its focus – not on the agencies nested within governmental-commercial militarism, but because it specifically focuses on the individual elite-males who control this public sector–private sector world. They do this in highly protected and continually legitimated ways, some of which are discussed in the preceding chapters. The anti-militarism protest we consider here took place in the National Gallery in London, itself a formidably elite institution, with its own hierarchically nested ranks of corporate sponsors and self-selecting boards and committees.

Without linking militarism and masculinity it is e
for anti-war cis-males to reproduce the legitimatin
that keep national and international militarism at th
of global political power. Hence, as testified by R
gender analysis that fails to connect the nested hier
some men over others within the military, with simil
hierarchies in non-military life – such as in business
which are both highly masculinized and masculinizii
cause internal contradictions within activist moven
particular, Rossdale reports that there is

> a fair amount of sexist (and homophobic, transphob
> behaviour in activist spaces. In my interviews, eve
> single non-male interviewee described experienc
> of being ignored, patronised and humiliated b
> men in the movement. They also called attentio
> to the prevalence of the 'alternative machismo ..
> which assesses people's commitment on the basi
> of how often they resist arrest or go to jail' and to
> the tendency of meetings and organising spaces to
> become dominated by male voices in what one
> interviewee referred to as a 'look at my huge dick
> of arms trade knowledge' contest.[86]

Even at an all-male workshop, designed and facilitated to disc
gender/sexuality politics, held at a Peace News Summer Car
the 'suggestion that people might form an all-male feminist gro
to explore possibilities for anti-militarist masculinities was n
with uncomfortable glances and sniggers'. Despite misgivin
expressed somewhat later within the groups, Rossdale conclud
that 'attitudes which dismiss suggestions of a relationship betwee
militarism and masculinity, and which presume the benign o
innocent nature of "men like us", are not uncommon'.[87]

What this tells us is that gender-feminism gets little traction
even with anti-militarist men, who have few incentives to see
exactly how much power masculinizing institutions have, and
how much that power depends on reinforcing the masculinities
that men are – more or less easily – inducted into. It isn't easy
for men to escape their somewhat varied identifications of

Without linking militarism and masculinity it is easy enough for anti-war cis-males to reproduce the legitimating strategies that keep national and international militarism at the pinnacle of global political power. Hence, as testified by Rossdale, a gender analysis that fails to connect the nested hierarchies of some men over others within the military, with similar, parallel hierarchies in non-military life – such as in business or sport, which are both highly masculinized and masculinizing – will cause internal contradictions within activist movements. In particular, Rossdale reports that there is

> a fair amount of sexist (and homophobic, transphobic) behaviour in activist spaces. In my interviews, every single non-male interviewee described experiences of being ignored, patronised and humiliated by men in the movement. They also called attention to the prevalence of the 'alternative machismo ... which assesses people's commitment on the basis of how often they resist arrest or go to jail' and to the tendency of meetings and organising spaces to become dominated by male voices in what one interviewee referred to as a 'look at my huge dick of arms trade knowledge' contest.[86]

Even at an all-male workshop, designed and facilitated to discuss gender/sexuality politics, held at a Peace News Summer Camp, the 'suggestion that people might form an all-male feminist group to explore possibilities for anti-militarist masculinities was met with uncomfortable glances and sniggers'. Despite misgivings expressed somewhat later within the groups, Rossdale concludes that 'attitudes which dismiss suggestions of a relationship between militarism and masculinity, and which presume the benign or innocent nature of "men like us", are not uncommon'.[87]

What this tells us is that gender-feminism gets little traction even with anti-militarist men, who have few incentives to see exactly how much power masculinizing institutions have, and how much that power depends on reinforcing the masculinities that men are – more or less easily – inducted into. It isn't easy for men to escape their somewhat varied identifications of

themselves as men, and to understand that their participation in these masculinizing and heteromasculinity-maintaining structures isn't merely a personal affair, even though that is the way it is experienced.

Making global change isn't so much a matter of working through individual male cathexes and disavowals as it is a matter of showing men – and everyone else – just how it is that normalized elite-male masculinizing hierarchies of destruction derive their power from the complicity and indifference of subordinated males, and further subordinated others. This is what makes resistance so difficult and risky.

'We can't even march straight'

A turn from male complicity and indifference to queer anti-militarism, which is set against and over-and-above the gender binary, might possibly help here. This could be a focus for anti-militarist activism such that masculinism/militarism snaps into focus as mutually constitutive. Rossdale gives three detailed case studies that are 'strong examples of how feminist and queer anti-militarists seek to contend with the banal or everyday dimensions of militarism while also targeting particular institutions'.[88] Some of the targeted institutions will be familiar from the preceding chapters, for example BAE Systems, which was enhancing its corporate image in a Pride parade in London, and also the Defence and Security Technology exhibition, where queer-identified protestors at the site suffered disproportionately at the hands of exhibition security and the Metropolitan Police.

However, one of the groups that Rossdale discusses is of particular interest here, because of its focus – not on the agencies nested within governmental-commercial militarism, but because it specifically focuses on the individual elite-males who control this public sector–private sector world. They do this in highly protected and continually legitimated ways, some of which are discussed in the preceding chapters. The anti-militarism protest we consider here took place in the National Gallery in London, itself a formidably elite institution, with its own hierarchically nested ranks of corporate sponsors and self-selecting boards and committees.

In the hushed and marbled sacred spaces of the national art collection, Sparkles Not Shrapnel performed a queer 'die-in', outfitted in military helmets and sparkly tops. They also declaimed an anti-war poem, written by the then – and first ever – female UK poet laureate, before falling to the floor 'dead'. After that they were ejected, as one would expect.

However, the queer protestors' object was rather more specific than merely staging a protest in public, because they were taking part in Disarm the Gallery, which was running concurrently as an ongoing anti-arms trade campaign. In particular the National Gallery's relationship with Finmeccanica as a sponsoring funder was targeted.[89] Now known as Leonardo, the company is part-owned by the Italian government and figures in the top ranks of the world's commercial defence, aeronautics, outer space and security contractors.

While 'tactical frivolity' could be deployed in a city street or public square, what is interesting here is how queer gender/sexuality mocks the imbrication of masculinity with violence via the top levels of organized commercial militarism. It does this in a zone where commercial, militarizing masculinity is repetitively legitimated at a hallowed institution. The National Gallery glorifies the nation-state and vice versa; the clue is in the name.

In that kind of mutually legitimating institutional setting, nation-state elites honour themselves at the highest levels, and also admit the public *gratis* to help them do it. Given that arms companies have a lot to hide, they can – in those venues – hide what they're doing in plain sight. In such sacred spaces they become moralized 'good' by the grandeur of the nation-state, its control over life and death, and its wealth and culture. Because elite benefactors and sponsors are moralized at that level, they are the eponymous 'great and good' men, along with a minority of functionally masculinized women. Exactly what they are doing there, celebrating themselves as national treasures in an international treasury of priceless artefacts, then covers over the moral deficits of their so-called 'private sector' wealth-generating enterprises. In fact these businesses are massively and quite openly funded and secured with public, taxpayer appropriations from congresses and parliaments.

Wrapping up/moving on

This book has shown how the effort to reveal gender as a binary *and* a hierarchy – making men *and* women visible as gendered beings, *and* making masculinity and femininity visible as practices of power – enables us to understand how certain subject positions can be created and renewed. In that way certain meanings are naturalized as inevitable, and certain practices are valorized and privileged. This study has therefore shown that gender is key to understanding *how* certain practices are repetitively legitimized – not just as normal everyday undertakings, but also as praiseworthy imbrications of commercialism and violence. As Stern explains: 'Because of their associations with the "natural", gendered divisions provide a powerful mechanism for creating seemingly stable categories. Evocations of masculinity and femininity masquerade as known entities – entities that carry the weight of history.'[90]

It is precisely an indifference to how gender really works, and therefore the invisibility of its workings, which allows it 'to function so effectively as a common denominator between apparently different discourses', in Rowley's words.[91] Without a clear understanding of gender as a power/knowledge construction, rather than simply talking about gender as a supposed synonym for the supposed male/female and supposed masculinity/femininity binary lines, it isn't possible even to ask *how* it is that the arms trade has become legitimized. That legitimized trade in weaponry is definitionally and practically constitutive of the nation-state, and therefore of great power politics.

In turn, not understanding exactly *how* gender works, in and through nested hierarchies of men presuming and enforcing the gender order, then the possibilities for delegitimization, and therefore imaginative transformation, are very limited. As registered, activisms that do not encourage their members, hence the general public, and indeed, elite-men and masculinized women, to address the imbrication of sex/gender/sexuality with militarism and weaponry can promise only limited results, if any.

Legitimacy is a crucial target in denaturalization and destabilization, because – under the liberal-minded principles promulgated and endorsed by the UN Charter, and reinforced in further declarations and resolutions – the rights that are enumerated therein can only exist when they are constitutive of governments. Those governments are then presumed to have secured the consent of their peoples, as otherwise they would not have been admitted to the international system.

When unconsent occurs, legitimacy seems less credible, state actions become rights violations, and the international community comes under pressure. UN declarations on gender, women – and only by implication, men, which is *not* an accidental omission – are rather less than clear on the subject of the gender-order hierarchy. In general it passes as simply a natural fact, or is even naturalized overtly through repetitive discursive construction. Those familiar strategies follow from the vested interests of national/international nested hierarchies of male-dominated, and in some cases male-exclusive, religious and political power structures. Those two hierarchies of authority are themselves more often imbricated than separated, whatever national constitutions may say.

In that context the various international treaties and protocols discussed above attempt to draw a line in international law between a legitimate arms trade and an illegitimate one. The dividing lines and sanctions policies expressed in those documents are made visible through the news media, which are attuned to what is considered important at the great power level. In implementing the treaty terms and sanctions, some men would lose opportunities. That would destabilize their elite identities that are invested in controlling, or trying to control, other men.

Of course we are leaving aside loopholes here, enforcement gaps, disavowal of responsibilities, mutual cover-ups, 'grey areas' of toleration, and suchlike. Protecting womenandchildren, or at least claiming to, might look like it requires effort and sacrifice, but those activities and risks are themselves constitutive of the masculinity that most men consent to, or at least overwhelmingly fail to dissent from. Or those men who do dissent don't often do it in very visible, and potentially destabilizing, terms. As feminists have persuasively argued, inclusion isn't empowerment.

Empowering women obviously threatens the gender-order hierarchy of privilege and graded subordinations, hence the many familiar social disciplines that are in place. Those practices teach everyone that masculinity is normal, and indeed essential to national and personal security. Acceptance of that framework constitutes consent, and with consent comes legitimacy. Thus male privilege remains in place even if, and perhaps when, the 'opposite' female yet masculinized body is not an exact match to the original ideas of male superiority. This is precisely because the full array of male vs female nakedly physical sex signifiers is less relevant to the business of militarism than is the body surface visibility of behavioural gender signifiers.

Commonplace gender/sex identification is most often a matter of clothing and deportment, together with racialized understandings of physiognomy. This is because the relevant genital markers are generally under wraps, and subject to strict protocols on unconsented views, or supposedly so. But in that way there is much more at stake than descriptive identifications and gender box-ticking. Masculinity and masculinization as behavioural normalizations are the exact means through which the gender-order hierarchy secures itself. It is in that way that male domination in the nation-states ensures that violence and destruction become their own rewards.

Starting from feminist perspectives – which is where critical masculinity studies originated – is essential to understanding militarism and thus to promoting effective activisms, since it is from within feminism that the legitimacy issue was raised in relation to male dominance. Properly understood, hegemony is domination *by consent*, the notion that has spurred masculinity studies and given it a focus on power. Note: *hegemony is not a synonym for domination – it is domination by consent.*

Whether a revisioned masculinity – 'eco' or 'caring' or otherwise – could challenge the gender-order hierarchy effectively, or would instead merely mitigate or mutate it, remains to be seen. A recent gender-focused study of climate change activism and institutional resistance – mentioned above – catalogues a considerable number of variant heteronormative masculinities in various agencies around the world.[92] There are also notable global movements to end men's violence against women, for example the White Ribbon campaign.[93] The focus there is interpersonal and individual, although a more structurally conscious approach could emerge. That could happen particularly via convergence with men's involvement in anti-militarism movements, such as Veterans for Peace[94] and the White Poppy campaign,[95] along with the activisms discussed above.

Definitive change can sometimes come suddenly and unpredictably, but then change has to come from somewhere. And some people have to be able to articulate the terms of transformation. The 'gays in the military' movement to end hetero-male exclusivity in some national ranks is a case in point. The U-turn in the American Congress and administration arrived quite suddenly and through seemingly contingent circumstances. But those contingencies arose only because years of articulate advocacy and repetitive issue-raising had sunk in, such that a very few men in power eventually took action, and others close to them chose to stand aside.[96]

Looking back on the history of varied kinds of inclusions by race, class and sexuality within some of the world's militaries, which are emblematic of the nation-state, and also of an international masculine ideal of citizen-hero, there is a certain serial intersectionality about the struggles as they add up. The Trump administration's attempts to reverse the inclusion of 'trans' as a material category of gender equality in the US military was a notable instance of a pushback that failed.[97]

This book has shown that the sharply legalistic dichotomies outlined above, which structure much of the arms control discourse in terms of legitimate vs illegitimate, or licit vs illicit, are in actuality blurry and porous. In discursive, public-facing terms, the masculinity and the weaponry are mutually legitimated as licit by characterizing the shadowy illicit trade as super-subordinated criminality. This enhances the supra-ordinated position of the dominant male elites who circulate through the public–private world of commercialized weaponry.

Yet racialized nefarious actors, alluded to in the arms control discourse and in corporate promotional videos, are, in fact, invited to arms fairs by the legitimate states that host them, such as the UK. The UK government was responsible for inviting state representatives to attend the Defence and Security Equipment International (DSEI) 2013 trade fair from Uzbekistan, Turkmenistan and Saudi Arabia, respectively then ranked 161 to 163 out of 167 nations listed in the EIU Democracy Index.[98] At these fairs, predominantly white, or more specifically, non-black, conceptions of militarized masculinity are celebrated and marketed.

However, the masculinities, through which weapons marketing at UK arms fairs are defined as legitimate, are not so different from those underpinning the proliferation of small arms and light weapons bought and sold in illegitimated contexts. The relevance of masculinities to weapons in war-torn/illegitimate contexts 'out there' is therefore the same as the masculinities found 'in here'. It is a militarized masculinity of protection and aggression, albeit with local variations. Notions of masculinity perpetuate gun cultures and the proliferation of small arms and light weapons in conflict zones, for example the Democratic Republic of the Congo, the favelas of urban Brazil, the borderlands of Mexico, and the United States more generally. These are part of the same dynamic that uses fetishized tropes of both commercial bourgeois-rational and military warrior-protector masculinities to sell weaponry.

While the gun cultures of the global south are increasingly pathologized by the politics of the global north, so the commercial and ideological complicities of the global north are normalized, and thus invisibilized.[99] The masculinity 'out there' looks different from the one 'in here' because it is racialized, 'othered' and barbarized in comparison to the sanitized, restrained, purportedly civilized self of empowered white male elites, such as the ones encountered at arms fairs.

And in the global north, the 'out there' also characteristically references marginalized, racialized and demonized groups within national boundaries. In actuality corruption and bribery are central to the global, white-dominated arms trade, so what is really made visible in these north–south hierarchies – even if denied as policy and practice – is the core–periphery relationship of unequal power relations, largely focused on race.[100] As Stravrianakis explains, rather than 'signalling a victory for human security, the International Arms Trade Treaty is better understood as facilitating legitimacy for some forms of fighting, and thus tactically off-siding others'.[101]

Repetitive legitimation naturalizes the current distributions of power, while delegitimizing low-tech violence, so that the hi-tech violence remains high-value commercially. As Cohn and Ruddick succinctly state: 'metaphors of masculinity' become entwined 'with judgements of legitimacy and power'.[102] Through repetitive performance 'mere' metaphors become activities and certainties, subsumed within the gender-order hierarchy of masculinity over femininity, some men over others. Focusing on gender in that way, by naming men as men, and by examining processes of legitimation, might stimulate unconsent to the arms trade. That would then begin to decouple the nation-state from both widespread complicity and elite male temptation.

That breakthrough could start to remake great power politics as the pursuit of non-violence. And it would make masculinity look different, because it would be different. That difference would be in relation to male dominance, not simply more varied ways of characterizing what men are like, when they do what they do. Looked at the other way, mobilizing small differences tactically in that direction – and targeting power, dominance and destruction – could have genuine rewards for humanity. That is because – at least to some degree – the gender-order hierarchy of male dominance would, mirror-like, then look less legitimate, too. Delegitimating the gender-order hierarchy completely is an even bigger project. But action against the arms trade – and in particular the legal or 'licit' arms trade – looks like an excellent site for contestation.

Further reading

Claire Duncanson (2015) 'Hegemonic masculinity and the possibility of change in gender relations', *Men and Masculinities*, 18(2): 231–48.

Katharine M. Millar and Joanna Tidy (2017) 'Combat as a moving target: Masculinities, the heroic soldier myth, and normative martial violence', *Critical Military Studies*, 3(2): 42–60.

Lucy Nicholas and Christine Agius (2018) *The Persistence of Global Masculinism: Discourse, Gender and Neo-Colonial Re-articulations of Violence*, Cham: Palgrave Macmillan.

Chris Rossdale (2021) *Resisting Militarism: Direct Action and the Politics of Subversion*, Edinburgh: Edinburgh University Press.

Marysia Zalewski, Paul Drummond, Elizabeth Prügl and Maria Stern (eds) (2020) *Sexual Violence against Men in Global Politics*, Abingdon: Routledge.

Notes

Chapter 1

1   For a starkly contrasting view, see Laura J. Shepherd (ed) (2014) *Gender Matters in Global Politics: A Feminist Introduction to International Relations*, Abingdon: Routledge.

2   As does Laura Shepherd in *Gender Matters* (2014).

3   For a discussion of gender hierarchies, see Mimi Schippers (2007) 'Recovering the feminine other: Masculinity, femininity and gender hegemony', *Theory & Society*, 36: 85–102.

4   See the discussion on feminism, gender and liberation in Judith Grant (1993) *Fundamental Feminism: Contesting the Core Concepts of Feminist Theory*, New York: Routledge, pp 188–91. All of Cynthia Enloe's books also make this point – see further references below.

5   Lisa Disch and Mary Hawkesworth (eds) (2018) *Oxford Handbook of Feminist Theory*, Oxford: Oxford University Press; this has 50 chapters, none addressing men and/or masculinity as such, and runs to 1,084 pages; the relevant index entries pick up a few dozen pages related to violence, crime and the law.

6   See Victor J. Seidler (ed) (2003) *Men, Sex and Relationships: Writings from Achilles Heel*, Abingdon: Routledge.

7   For a synoptic view, see Cynthia Enloe (2016) *Globalization and Militarism: Feminists Make the Link* (2nd edn), Lanham, MD: Rowman & Littlefield.

8   And sometimes, in recent years, with some additional options and opt-outs.

9   For a global survey of wealth and power distributed by gender, see Joni Seager (2018) *The Women's Atlas*, Brighton: Myriad; while that book focuses on women's share, simple subtraction generates men's; this is discussed in relation to race/ethnicity and similar discriminatory ascriptions later on in this chapter.

10 See Caroline Criado-Perez (2019) *Invisible Women: Exposing Data Bias in a World Designed for Men*, London: Chatto & Windus.

11 See the classic study by Jean Bethke Elshtain (1993) *Public Man/Private Woman: Women in Social and Political Thought* (2nd edn), Princeton, NJ: Princeton University Press.

12 For a particularly analytical discussion, see Raia Prokhovnik (1999) *Rational Woman: A Feminist Critique of Dichotomy*, London: Routledge.

13 Judith Butler (1999) *Gender Trouble: Feminism and the Subversion of Identity* (2nd edn), Abingdon: Routledge.

14 See Anne Fausto-Sterling (2000) *Sexing the Body*, Philadelphia, PA: Temple University Press.

15 Judith Butler (2011) *Bodies that Matter: On the Discursive Limits of Sex*, Abingdon: Routledge.

16 For a classic account, see Jeff Hearn (1987) *The Gender of Oppression: Men, Masculinity and the Critique of Marxism*, Brighton: Wheatsheaf.

17 The classic was William Foote Whyte (1993) *Street Corner Society* (4th edn), Chicago, IL: University of Chicago Press [first published in 1943, originally with the subtitle *The Social Structure of an Italian Slum*].

18 See J. Ann Tickner (1992) *Gender in International Relations: Feminist Perspectives on Achieving Global Security*, New York: Columbia University Press.

19 See James Martin (1998) *Gramsci's Political Analysis: A Critical Introduction*, London: Palgrave Macmillan.

20 See Jeff Hearn (2015) *Men of the World: Genders, Globalizations, Transnational Times*, London: Sage Publications.

21 For a discussion of the 'patriarchal dividend', see Raewyn Connell (1987) *Gender and Power: Society, the Person and Sexual Politics*, Cambridge: Polity, pp 142–3.

22 See Mary Hawkesworth (2018) *Globalization and Feminist Activism* (2nd edn), Lanham, MD: Rowman & Littlefield.

23 For a recent discussion, see Peter Beinart (2019) 'The new authoritarians are waging a war on women', *The Atlantic*, January–February, www.theatlantic.com/magazine/archive/2019/01/authoritarian-sexism-trump-duterte/576382

24 See, for example, Marie Evertsson (2014) 'Gender ideology and the sharing of housework and childcare in Sweden', *Journal of Family Studies*, 35(7): 927–49.

25 Ian Hurd (2008) *After Anarchy: Legitimacy and Power in the United Nations Security Council*, Princeton, NJ: Princeton University Press, p 2.

26 Hurd (2008) *After Anarchy*, p 3.

27 Raewyn W. Connell (2006) *Masculinities* (2nd edn), Cambridge: Polity.

28 For the classic analysis of power, see Steven Lukes (2004) *Power: A Radical View* (2nd edn), London: Palgrave Macmillan.

29 See Anne Fausto-Sterling (2000) *Sexing the Body*, Philadelphia, PA: Temple University Press.

30 See Kimberlé Crenshaw (1991) 'Mapping the margins: Intersectionality, identity politics, and violence against women of color', *Stanford Law Review*, 43(6): 1299–59.

31 For a discussion of masculinity/masculinization as dominance, see Judith (now Jack) Halberstam (1998) *Female Masculinity*, Durham, NC: Duke University Press.

32 For an overview, see Lukas Gottzén, Ulff Mellström and Tamara Shefer (eds) (2019) *Routledge International Handbook of Masculinity Studies*, Abingdon: Routledge.

33 For the classic study, see J.P. Plamenatz (1968) *Consent, Freedom and Obligation* (2nd edn), Oxford: Oxford University Press.

34 See James Martin (2014) *Politics and Rhetoric: A Critical Introduction*, Abingdon: Routledge.

35 Edward S. Herman and Noam Chomsky (2008) *Manufacturing Consent: The Political Economy of the Mass Media*, London: Bodley Head.

36 The classic argumentative study is Cynthia Enloe (2014) *Bananas, Beaches, and Bases: Making Feminist Sense of International Politics* (2nd edn), Berkeley, CA: University of California Press.

Chapter 2

1 Onur Ulas Ince (2018) *Colonial Capitalism and the Dilemmas of Liberalism*, Oxford: Oxford University Press.

2 For the classic definition, see Judith Stiehm (1982) *Women and Men's Wars*, Oxford: Pergamon.

3 See Kim Lane Scheppele (2013) 'From a war on terrorism to global security law', Princeton, NJ: Institute for Advanced Study, Social Science, www.ias.edu/ideas/2013/scheppele-terrorism

4 For a synoptic discussion, see Charles Beitz (1999) *Political Theory and International Relations* (revised edn), Princeton, NJ: Princeton University Press.

5 For the classic account, see Kenneth Waltz (1979) *Theory of International Politics*, New York: McGraw-Hill. This is reprised and critically updated in John Baylis, Steve Smith and Patricia Owens (eds) (2020) *The Globalization of World Politics: An Introduction to International Relations* (8th edn), Oxford: Oxford University Press.

6 For an analytical alignment of political and commercial masculinized elites, see Charlotte Hooper (1999) *Manly States: Masculinities, International Relations, and Gender Politics*, New York: Columbia University Press.

7 For a critical analysis, see Mark Duffield (2018) *Post-Humanitarianism: Governing Precarity in the Digital World*, Cambridge: Polity.

8 Jill Steans (2006) *Gender and International Relations: Issues, Debates and Future Directions* (2nd edn), Cambridge: Polity, p 55.

9 Carol Cohn and Sara Ruddick (2003) *A Feminist Ethical Perspective on Weapons of Mass Destruction*, Working Paper No 104/2003, Boston, MA: Boston Consortium on Gender, Security and Human Rights, http://genderandsecurity.org/sites/default/files/carol_cohn_and_sara_ruddick_working_paper_104.pdf, p 7.

10 John Hopton (2003) 'The State and Military Masculinity', in Paul Higate (ed) *Military Masculinities: Identity and the State*, Westport, CT: Praeger Publishers, pp 111–24, p 115.

11 Cohn and Ruddick (2003) *A Feminist Ethical Perspective*, p 7.

12 For a classic analytical discussion, see Carole Pateman (2018) *The Sexual Contract* (30th anniversary edn), Stanford, CA: Stanford University Press.

13 Cynthia Enloe (2007) *Globalization and Militarism: Feminists Make the Link*, Lanham, MD: Rowman & Littlefield, p 39.

14 Cynthia Weber (1998) 'Peformative states', *Millennium: Journal of International Relations*, 27(1): 77–95, pp 93–4.

15 Tim Dunne (2020) 'Liberal Internationalism', in Baylis, Smith and Owens (eds) *Globalization of World Politics*, pp 103–14.

16 Cynthia Weber (2014) 'Why is there no queer international theory?', *European Journal of International Relations*, 21(1): 27–51.

17 Weber (1998) 'Performative states', pp 93–4.

18 Alexander Wendt (2004) 'The state as person in international theory', *Review of International Studies*, 30(2): 289–316.

19 David Campbell (1992) *Writing Security: United States Foreign Policy and the Politics of Identity*, Manchester: Manchester University Press, p 9.

20 Wendt (2004) 'State as person', p 289; emphasis in the original.

21 Erik Ringmar (1996) 'On the ontological status of the state', *European Journal of International Relations*, 2(4): 439–66, p 443.

22 Wendt (2004) 'State as person', p 289.

23 George Lakoff and Mark Johnson (1980) *Metaphors We Live By*, Chicago, IL: University of Chicago Press, p 29.

24 See Matthew Longo (2017) *The Politics of Borders: Sovereignty, Security and the Citizen after 9/11*, New York: Cambridge University Press.

25 *The Economist* (2010) 'More than a slapped wrist?', 23 March, www.economist.com/node/15763761?story_id=15763761

26 Weber (1998) 'Performative states', p 78.

27 Cynthia Weber (1999) *Faking It: US Hegemony in a 'Post-Phallic' Era*, Minneapolis, MN: University of Minnesota Press, p 90.

28 Laura Mulvey (1975) 'Visual pleasure and narrative cinema', *Screen*, 16(3): 6–18.

29 Weber (1999) *Faking It*, p 90.

30 Jonathan D. Wadley (2010) 'Gendering the State: Performativity and Protection in International Security', in Laura Sjoberg (ed) *Gender and International Security: Feminist Perspectives*, Abingdon: Routledge, pp 38–57, p 39.

31 See J. Samuel Barkin and Laura Sjoberg (2021) 'The queer art of failed IR?', *Alternatives*, 45(4), 10 February, https://doi.org/10.1177/0304375421989572

32 Campbell (1992) *Writing Security*, p 91.

33 Carol Cohn (ed) (2013) *Women and Wars: Contested Histories, Uncertain Futures*, Malden, MA: Polity, p 14.

34 Jan Jindy Pettman (1996) *Worlding Women: A Feminist International Politics*, London: Routledge, p 4.

35 Iris Marion Young (2003) 'The logic of masculine protection: Reflections on the current security state', *Signs*, 29(1): 1–25, p 2.

36 Young (2003) 'The logic of masculine protection', p 8.

NOTES

37 Cynthia Enloe (1990) 'Womenandchildren: Making feminist sense of the Persian Gulf crisis', *Village Voice*, 25 September.

38 For a novel discussion of class politics, see Petrus Liu (2015) *Queer Marxism in Two Chinas*, Durham, NC: Duke University Press.

39 Jasbir Puar (2007) *Terrorist Assemblages: Homonationalism in Queer Times. Next Wave*, Durham, NC: Duke University Press, p 48.

40 See Paul Amar (2021) 'Insurgent African intimacies in pandemic times: Deimperial queer logics of China's new global families in *Wolf Warrior 2*', *Feminist Studies*, 47(2): 419–49.

41 See Stevi Jackson's pioneering work (1999) *Heterosexuality in Question*, London: Sage Publications.

42 V. Spike Peterson (1999) 'Sexing political identities/nationalism as heterosexism', *International Feminist Journal of Politics*, 1(1): 34–65, p 52.

43 For a foundational study, see Alan Petersen (1998) *Unmasking the Masculine: 'Men' and 'Identity' in a Sceptical Age*, Thousand Oaks, CA: Sage Publications.

44 Aaron Belkin (2012) *Bring Me Men: Military Masculinity and the Benign Facade of American Empire, 1898–2001*, New York: Columbia University Press.

45 Belkin (2012) *Bring Me Men*, p 4.

46 Cynthia Weber (1998) 'Something's Missing: Male Hysteria and the US Invasion of Panama', in Marysia Zalewski and Jane Parpart (eds) *The 'Man' Question in International Relations*, Boulder, CO: Westview Press, pp 150–68, p 158.

47 See Hannah Fenichel Pitkin (1999) *Fortune is a Woman: Gender and Politics in the Thought of Niccolò Machiavelli*, Chicago, IL: University of Chicago Press.

48 Puar (2007) *Terrorist Assemblages*, p 47.

49 Weber (1999) *Faking It*, p 90.

50 Puar (2007) *Terrorist Assemblages*, p 47.

51 Belkin (2012) *Bring Me Men*, pp 85, 98.

52 Belkin (2012) *Bring Me Men*, pp 97–102.

53 Puar (2007) *Terrorist Assemblages*, p 47.

54 Belkin (2012) *Bring Me Men*, pp 80–99.

55 Acknowledgement to Harry Enfield at www.youtube.com/watch?v=5mtkciKpvnM

56 For an analytical discussion, see Lauren B. Wilcox (2015) *Bodies of Violence: Theorizing Embodied Subjects in International Relations*, Oxford: Oxford University Press.

57 For a synoptic view, see Helen Kinsella (2011) *The Image before the Weapon: A Critical History of the Distinction between Combatant and Civilian*, Ithaca, NY: Cornell University Press.

58 See Cynthia Weber (2016) *Queer International Relations: Sovereignty, Sexuality and the Will to Knowledge*, Oxford: Oxford University Press.

59 Jasbir K. Puar and Amit S. Rai (2002) 'Monster, terrorist, fag: The war on terrorism and the production of docile patriots', *Social Text*, 72(20/3): 117–48, 126, 135, 137.

60 See Mimi Schippers (2007) 'Recovering the feminine other: Masculinity, femininity and gender hegemony', *Theory & Society*, 36: 85–102.

61 Jasbir K. Puar (2018) 'Queer times, queer assemblages', *Social Text*, 23(3–4): 84–5, http://jasbirkpuar.com/wp-content/uploads/2018/08/Queer-Times-Queer-Assemblages-1.pdf

62 Puar (2007) *Terrorist Assemblages*, pp 47–50.

63 Krista Hunt and Kim Rygiel (2006) '(En)Gendered War Stories and Camouflaged Politics', in Krista Hunt and Kim Rygiel (eds) *(En)Gendering the War on Terror: War Stories and Camouflaged Politics*, Farnham: Ashgate, pp 1–23, p 9.

64 See Steve Niva (1998) 'Tough and Tender: New World Order Masculinity and the Gulf War', in Zalewski and Parpart, *The 'Man' Question*, pp 109–28.

65 Laura J. Shepherd (2006) 'Veiled references: Constructions of gender in the Bush administration discourse on the attacks on Afghanistan post-9/11', *International Feminist Journal of Politics*, 8(1): 19–41.

66 Jill Steans (2006) *Gender and International Relations*, Cambridge: Polity, pp 28, 52.

67 Timothy Kaufman-Osborn (2005) 'Gender trouble at Abu Ghraib?', *Politics and Gender*, 1(4): 597–619, 597.

68 Kaufman-Osborn (2005) 'Gender trouble at Abu Ghraib', p 599.

69 Kaufman-Osborn (2005) 'Gender trouble at Abu Ghraib', p 605.

70 Zillah Eisenstein (2006) 'Resexing Militarism for the Globe', in Robin L. Riley, Minnie Bruce Platt and Chandra Talpade Mohanty (eds) *Feminism and War: Confronting US Imperialism*, New York: Zed Books, pp 27–46, p 51.

71 Nicholas Mirzoeff (2006) 'Papers presented at a Visual Culture Gathering, November 5–7, 2004', *Visual Arts Research*, 32(2): 38–42, 40. [The published article was entitled 'Invisible empire: Abu Ghraib and embodied spectacle'.]

72 Eisenstein (2006) 'Resexing Militarism for the Globe', p 33.

73 Melisa Brittain (2006) 'Benevolent Invaders, Heroic Victims and Depraved Villains: White Femininity in Media Coverage of the Invasion of Iraq', in Hunt and Rygiel, *(En)Gendering the War on Terror*, pp 73–96, p 89.

74 *The Economist* (2009) 'The odd couple', 22 October, www.economist.com/node/14699593

75 The occasion was the visit of the US president to China for wide-ranging state-to-state talks in November 2009.

76 See Gayle Rubin (1975) 'The Traffic in Women: Notes on the Political Economy of Sex', in Rayna Reiter (ed) *Toward an Anthropology of Women*, New York: Monthly Review, pp 157–210.

77 Raewyn W. Connell, *Masculinities* (2nd edn), Cambridge: Polity, pp 77–8.

78 See Judith Butler (2002) *Antigone's Claim: Kinship Between Life and Death*, New York: Columbia University Press.

79 *The New York Times* (2018) 'Trump and Putin: A love story', 25 June, www.nytimes.com/2018/06/25/opinion/trump-bites-putin-love-story. html

80 Ryan Butcher (2018) 'Depicting Trump and Putin in a romantic relationship isn't funny – it just makes you a homophobe', *Independent*, 17 July, www.independent.co.uk/voices/trump-putin-new-york-times-homophobia-relationship-a8451151.html

81 Ryan Butcher (2018) 'Depicting Trump and Putin in a romantic relationship isn't funny'.

82 See *The Washington Post*, where Meredith Loken also refers to articles in the US media that depict the relationship between Trump and Kim Jong-un in romantic terms: Meredith Loken (2018) 'No, your Trump-is-gay-for-Putin jokes aren't funny', *The Washington Post*, 17 July, www.washingtonpost. com/news/posteverything/wp/2018/07/17/no-your-trump-is-gay-for-putin-jokes-arent-funny

83 Jonathan D. Mackintosh (2011) *Homosexuality and Manliness in Postwar Japan*, Abingdon: Routledge.

84 Carol Cohn (1998) 'Gays in the Military: Texts and Subtexts', in Zalewski and Parpart, *The 'Man' Question*, pp 129–49.

85 Puar (2007) *Terrorist Assemblages*, p 49.

86 Puar (2007) *Terrorist Assemblages*, p 50.

87 Belkin (2012) *Bring Me Men*, pp 80, 81.

88 Weber (1999) *Faking It*, p 86.

89 Mark Duffield (2007) *Development, Security and Unending War*, Cambridge: Polity, p 160.

90 Harry Enfield, at: www.youtube.com/watch?v=5mtkciKpvnM

91 Carol Cohn and Cynthia Enloe (2003) 'A conversation with Cynthia Enloe: Feminists look at masculinity and the men who wage war', *Signs: Journal of Women in Culture and Society*, 28(4): 1187–1207, 1204.

92 John Hopton (2003) 'The State and Military Masculinity', in Paul R. Higate (ed) *Military Masculinities: Identity and the State*, Westport, CT: Praeger, pp 111–24, p 115.

93 For inspiration, see Cynthia Enloe (2004) *The Curious Feminist: Searching for Women in a New Age of Empire*, Berkeley, CA: University of California Press.

94 Cynthia Enloe (2014) 'A conversation with Cynthia Enloe on curiosity, confidence, and feminist questions', *Fletcher Forum*, 38(2): 13–22.

95 Laura Sjoberg (2012) 'Towards transgendering international relations', *International Political Sociology*, 6(4): 337–54, 347; see also Melanie Richter-Montpetit (2018) 'Everything you always wanted to know about sex (in IR) but were afraid to ask: The "queer turn' in international relations', *Millennium: Journal of International Relations*, 46(2): 220–40.

96 *The Economist* (2002) 'The challenge to paternalism', 4 April, www. economist.com/the-americas/2002/04/04/the-challenge-to-paternalism

97 Hooper (1999) *Manly States*, p 151.

98 *The Economist* (2002) 'The challenge to paternalism'.

99 Sjoberg (2012) 'Towards transgendering', p 344.

100 Alison Brysk (2005) 'Global good Samaritans? Human rights foreign policy in Costa Rica', *Global Governance*, 11(4): 445–66.

101 Brysk (2005) 'Global good Samaritans?', p 446.

102 See Paul Amar (2013) *The Security Archipelago: Human-Security States, Sexuality Politics, and the End of Neoliberalism*, Durham, NC: Duke University Press, pp 1–38.

103 Carlos Sandoval-García (2005) 'Forging nationhood and masculinities in Costa Rica', *International Journal of the History of Sport*, 22(2): 212–30.

104 Sandoval-García (2005) 'Forging nationhood', p 220.

105 Advance Local Media (2014) 'Costa Rica's army: Soccer team represents tiny Central American nation in World Cup quarterfinals on Saturday', 6 March , www.al.com/entertainment/2014/07/costa_ricas_army_soccer_team_r.html

106 NDTV (2014) 'Costa Rica walking tall out of FIFA World Cup door', https://sports.ndtv.com/fifa-world-cup-2014/costa-rica-walking-tall-out-of-fifa-world-cup-door-1516178

107 David Boddiger, editor in chief of *The Tico Times*, a rebuttal to a *Wall Street Journal* editor's call for US World Cup fans to ignore Costa Rica.

108 Advance Local Media (2014) 'Costa Rica's army'.

109 Jo Tuckman (2014) 'World Cup 2014: "We showed them who we are. Costa Rica is proud of its team"', *The Guardian*, 22 June, www.theguardian.com/world/2014/jun/22/costa-rica-world-cup-football-triumph-society-values

110 Russ Wellen (2010) 'Costa Rica's love–hate relationship with heavy US military footprint', Foreign Policy in Focus, 8 July, www.fpif.org/blog/costa_ricas_love-hate_relationship_with_heavy_us_military_footprint

111 Belkin (2012) *Bring Me Men*, pp 84–5.

112 Maria Eriksson Baaz and Maria Stern (2009) 'Why do soldiers rape? Masculinity, violence, and sexuality in the armed forces in the Congo (DRC)', *International Studies Quarterly*, 53(2): 495–518.

113 Mike Donaldson (1993) *What is Hegemonic Masculinity?*, University of Wollongong, Faculty of Arts Papers – Archive, https://ro.uow.edu.au/cgi/viewcontent.cgi?article=1149&context=artspapers

114 Johanna Kantola (2007) 'The gendered reproduction of the state in international relations', *British Journal of Politics and International Relations*, 9(2): 270–83, 274, 275.

115 Hunt and Rygiel (2006) '(En)gendered War Stories', p 17.

Chapter 3

1 See, for example, the film *GI Jane*, directed by Ridley Scott, and released in 1997.

2 See Cynthia Enloe (2014) *Bananas, Beaches and Bases: Making Feminist Sense of International Politics* (2nd edn), Berkeley, CA: University of California Press.

3 See Cynthia Enloe (1983) *Does Khaki Become You? The Militarization of Women's Lives*, London: Pluto.

4   For a conception of 'martial politics' that critiques militarization, see Allison Howell (2018) 'Forget "militarization": Race, disability and the "martial politics" of the police and of the university', *International Feminist Journal of Politics*, 20(2): 117–36.

5   See Cynthia Enloe (2016) *Globalization and Militarism: Feminists Make the Link* (2nd edn), Lanham, MD: Rowman & Littlefield.

6   Scott Stedjan (2012) 'What's the deal with bananas and the global arms trade? Politics of poverty', Oxfam, 26 June, http://politicsof poverty.oxfamamerica.org/2012/06/comparing-bananas-to-the-global-arms-trade

7   Hazel Sheffield (2015) 'Syria air strikes see shares rise at BAE systems, Thales other weapons manufacturers', *Independent*, 12 April, www.independent.co.uk/news/business/news/syria-air-strikes-see-bae-systems-and-other-weapons-manufacturers-share-prices-spike-a6760641.html

8   Chris Wrigley (2001) *The Arms Industry*, London: Campaign Against Arms Trade.

9   See R. Claire Snyder (1999) *Citizen Soldiers and Manly Warriors: Military Service and Gender in the Civic Republican Tradition*, Lanham, MD: Rowman & Littlefield.

10   Campaign Against Arms Trade (2021) 'The arms trade', https://caat.org.uk/challenges/the-arms-trade

11   See Anna Stavrianakis (2010) *Taking Aim at the Arms Trade: NGOs, Global Civil Society and the World Military Order*, London: Zed Books.

12   Oxfam (no date) 'Why we need a global Arms Trade Treaty', www.oxfam.org/en/why-we-need-global-arms-trade-treaty

13   Roxanne L. Doty (1993) 'Foreign policy as social construction: A post-positivist analysis of US counterinsurgency policy in the Philippines', *International Studies Quarterly*, 37(3): 297–320, 297.

14   Terrell Carver (2008) 'Real Construction through Metaphorical Language: How Animals and Machines (amongst other Metaphors) Makest (Hu)man what "He" Is', in Terrell Carver and Jernej Pikalo (eds) *Political Language and Metaphor: Interpreting and Changing the World*, New York: Routledge, pp 151–64, p 161.

15   See Anna Stavrianakis (2011) 'Small arms control and the reproduction of imperial relations', *Contemporary Security Policy*, 32(1): 193–214.

16   V. Spike Peterson (2010) 'International/Global Political Economy', in Laura J. Shepherd (ed) *Gender Matters in Global Politics: A Feminist Introduction to International Relations*, Abingdon: Routledge, p 208.

17   V. Spike Peterson (2010) 'Gendered Identities, Ideologies and Practices in the Context of War and Militarism', in Laura Sjoberg and Sandra Via (eds) *Gender, War, and Militarism: Feminist Perspectives*, Santa Barbara, CA: Praeger, pp 17–29, p 19.

18   Christina Rowley (2010) 'An intertextual analysis of Vietnam War films and US presidential speeches', Unpublished PhD dissertation, University of Bristol, p 310.

19 Raewyn W. Connell (1995) *Masculinities* (2nd edn), Cambridge: Polity, p 107.
20 Carver (2008) 'Real Construction through Metaphorical Language', pp 161–2.
21 Iris Marion Young (2003) 'The logic of masculine protection: Reflections on the current security state', *Signs*, 29(1): 1–25.
22 Stavrianakis (2011) 'Small arms control', p 199.
23 Anna M. Agathangelou and Heather M. Turcotte (2010) 'Postcolonial Theories and Challenges to "First World-ism"', in Laura J. Shepherd (ed) *Gender Matters in Global Politics: A Feminist Introduction to International Relations*, Abingdon: Routledge, pp 44–58, p 51.
24 Aaron Belkin and Terrell Carver (2012) 'Militarized masculinities and the erasure of violence: Aaron Belkin in conversation with Terrell Carver', *International Feminist Journal of Politics*, 14(4): 558–67.
25 CITS-UGA (Center for International Trade and Security, University of Georgia) (2010) 'The international Arms Trade Treaty: A win–win for the defense industry', University of Georgia, www.armscontrol.org/system/files/CITSIndustry.pdf
26 Arms Control Association (2008) 'About the Arms Control Association', www.armscontrol.org/about
27 CITS-UGA (2010) 'The international Arms Trade Treaty'.
28 See James Martin (2014) *Politics and Rhetoric: A Critical Introduction*, Abingdon: Routledge.
29 CITS-UGA (2010) 'The international Arms Trade Treaty'.
30 CITS-UGA (2010) 'The international Arms Trade Treaty'.
31 John Locke (1689) *Two Treatises of Government*, Second Treatise, §87.
32 CITS-UGA (2010) 'The international Arms Trade Treaty'.
33 CITS-UGA (2010) 'The international Arms Trade Treaty'.
34 Michelle M. Lazar (2007) 'Feminist critical discourse analysis: Articulating a feminist discourse praxis', *Critical Discourse Studies*, 4(2): 141–64, 142.
35 See Raewyn W. Connell (2005) 'Globalization and business masculinities', *Men and Masculinities*, 7(4): 347–64.
36 Cameron McAuliffe (2007) 'Visible Minorities: Constructing and Deconstructing the "Muslim Iranian" Diaspora', in Cara Aitchison, Peter Hopkins and Mei-Po Kwan (eds) *Geographies of Muslim Identities: Diaspora, Gender and Belonging*, Farnham: Ashgate, pp 29–56, p 39.
37 See Gayatri Chakravorty Spivak (1994) 'Can the Subaltern Speak?', in Patrick Williams and Laura Chrisman (eds) *Colonial Discourse and Post-Colonial Theory: A Reader*, London: Routledge, Chapter 4.
38 See Sahar Ghumkhor (2012) 'The veil and modernity: The case of Tunisia', *Interventions*, 14(4): 493–514, 505.
39 See Chandra Mohanty (1988) 'Under Western eyes: Feminist scholarship and colonial discourses', *Feminist Review*, 30(1): 61–88.
40 Kiran Grewal (2012) 'Reclaiming the voice of the "third world woman": But what do we do when we don't like what she has to say? The tricky case of Ayaan Hirsi Ali', *Interventions*, 14(4): 569–90, 588.

41 Young (2003) 'The logic of masculine protection', p 4.
42 For a discussion of these discursive logics, see David Howarth (2000) *Discourse*, Milton Keynes: Open University Press.
43 Maria Stern (2011) 'Gender and race in the European security strategy: Europe as a "force for good"?', *Journal of International Relations and Development*, 14(1): 28–59, 48.
44 See, for example, UK Parliament, Early Day Motions, 'Saudi Arabia and violations of international law', https://edm.parliament.uk/early-day-motion/52198/saudi-arabia-and-violations-of-international-law
45 See Rachel Stohl and Suzette Grillot (2009) *The International Arms Trade: War and Conflict in the Modern World*, Cambridge: Polity.
46 See J. Ann Tickner (2014) *A Feminist Voyage through International Relations*, New York: Oxford University Press.
47 See Raewyn W. Connell (2016) 'Masculinities in global perspective: Hegemony, contestation, and changing structures of power', *Theory & Society*, 45(4): 303–18.
48 Dana P. Eyre and Mark C. Suchman (1996) 'Status, Norms and the Proliferation of Conventional Weapons: An Institutional Theory Approach', in Peter J. Katzenstein (ed) *The Culture of National Security: Norms and Identity in World Politics*, New York: Columbia University Press, pp 79–113, pp 86–7.
49 Rodney W. Jones and Steven Hildreth, quoted in Eyre and Suchman (1996) 'Status, Norms and the Proliferation of Conventional Weapons', p 85.
50 Eyre and Suchman (1996) 'Status, Norms and the Proliferation of Conventional Weapons', pp 79–113, pp 85–6.
51 See Anna Stavrianakis (2005) 'Analysis: (Big) business as usual. Sustainable development, NGOs and UK arms export policy', *Conflict, Security and Development*, 5(1): 45–67.
52 Enloe (2016) *Globalization and Militarism*, p 158.
53 Anna Stavrianakis (2015) 'Thinking internationally about the arms trade', The Disorder of Things, 2 October, http://thedisorderofthings.com/2015/10/02/thinking-internationally-about-the-arms-trade
54 Gideon Burrows (2002) *The No Nonsense Guide to the Arms Trade*, Oxford: New Internationalist, p 90.
55 Enloe (2016) *Globalization and Militarism*, p 158.
56 Harry Blain (2015) 'Confronting Britain's military-industrial complex', Open Democracy UK, 1 May, www.opendemocracy.net/en/opendemocracyuk/confronting-britains-militaryindustrial-complex
57 UKTI DSO verbal briefing at the Defence Procurement Research Technology & Exportability exhibition (DPRTE 2014), held at Motorpoint, Cardiff, 8 October 2014.
58 Damien Gayle (2016) 'BAE chairman to peace activists: "Weapons sales encourage peace"', *The Guardian*, 5 April, www.theguardian.com/business/2016/may/04/peace-activists-bae-systems-agm-saudi-arms-sales

[59]   UK Ministry of Defence (2005) *Defence Industrial Strategy, Defence White Paper*, Executive Summary, para vii.

[60]   See Anna Stavrianakis (2008) *The Facade of Arms Control: How the UK's Export Licensing System Facilitates the Arms Trade*, Campaign Against Arms Trade, Goodwin paper #6, pp 1–25 [Reviewed in https://caat.org.uk/ wp-content/uploads/2020/09/caatnews206.pdf].

[61]   Wrigley (2001) *The Arms Industry*.

[62]   Blain (2015) 'Confronting Britain's military-industrial complex'.

[63]   Jill Steans (ed) (2006) *Gender and International Relations: Issues, Debates and Future Directions* (2nd edn), Cambridge: Polity, p 55.

[64]   Burrows (2002) *The No Nonsense Guide to the Arms Trade*, p 90.

[65]   James Vincent (2015) 'Shopping for drones and missiles with the world's armies', *The Verge*, 28 September, www.theverge. com/2015/9/28/9410525/shopping-for-drones-and-missiles-at-dsei

[66]   See David Brown (2019) 'How women took over the military-industrial complex', Politico, 1 February, www.politico.com/story/2019/01/02/ how-women-took-over-the-military-industrial-complex-1049860

[67]   Henri Myrttinen (2003) 'Disarming masculinities', *Disarmament Forum: Women, Men, Peace and Security*, 4: 37–46.

[68]   John Ficenec (2014) 'How Radway Green keeps its bullets at the cutting edge', *The Telegraph*, 25 May, www.telegraph.co.uk/finance/newsbysector/ industry/defence/10855488/How-Radway-Green-keeps-its-bullets-at- the-cutting-edge.html

[69]   Wrigley (2001) *The Arms Industry*.

[70]   Stavrianakis (2011) 'Small arms control', p 205.

[71]   UK Government (2013) 'Adoption of Arms Trade Treaty welcomed by Prime Minister Cameron', Prime Minister's Office, 2 April, www.gov.uk/ government/news/adoption-of-arms-trade-treaty-welcomed-by-prime- minister-cameron

[72]   Quoted in Steans (2006) *Gender and International Relations*, p 71.

[73]   Amnesty International UK (2015) 'Government breaking the law supplying arms to Saudi say leading lawyers', Press release, 17 December, www. amnesty.org.uk/press-releases/government-breaking-law-supplying-arms- saudi-say-leading-lawyers

[74]   Owen Bowcott (2015) 'UK and Saudi Arabia "in secret deal" over human rights council place', *The Guardian*, 29 September, www.theguardian.com/ uk-news/2015/sep/29/uk-and-saudi-arabia-in-secret-deal-over-human- rights-council-place

[75]   See Dan Sabbogh (2021) 'UK authorised £1.4bn of arms sales to Saudi Arabia after exports resumed', *The Guardian*, 9 February, www.theguardian. com/world/2021/feb/09/uk-authorised-14bn-of-arms-sales-to-saudi- arabia-after-exports-resumed

[76]   Victoria M. Basham (2016) 'Gender, race, militarism and remembrance: The everyday geopolitics of the poppy', *Gender, Place & Culture*, 23(6): 883–96, 887.

77 Steve Niva (1998) 'Tough and Tender: New World Order Masculinity and the Gulf War', in Marysia Zalewski and Jane Parpart (eds) *The 'Man' Question in International Relations*, Boulder, CO: Westview, pp 109–28.

78 Laura J. Shepherd (2006) 'Veiled references: Constructions of gender in the Bush administration discourse on the attacks on Afghanistan post-9/11', *International Feminist Journal of Politics*, 8(1): 19–41, 29.

79 Jane Mayer (2007) 'Whatever it takes', *The New Yorker*, 83(1): 66–82, www.newyorker.com/magazine/2007/02/19/whatever-it-takes

80 See Regina F. Titunik (2009) 'Are we all torturers now? A reconsideration of women's violence at Abu Ghraib', *Cambridge Review of International Affairs*, 22(2): 257–77.

81 John Tosh (2004) 'Hegemonic Masculinity and the History of Gender', in Stefan Dudink, Karen Hagemann and John Tosh (eds) *Masculinities in Politics and War: Gendering Modern History*, Manchester: Manchester University Press, pp 41–59, p 44.

82 Steve Smith (1998) '"Unacceptable Conclusions" and the "Man" Question: Masculinity, Gender, and International Relations', in Marysia Zalewski and Jane Parpart (eds) *The 'Man' Question in International Relations*, Boulder, CO: Westview, pp 55–72, p 66.

83 Quoted in Nicola Slawson (2015) 'David Cameron insists UK must have close ties with Saudi Arabia', *The Guardian*, 6 October, www.theguardian.com/politics/2015/oct/06/david-cameron-insists-uk-ties-saudi-arabia

84 Ewen MacAskill (2016) 'UN report into Saudi-led strikes in Yemen raises questions over UK role', *The Guardian*, 27 January, www.theguardian.com/world/2016/jan/27/un-report-into-saudi-led-strikes-in-yemen-raises-questions-over-uk-role

85 Saferworld (2007) *The Good, the Bad and the Ugly: A Decade of Labour's Arms Exports*, www.saferworld.org.uk/resources/publications/264-the-good-the-bad-and-the-ugly---a-decade-of-labours-arms-exports, p 7.

86 Stavrianakis (2008) *The Facade of Arms Control*.

87 See Cerelia Athanassiou (2014) '"Gutsy" decisions and passive processes: The warrior decision-maker after the global war on terror', *International Feminist Journal of Politics*, 16(1): 6–25.

88 Jenny Nordberg (2015) 'Who's afraid of a feminist foreign policy?', *The New Yorker*, 15 April, www.newyorker.com/news/news-desk/swedens-feminist-foreign-minister

89 See Dan Sabbagh (2021) 'High court to hear legal battle over UK arms sales to Saudi Arabia', *The Guardian*, 22 April, www.theguardian.com/world/2021/apr/22/campaigners-to-challenge-decision-to-resume-selling-arms-to-saudi-in-high-court

90 Basham (2016) 'Gender, race, militarism and remembrance', p 887.

91 Blain (2015) 'Confronting Britain's military-industrial complex'.

Chapter 4

1 Mark Thomas (2007) *As Used on the Famous Nelson Mandela: Underground Adventures in the Arms and Torture Trade*, London: Ebury, p 282.

2   Laura Lyddon's observations, incorporated *passim* in this chapter, derive from her visits to the Counter-Terror Expo 2012, held at London-Olympia; DPRTE 2014, held at Motorpoint Cardiff; and DSEI 2015, held at ExCeL London. In all these instances she obtained participant status as a self-declared researcher.

3   Clarion Events (2015) 'Clarion Events Defence and Security Portfolio', www.itec.co.uk/Content/Clarion-Events-Defence-and-Security-Portfolio/1_55

4   Jill Gibbon (2018) *The Etiquette of the Arms Trade: Undercover Drawings*, Nottingham: Beam Editions.

5   See J. Ann Tickner (1992) *Gender in International Relations: Feminist Perspectives on Achieving Global Security*, New York: Columbia University Press.

6   Counter Terror Expo, 'Welcome to Security & Counter Terror Expo 2016', www.counterterrorexpo.com

7   MOD Defence Contractors Online (2014) 'Unique Access to Defence Procurement Buyers at DPRTE 2014', www.contracts.mod.uk/blog/unique-access-to-defence-procurement-buyers-at-dprte-2014/ (accessed 1 December 2015; no longer available).

8   Information taken from promotional materials at the time (DSEI, 2015), www.dsei.co.uk

9   CAAT (Campaign Against Arms Trade) (2015) 'Arms fairs: UK Arms fairs', www.caat.org.uk/issues/arms-fairs

10 Information taken from promotional materials at the time (DSEI, 2015), www.dsei.co.uk

11 Jutta Joachim and Andrea Schneiker (2012) 'Of "true professionals" and "ethical hero warriors": A gender-discourse analysis of private military and security companies', *Security Dialogue*, 43(6): 495–512, 499.

12 Raewyn W. Connell (2005) 'Globalization and business masculinities', *Men and Masculinities*, 7(4): 347–64.

13 Cristina Masters (2005) 'Bodies of technology: Cyborg soldiers and militarized masculinities', *International Feminist Journal of Politics*, 7(1): 112–32.

14 Cynthia Enloe (2007) *Globalization and Militarism: Feminists Make the Link*, Lanham, MD: Rowman & Littlefield.

15 Gibbon (2018) *The Etiquette of the Arms Trade*, no page.

16 For a well-documented account of the global militarization of policing, see Paul Amar (2013) *The Security Archipelago: Human Security States, Sexuality Politics, and the End of Neo-Liberalism*, Durham, NC: Duke University Press.

17 James Vincent (2015) 'Shopping for drones and missiles with the world's armies', *The Verge*, 28 September, www.theverge.com/2015/9/28/9410525/shopping-for-drones-and-missiles-at-dsei

18 Dorothy E. Smith (1987) *The Everyday World as Problematic: A Feminist Sociology*, Boston, MA: Northeastern University Press, p 30.

19 Rob Young (2011) *Power Dressing: First Ladies, Women Politicians and Fashion*, London: Merrell, Foreword by Pamela Golbin.

20 Joanne Entwistle (2015) *The Fashioned Body: Fashion, Dress and Modern Social Theory* (2nd edn), Cambridge: Polity Press, p xxii.
21 Jennifer Craik (2003) 'The cultural politics of the uniform', *Fashion Theory: Journal of Dress, Body & Culture*, 7(2): 127–47, 136; emphasis added.
22 Connell (2005) 'Globalization and business masculinities'.
23 Thomas (2007) *As Used on the Famous Nelson Mandela.*
24 Gibbon (2018) *The Etiquette of the Arms Trade*, no page.
25 See Carol Cohn (1999) 'Gays in the military: Texts and subtexts', in Marysia Zalewski and Jane Parpart (eds) *The 'Man' Question in International Relations*, Abingdon: Routledge, pp 129–49.
26 Craik (2003) 'The cultural politics of the uniform', p 129.
27 Erynn Masai de Casanova (2015) *Buttoned Up: Clothing, Conformity, and White-Collar Masculinity*, Ithaca, NY: Cornell University Press, p 4.
28 Craik (2003) 'The cultural politics of the uniform', p 131.
29 Information taken from promotional materials at the time (DSEI, 2015), www.dsei.co.uk
30 See John Hopton (2003) 'The State and Military Masculinity', in Paul Higate (ed) *Military Masculinities: Identity and the State*, Westport, CT: Praeger Publishers, pp 111–24.
31 Raewyn W. Connell (2005) *Masculinities* (2nd edn), Cambridge: Polity.
32 Gibbon (2018) *The Etiquette of the Arms Trade*, no page.
33 Laura Sjoberg (2015) 'Seeing sex, gender, and sexuality in international security', *International Journal: Canada's Journal of Global Policy Analysis*, 70(3): 434–53.
34 Jill Gibbon (2011) 'An insider's guide to DSEI: Dress', *Peace News*, http://peacenews.info/node/6117/insiders-guide-dsei-dress
35 Kimberlé Crenshaw (1991) 'Mapping the margins: Intersectionality, identity politics, and violence against women of color', *Stanford Law Review*, 43(6): 1241–99.
36 Gibbon (2018) *The Etiquette of the Arms Trade*, no page.
37 See Nick Turse (2008) *The Complex: How the Military Invades our Everyday Lives*, London: Faber and Faber; Susan Carruthers (2003) 'Bringing it all back home: Hollywood returns to war', *Small Wars & Insurgencies*, 14(1): 167–82; see also Gibbon (2018) *The Etiquette of the Arms Trade*, no page.
38 Marcus Power (2007) 'Digitized virtuosity: Video war games and post-9/11 cyber-deterrence', *Security Dialogue*, 38(2): 271–88, 274.
39 Power (2007) 'Digitized virtuosity', p 275.
40 Carol Cohn (1987) 'Sex and death in the rational world of defense intellectuals', *Signs: Journal of Women in Culture and Society*, 12(4): 687–718.
41 James Vincent (2015) 'Shopping for drones and missiles with the world's armies', *The Verge*, 28 September, www.theverge.com/2015/9/28/9410525/shopping-for-drones-and-missiles-at-dsei
42 Gibbon (2018) *The Etiquette of the Arms Trade*, no page.
43 Dominic Gronning (2015) 'A report from London's big arms fair from a guilt-ridden arms industry insider', *Vice*, 18 September, http://www.vice.com/en_uk/read/dsei-arms-fair-insider-849

44 Vincent (2015) 'Shopping for drones'.
45 Gibbon (2018) *The Etiquette of the Arms Trade*, no page.
46 Thomas (2007) *As Used on the Famous Nelson Mandela*, p 282.
47 Gibbon (2018) *The Etiquette of the Arms Trade*, no page.
48 Lucie Béraud-Sudreau, Alexandra Marksteiner, Diego Lopes da Silva, Nan Tian, Alexandra Kuimova, Pieter D. Wezeman and Siemon T. Wezeman (2020) 'Mapping the international presence of the world's largest arms companies', SIPRI Insights on Peace and Security, No 2020/12, December, www.sipri.org/sites/default/files/2020-12/sipriinsight2012_mapping_the_international_presence_of_the_worlds_largest_arms_companies.pdf
49 See Statista, 'The world's largest arms-producing companies', www.statista.com/chart/12221/the-worlds-biggest-arms-companies
50 BAE Systems, Inc (2012) 'On the next front', YouTube, 12 October, www.youtube.com/watch?v=tvK3WZ6BADo; BAE Systems (2014) 'Inside BAE Systems – Our new global video', YouTube, 7 May, www.youtube.com/watch?v=MCfU0JzxnlA (the latter video has subsequently been removed but is still available to view via another You Tube account at www.youtube.com/watch?v=5LruU__n7O8).
51 Dianne Otto (2004) *Securing the Gender Legitimacy of the UN Security Council: Prising Gender from its Historical Moorings*, Social Sciences Research Network, http://papers.ssrn.com/sol3/papers.cfm?abstract_id=585923
52 Geeta Chowdhury and Sheila Nair (2002) 'Introduction: Power in a Postcolonial World: Race, Gender and Class in International Relations', in Geeta Chowdhury and Sheila Nair (eds) *Power, Postcolonialism and International Relations*, London: Routledge, pp 1–32, p 2.
53 Jutta Weldes (1999) *Constructing National Interests: The United States and the Cuban Missile Crisis*, Minneapolis, MN: University of Minnesota Press, p 163.
54 Anna Stavrianakis and Jan Selby (eds) (2013) *Militarism and International Relations: Political Economy, Security and Theory*, New York: Routledge, p 12.
55 Kevin Lewis O'Neill (2007) 'Armed citizens and the stories they tell: The National Rifle Association's achievement of terror and masculinity', *Men and Masculinities*, 9(4): 457–75, 459.
56 William Hartung (2021) 'Afghanistan is just the latest case of US arms ending up with US adversaries', *Forbes*, 27 August, www.forbes.com/sites/williamhartung/2021/08/27/afghanistan-is-just-the-latest-case-of-us-arms-ending-up-with-us-adversaries/?sh=27af447a6685
57 CAAT (2015) 'Arms fairs'.
58 Cynthia Enloe (2015) 'The recruiter and the sceptic: A critical feminist approach to military studies', *Critical Military Studies*, 1(1): 3–10.
59 BAE Systems (2002) 'Corporate Responsibility Report 2002'.
60 Zillah Eisenstein (2007) *Sexual Decoys: Gender, Race and War in Imperial Democracy*, Melbourne: Spinifex Press, p 17.
61 Michael S. Kimmel and Abby L. Ferber (eds) (2010) *Privilege: A Reader*, Boulder, CO: Westview Press, p xi.

62 Kamesha Spates and Brittany C. Slatton (2014) 'Introduction: Blackness, Maleness, and Sexuality as Interwoven Identities: Toward an Understanding of Contemporary Black Male Identity Formation', in Brittany C. Slatton and Kamesha Spates (eds) *Hyper Sexual, Hyper Masculine? Gender, Race and Sexuality in the Identities of Contemporary Black Men*, Farnham: Ashgate, pp 1–5, pp 2, 3.

63 Paul Amar (2011) 'Middle East masculinity studies: Discourses of "men in crisis", industries of gender in revolution', *Journal of Middle East Women's Studies*, 7(3): 36–70.

64 Frank Rudy Cooper (2009) *Our First Unisex President? Black Masculinity and Obama's Feminine Side*, Suffolk University Law School Legal Studies Research Paper Series 09-01, p 636.

65 See Manning Marable (2001) 'The Black Male: Searching Beyond Stereotypes', in Michael S. Kimmel and Michael A. Messner (eds) *Men's Lives* (5th edn), New York: Allyn & Bacon, pp 17–23.

66 *Urban Dictionary*, www.urbandictionary.com/define.php?term=white%20wash

67 Sara Ahmed (2007) 'A phenomenology of whiteness', *Feminist Theory*, 8(2): 149–68, 158.

68 Ahmed (2007) 'A phenomenology of whiteness', p 156.

69 Charles W. Mills (2017) 'White Ignorance', in Charles W. Mills, *Black Rights/White Wrongs: The Critique of Racial Liberalism*, Oxford: Oxford University Press, pp 49–71.

70 BAE Systems, Inc (2014) 'Inspired work: More than a tagline', YouTube, www.youtube.com/watch?v=StZtD6O_xrc (accessed 11 November 2015).

Chapter 5

1 For a historical view from that perspective, see Priya Satia (2018) *Empire of Guns: The Violent Making of the Industrial Revolution*, Harmondsworth: Penguin.

2 L.H.M. Ling (2008) 'Borderlands: A Postcolonial-Feminist Alternative to Neoliberal Self/Other Relations', in H. Brabandt, B. Ross and S. Zwingel (eds) *Mehrheit am Rand?*, Wiesbaden: VS Verlag für Sozialwissenschaften, pp 105–24, p 106, http://link.springer.com/10.1007/978-3-531-91097-0_6

3 Henry David Thoreau (2017) *Civil Disobedience*, Los Angeles, CA: Enhanced Media Publishing; W.E.B. Du Bois (1945) *Color and Democracy: Colonies and Peace*, New York: Harcourt Brace.

4 Charlotte Hooper (2001) *Manly States: Masculinities, International Relations, and Gender Politics*, New York: Columbia University Press.

5 See Daniel Conway (2012) *Masculinities, Militarisation and the End Conscription Campaign: War Resistance in Anti-Apartheid South Africa*, Manchester: Manchester University Press.

6 Ana Jordan (2019) *The New Politics of Fatherhood: Men's Movements and Masculinities*, London: Palgrave.

7   Judith Butler (1999) *Gender Trouble: Feminism and the Subversion of Identity*, Abingdon: Routledge.

8   See Katharine M. Millar and Joanna Tidy (2017) 'Combat as a moving target: Masculinities, the heroic soldier myth, and normative martial violence', *Critical Military Studies*, 3(2): 42–60.

9   Rachel Stohl and Suzette Grillo (2009) *The International Arms Trade: War and Conflict in the Modern World*, Cambridge: Polity, pp 14–15.

10 David G. Anderson (1992) 'The international arms trade: Regulating conventional arms transfers in the aftermath of the Gulf War', *American University International Law Review*, 7(4): 749–805, 759.

11 Article 8[5], quoted in Anderson (1992) 'The international arms trade', p 759.

12 David Edgerton (2008) 'The British military-industrial complex in history: The importance of political economy', *The Economics of Peace & Security*, 3(1): 6–10, 7.

13 David G. Anderson (1994) 'British rearmament and the "merchants of death": The 1935–36 Royal Commission on the manufacture of and trade in armaments', *Journal of Contemporary History*, 29(1): 5–37, 6–7.

14 For very useful overviews of current research, see Jill Steans and Daniela Tepe (eds) (2013) *Handbook on Gender in World Politics*, Cheltenham: Edward Elgar; Lisa Disch and Mary Hawkesworth (eds) (2018) *Oxford Handbook of Feminist Theory*, Oxford: Oxford University Press; and Laura J. Shepherd (ed) (2018) *Building Peace: Feminist Perspectives*, Abingdon: Routledge.

15 See Stefan Horlacher and Kevin Floyd (eds) (2017) *Contemporary Masculinities in the UK and US: Between Bodies and Systems*, New York: Palgrave Macmillan.

16 See Lucy Nicholas and Christine Agius (2018) *The Persistence of Global Masculinism: Discourse, Gender and Neo-Colonial Re-articulations of Violence*, Cham: Palgrave Macmillan.

17 See Judith Halberstam (2018) *Female Masculinity* (20th anniversary edn), Durham, NC: Duke University Press.

18 Finn Mackay (2021) 'What toxic men can learn from masculine women', *The Guardian*, 5 November, www.theguardian.com/commentisfree/2021/nov/05/what-toxic-men-can-learn-from-masculine-women

19 Cynthia Enloe (2014) *Bananas, Beaches, and Bases: Making Feminist Sense of International Politics* (2nd edn), Berkeley, CA: University of California Press.

20 Raewyn W. Connell (2005) *Masculinities* (2nd edn), Oxford: Polity, pp 77–8.

21 Mimi Schippers (2007) 'Recovering the feminine other: Masculinity, femininity, and gender hegemony', *Theory & Society*, 36(1): 85–102, 96.

22 Cynthia Cockburn and Cynthia Enloe (2012) 'Militarism, patriarchy and peace movements', *International Feminist Journal of Politics*, 14(4): 550–7.

23 Chris Rossdale (2021) *Resisting Militarism: Direct Action and the Politics of Subversion*, Edinburgh: Edinburgh University Press, p 68.

24 Cynthia Cockburn (2010) 'Gender relations as causal in militarization and war', *International Feminist Journal of Politics*, 12(2): 139–57, 140.

25 Cockburn (2010) 'Gender relations as causal', p 142.

26 Cockburn (2010) 'Gender relations as causal', p 142.

27 Ray Acheson (2019) 'The nuclear ban and the patriarchy: A feminist analysis of opposition to prohibiting nuclear weapons', *Critical Studies on Security*, 7(1): 78–82, 79.

28 Reaching Critical Will, 'Who we are', www.reachingcriticalwill.org/about-us/who-we-are

29 Helen Caldicott (1986) *Missile Envy: The Arms Race and Nuclear War*, Toronto: Bantam Books.

30 Carol Cohn (1987) 'Sex and death in the rational world of defense intellectuals', *Signs*, 12(4): 687–718, 692; see also Carol Cohn and Sara Ruddick (2012) *A Feminist Ethical Perspective on Weapons of Mass Destruction*, Cambridge: Cambridge University Press.

31 Acheson (2019) 'The nuclear ban and the patriarchy', p 78.

32 Anna Stavrianakis (2019) 'Controlling weapons circulation in a postcolonial militarised world', *Review of International Studies*, 45(1): 57–76, 57.

33 For an enlightening discussion, see Jairus Grove (2016) 'An insurgency of things: Foray into the world of improvised explosive devices', *International Political Sociology*, 10(4): 332–51.

34 bpb/bicc (Bundeszentrale für politische Bildung/Bonn International Centre for Conversion) (2006) 'Small arms and light weapons – The real weapons of mass destruction', Bonn, www.warpp.info/en/m5/articles/small-arms-and-light-weapons-the-real-weapons-of

35 United Nations (2013) 'The Arms Trade Treaty', p 6, www.thearmstradetreaty.org/hyper-images/file/TheArmsTradeTreaty1/TheArmsTradeTreaty.pdf

36 For an introductory overview, see Jacqui True (2020) *Violence against Women: What Everyone Needs to Know*, Oxford: Oxford University Press.

37 Caroline Green, Deepayan Ray Basu, Claire Mortimer and Kate Stone (2013) 'Gender-based violence and the Arms Trade Treaty: Reflections from a campaigning and legal perspective', *Gender & Development*, 21(3): 551–62, 553.

38 Jutta Weldes and Christina Rowley (2015) 'So, how does popular culture relate to world politics?', *e-International Relations*, www.e-ir.info/2015/04/29/so-how-does-popular-culture-relate-to-world-politics

39 Centre for Humanitarian Dialogue (2007) *Missing Pieces: A Guide for Reducing Gun Violence through Parliamentary Action*, Handbook for Parliamentarians, No 12, www.ipu.org/PDF/publications/missing_en.pdf, p 81

40 Centre for Humanitarian Dialogue (2006) *Hitting the Target: Men and Guns*, https://reliefweb.int/report/world/hitting-target-men-and-guns, p 2.

41 See Inderpal Grewal (2020) 'Authoritarian patriarchy and its populism', *English Studies in Africa*, 63(1): 179–98.

[42] Marysia Zalewski, Paul Drummond, Elizabeth Prügl and Maria Stern (eds) (2020) *Sexual Violence against Men in Global Politics*, Abingdon: Routledge.

[43] Paul Amar (2011) 'Middle East masculinity studies: Discourses of "men in crisis", industries of gender in revolution', *Journal of Middle East Women's Studies*, 7(3): 36–71, 40.

[44] Vanessa Farr, Henri Myrttinen and Albrecht Schnabel (eds) (2009) *Sexed Pistols: The Gendered Impacts of Small Arms & Light Weapons*, Tokyo: United Nations University Press.

[45] See Amanda Chisolm and Joanna Tidy (eds) (2019) *Masculinities at the Margins: Beyond the Hegemonic in the Study of Militaries, Masculinities and War*, Abingdon: Routledge.

[46] Laura J. Shepherd (2016) 'Making war safe for women? National action plans and the militarisation of the women, peace and security agenda', *International Political Science Review*, 37(3): 324–35, 327, 333; see also Caron E. Gentry, Laura J. Shepherd and Laura Sjoberg (eds) (2019) *Routledge Handbook of Gender and Security*, Abingdon: Routledge.

[47] Diana Otto (2004) *Securing the Gender Legitimacy of the UN Security Council: Prising Gender from its Historical Moorings*, Social Sciences Research Network, http://papers.ssrn.com/sol3/papers.cfm?abstract_id=585923; see also Henri Myrttinen, Lana Khattab and Jana Naujoks (2017) 'Rethinking hegemonic masculinities in conflict-affected contexts', *Critical Military Studies*, 3(2): 103–19.

[48] Martin Hultman (2017) 'Natures of Masculinities: Conceptualising Industrial, Ecomodern and Ecological Masculinities', in Susan Buckingham and Virginie Le Masson (eds) *Understanding Climate Change through Gender Relations*, Abingdon: Routledge, pp 87–103, p 87.

[49] Cynthia Enloe (2013) *Seriously! Investigating Crashes and Crises as if Women Mattered*, Berkeley, CA: University of California Press, pp 79–80.

[50] See David Duriesmith (2017) *Masculinity and New War: The Gendered Dynamics of Contemporary Armed Conflict*, Abingdon: Routledge.

[51] Chris Dolan (2002) 'Collapsing Masculinities and Weak States – A Case Study of Northern Uganda', in Frances Cleaver (ed) *Masculinities Matter! Men, Gender and Development*, London: Zed Books, pp 57–83, p 60.

[52] Joyce Marlow (2000) *Votes for Women: The Virago Book of Suffragettes*, London: Virago.

[53] David Crouch (2015) 'Swedish frustration with Saudis over speech may jeopardise arms agreement', *The Guardian*, 9 March, www.theguardian.com/world/2015/mar/09/swedish-foreign-minister-margot-wallstrom-saudi-arabia-blocked-speech-human-rights

[54] Crouch (2015) 'Swedish frustration'.

[55] David Crouch (2015) 'Saudia Arabia recalls ambassador to Sweden as diplomatic row deepens', *The Guardian*, 10 March, www.theguardian.com/world/2015/mar/10/sweden-tears-up-arms-agreement-with-saudi-arabia-over-blocked-speech

[56] Crouch (2015) 'Saudia Arabia recalls ambassador'.

57 Nick Cohen (2015) 'Sweden's feminist foreign minister has dared to tell the truth about Saudi Arabia. What happens now concerns us all', *Spectator*, 28 March, www.spectator.co.uk/article/sweden-s-feminist-foreign-minister-has-dared-to-tell-the-truth-about-saudi-arabia-what-happens-now-concerns-us-all-31-december-2015

58 Jacqui True (2015) 'Why we need a feminist foreign policy to stop war', openDemocracy, 20 April, www.opendemocracy.net/5050/jacqui-true/why-we-need-feminist-foreign-policy-to-stop-war

59 Women's International League for Peace and Freedom Sweden (2015) 'Feminist victory stops Swedish military deal with Saudi Arabia', www.wilpf.org/feminist-victory-stops-swedish-military-deal-with-saudi-arabia

60 Cohen (2015) 'Sweden's feminist foreign minister'.

61 United Nations (2013) 'The Arms Trade Treaty', https://unoda-web.s3.amazonaws.com/wp-content/uploads/2013/06/English7.pdf, p 6.

62 United Nations (1993) 'General Assembly Resolution 48/104 Declaration on the Elimination of Violence against Women', Article 1.

63 True (2015) 'Why we need a feminist foreign policy'.

64 ATT Monitor (2019) *ATT Monitor Report 2019*, New York, https://attmonitor.org/wp-content/uploads/2020/07/EN_ATT_Monitor-Report-2019_Online.pdf, p 19.

65 Twitter posting, Paul Kirby (@ProfPCK), Twitter post, 10.07 am, 30 January 2018, available at: https://twitter.com/ProfPCK/status/958401293462142976, quoted in Stavrianakis (2019) 'Controlling weapons circulation', p 72.

66 Claire Duncanson (2015) 'Hegemonic masculinity and the possibility of change in gender relations', *Men and Masculinities*, 18(2): 231–48.

67 Andrew Feinstein (2012) *The Shadow World: Inside the Global Arms Trade*, Harmondsworth: Penguin; Nicholas Gilby (2016) 'Might the Arms Trade Treaty be useful in stopping the worst arms exports?', Deception in High Places: A History of Bribery in Britain's Arms Trade, 16 January, https://deceptioninhighplaces.com/author/nicholas

68 Loren Thompson (2012) 'Rise of women transforms defense industry', *Forbes*, 30 July, www.forbes.com/sites/lorenthompson/2012/07/30/rise-of-women-transforms-defense-industry

69 Laura Williams-Tracy (2015) 'Linda Hudson: An agent of change in a man's world', *bizwomen: The Business Journals*, 27 July, www.bizjournals.com/bizwomen/news/profiles-strategies/2015/07/linda-hudsonan-agent-of-change-in-a-man-s-world.html?page=all

70 David Brown (2019) 'How women took over the military industrial complex', *Politico*, 1 February, www.politico.com/story/2019/01/02/how-women-took-over-the-military-industrial-complex-1049860

71 Cynthia Enloe speaking with Julian Hayda (2019) 'Women now at top of military-industrial complex. A feminist reaction', WBEZ 91.5, Chicago, National Public Radio, 8 January, www.wbez.org/stories/women-now-at-top-of-military-industrial-complex-a-feminist-reaction/900b5028-9f25-4fe0-b778-24b04f4a6115

72   Marillyn Hewson (2015) '3 ways leaders can help women succeed in business', LinkedIn, www.linkedin.com/pulse/3-ways-leaders-can-help-women-succeed-business-marillyn-hewson?published=t&sf14845082=1

73   Adrienne Roberts (2015) 'The political economy of "transnational business feminism": Problematizing the corporate-led gender equality agenda', *International Feminist Journal of Politics*, 17(2): 209–31, 212–14.

74   Quoted in Sarah Masters (2010) 'UN business: Women, guns and small arms control', openDemocracy, 25 October, www.opendemocracy. net/5050/sarah-masters/un-business-women-guns-and-small-arms-control

75   BAE Systems (no date) 'Our approach strategy: Why diversity matters'.

76   Roberts (2015) 'The political economy of "transnational business feminism"', p 211.

77   Ray Acheson (2021) *Banning the Bomb: Smashing the Patriarchy*, Lanham, MD: Rowman & Littlefield, p 28.

78   Cynthia Enloe, speaking with Julian Hayda (2019) 'Women now at top'.

79   Nancy Fraser (2009) 'Feminism, capitalism and the cunning of history', *New Left Review*, 56: 97–117.

80   Heike Schotten and Haneen Maikey (2012) 'Queers resisting Zionism: On authority and accountability beyond homonationalism', *Jadaliyya*, 10 October, www.jadaliyya.com/Details/27175/Queers-Resisting-Zionism-On-Authority-and-Accountability-Beyond-Homonationalism

81   Jasbir K. Puar (2017) *Terrorist Assemblages: Homonationalism in Queer Times*, Durham, NC: Duke University Press.

82   Rossdale (2021) *Resisting Militarism*, pp 77, 79.

83   Rossdale (2021) *Resisting Militarism*, p 69.

84   Rossdale (2021) *Resisting Militarism*, pp 65, 69, 71, 74.

85   Cynthia Enloe (2007) *Globalization and Militarism: Feminists Make the Link*, Lanham, MD: Rowman & Littlefield.

86   Rossdale (2021) *Resisting Militarism*, p 69.

87   Rossdale (2021) *Resisting Militarism*, p 70.

88   Rossdale (2021) *Resisting Militarism*, p 80.

89   Rossdale (2021) *Resisting Militarism*, pp 49–51.

90   Maria Stern (2011) 'Gender and race in the European security strategy: Europe as a "force for good"?', *Journal of International Relations and Development*, 14(1): 28–59, 32.

91   Christina Rowley (2010) 'An intertextual analysis of Vietnam war films and US presidential speeches', Unpublished PhD thesis, University of Bristol, pp 30–1.

92   Susan Buckingham and Virginie Le Masson (eds) (2017) *Understanding Climate Change through Gender Relations*, Abingdon: Routledge.

93   White Ribbon campaign, www.whiteribbon.org.uk/what-we-do

94   Veterans for Peace, https://vfpuk.org

95   White Poppy campaign, www.ppu.org.uk/remembrance-white-poppies

96   Aaron Belkin (2011) '"How we won": Progressive lessons from the repeal of "Don't ask, don't tell"', *Huffington Post*, 6 September, www.huffpost. com/entry/how-we-won-progressive-le_n_951175

[97] Samantha Allen (2018) 'How Trump's trans military ban backfired spectacularly', *Daily Beast*, 23 April, www.thedailybeast.com/how-trumps-trans-military-ban-backfired-spectacularly

[98] Cahal Milmo (2013) 'Where the worst dictators love to shop: World's largest arms fair comes to London', *Independent*, 9 October, www.independent.co.uk/news/uk/home-news/where-the-worst-dictators-love-to-shop-world-s-largest-arms-fair-comes-to-london-8807277.html

[99] For a discussion of the arms trade as the trade in 'martial' men, see Paul Higate (2012) 'Martial races and enforcement masculinities of the global south: Weaponising Fijian, Chilean and Salvadorean postcoloniality in the mercenary sector', *Globalizations*, 9(1): 35–52.

[100] Anna Stavrianakis (2015) 'Thinking internationally about the arms trade', The Disorder of Things, 2 October, http://thedisorderofthings.com/2015/10/02/thinking-internationally-about-the-arms-trade

[101] Anna Stavrianakis (2016) 'Legitimising liberal militarism: Politics, law and war in the Arms Trade Treaty', *Third World Quarterly*, 37(5): 840–65, 840.

[102] Cohn and Ruddick (2012) *A Feminist Ethical Perspective*.

Index

patriarchy 2, 22, 28–9, 35, 36–7,
134, 137–8, 149, 158
see also gender-order hierarchy
PATRIOT Act (US) 35
peace movements *see* activism/
activists
Peace News Summer Camp 161
peacefulness 17, 18, 19, 22, 48, 50,
53
see also activism/activists
penetration
contradictions surrounding 31–2,
45
Costa Rica 48, 52
Global War on Terror (GWOT)
33–5
queerness 52
rape 30–2, 38
sodomy 31–2, 34, 38, 39
of and by states/nations 30–2,
34–6, 45, 48, 52
torture of Iraqis 37–40
perpetrator–victim model 141–2
personification of the state 22,
25–8
Persson, Stefan 151
Peterson, V. Spike 64
Pettman, Jan Jindy 28
pink-washing 159
political repression 93
popular culture 22, 104–5, 116, 133
postcolonialism 64, 86
Power, Marcus 104
power
and consent 9
and legitimacy 7–9
systems of 134
see also gender-order hierarchy
prisoners of war 37–40
promotional videos 109–25
protestors
arms fairs 91, 96, 162
equipment for repressing 93
see also activism/activists

Puar, Jasbir 31, 33–4, 45
purple-washing 157–8
Putin, Vladimir 44

Q
queerness
anti-militarism activists 162–3
arms fairs 97
arms industry 159
containing the normal 23–5
Costa Rica 47–52
Global War on Terror (GWOT)
32–7
and heterosexual masculinity
40–3
and heterosexual norm 29–30
and homonationalism 34, 159
and hypermasculinity 44–5
and manliness 44–5
and the media 40–4
and military service 167
overt 43–7
and rape 30–2, 47–52
and states 23–5, 29–30, 40–5,
47–53, 159
and torture 40

R
race
arms fairs 168
arms industry 110, 118, 119,
120–5
arms trade 62–4, 65, 69, 70–1,
72
Global War on Terror (GWOT)
33–4, 36
north–south hierarchies 168–9
othering 64
Rafael 94
Rai, Amit S. 33–4
Rand Corporation 105
rape 30–2, 38